PENGUIN BOOKS

Brought to Book

Ian Breakwell regularly exhibits at the Anthony Reynolds Gallery in London. His artworks hang in public collections including the Tate Gallery. His illustrated fiction has been published as *The Artist's Dream*; he has also co-edited with Paul Hammond *Seeing in the Dark: A Compendium of Cinemagoing*. His *Diaries* (1985) were serialized on Radio 3 in 1990 and in twenty-nine television programmes by Channel 4, who also broadcast his five-part series *Public Face Private Eye* in 1991. During 1993 his photographic works, paintings and drawings were exhibited at Ffotogallery and Oriel, Cardiff and John Hansard Gallery, Southampton, his prints and publications at the Victoria and Albert Museum, London and his films and videotapes at the ICA, London.

Born and bred, like his co-editor, in Derby, Paul Hammond had a state education followed by eight years at art school, after which he gave up the brush for the pen. His first book, *Marvellous Méliès*, a study of the pioneer French filmmaker, was published in 1974. Since then he has written a potboiler about erotic postcards, *French Undressing* (1976); *Upon the Pun* (1978, with Patrick Hughes); and edited a volume of Surrealist writing on cinema, *The Shadow and Its Shadow* (1978; 2nd edition 1991). He now lives in Barcelona where, apart from asking what happened to the 1980s, he has resumed painting. His life of Riley is also devoted to translating, keeping a journal, reading and contemplating the ideas of Surrealism, his great and abiding passion.

Brought to Book

Edited by Ian Breakwell and Paul Hammond

PENGUIN BOOKS

PENGUIN BOOKS

Published by the Penguin Group
Penguin Books Ltd, 27 Wrights Lane, London w8 5tz, England
Penguin Books USA Inc., 375 Hudson Street, New York, New York 10014, USA
Penguin Books Australia Ltd, Ringwood, Victoria, Australia
Penguin Books Canada Ltd, 10 Alcorn Avenue, Toronto, Ontario, Canada m4v 3b2
Penguin Books (NZ) Ltd, 182–190 Wairau Road, Auckland 10, New Zealand

Penguin Books Ltd, Registered Offices: Harmondsworth, Middlesex, England

Published in Penguin Books 1994
10 9 8 7 6 5 4 3 2 1

Set in 10.75/14 pt Monophoto Janson
Filmset by Datix International Limited, Bungay, Suffolk
Printed in England by Clays Ltd, St Ives plc

Introduction

'Books take you out of yourself' is an often-heard phrase, but an ambiguous one. Does it mean that reading a book provides a temporary escape from humdrum workaday life into an exciting world of make-believe? Conversely, might it suggest that the reader is lifted out of self-centred introspection to a heightened awareness of the world around? Or – and this is where we come in – could its latent double meaning encompass both transformations and reveal them to be two sides of the same coin? So that, however private and intimate, contact with books simultaneously makes the most remarkable connection with the social world of which books are an integral and reflective part?

In order to find out we invited the contributors to *Brought to Book* to explore how books, in a myriad of tangential, curious, funny, sad, disturbing and surreal ways, have been influential or catalytic in revealing their lives to them. And through these accounts to us. We hope you will recognize your own selves in the pages that follow, for everything herein is true, especially the lies. There is no linear argument. The texts and pictures are arranged according to an intuitive and idiosyncratic method, a montage of attractions.

Anything with pages, spine and cover is a book. As well as the connection of people's lives with novels, thrillers, essays, histories, poetry, biographies, porn and all other forms of fiction and non-fiction, we asked our writers to consider the collision of their experiences and imaginations with schoolbooks, rent books, cookbooks, hymn and prayer books, law books, medical books, A–Zs, DIY manuals, notebooks, scrapbooks, etiquette and moral guidance books, mail order catalogues, tourist phrase books,

quiz and crossword books, Braille and talking books, almanacs, ledgers and registers, Books of Remembrance, Baby's Golden Footsteps, songbooks, logbooks, ration books, cult books, proscribed books, timetables, atlases: whatever triggered the story, poem or anecdote.

And so the subject matter in *Brought to Book* spans the spectrum: of childhood memories; of reading rituals; fetishism; stealing, eating, cooking and burning books; books as status symbols, furnishing, food for termites, aids to seduction, smuggling and espionage; books associated with journeys, falling in and out of love, marriage, sex, imprisonment, freedom, war and death; books and their relationship to night dreams and daydreams, religion, masturbation, the law and illness.

Some of us may be bibliomaniacs, cocooning ourselves with more books than we can possibly read in a lifetime, a bit like those postal workers who don't deliver the mail but stow it away unopened in their houses. Few of us, however, could claim to equal Abdul Kassem Ismail, a tenth-century Persian vizier, who travelled the desert by camel with his huge collection of books. His librarians could quickly lay hands on any volume since the animals had been trained to walk in alphabetical order.[1] Yes, the desert is a daunting place, but even in your own home you have to be careful. Alkan, the mystical French composer, died of a fractured skull in his library after a volume of the Torah fell from a high shelf.

Stepping out of the door can be just as risky. Legend has it that Woody Allen was walking down a New York street when he was struck on the chest by a Bible thrown from a thirty-third-floor window, and had it not been for the bullet in his vest pocket he wouldn't have survived to tell the tale. Woody was lucky: books are dangerous. Especially in the hands of crazed readers. Mark Chapman always carried a copy of *The Catcher in the Rye* and it told him to shoot John Lennon. The printed word of gods of all religions, and of secular gurus like Hitler and Stalin, have been responsible for much of history's record of war and genocide.

Books can be fraught with danger on a more local level. In medieval England John Leycestre and his wife Cecilia were hanged for stealing a volume from Stafford church. Even in London's Swinging Sixties, Joe Orton and Kenneth Halliwell did time for defacing library books. Perhaps what really raised the hackles of Islington Public Libraries was that these amoral pranksters combined three forms of book crime in one. For if, to quote the book trade's lingo, a biblioklept steals books and a biblioclast cuts pages out of them and a grangeriser sticks things into them, then Orton and Halliwell, by removing books from libraries and scurrilously embellishing their dustjackets before returning them, were guilty, presumably, of 'bibliokleptograngerclasm'. Call it what you will, it landed them in Wormwood Scrubs.

To be fair, public librarians are a long-suffering bunch. In the television programme 'The Missing Page' poor Hugh Lloyd dutifully brings four rare and heavy tomes, only for borrower Tony Hancock to use them as a step ladder to reach *Lady Don't Fall Backwards* on the top shelf.

Perhaps it's a folk myth that bacon rashers are a favoured form of bookmark, but a recent survey among 3,000 librarians in the United Kingdom revealed that other handy items for marking the page included a razor blade, a used condom, banana peel and a smelly rugby sock. Books never ever borrowed included *Gay Bulgaria, Brown Girl in the Ring: The Lyrics of Boney M* and *The History of the Handkerchief.* Lamest excuses for the late return of a library book included, 'My mum won't let me out after dark alone'; 'My mother was wallpapering and I think the book is behind the wallpaper'; and 'I didn't know you wanted it back.'[2]

Stories of eccentric behaviour brought on through the possession of and by books are legion. Holbrook Jackson speaks of a German scholar who had Homer printed on india rubber so that it could be read in the bath.[3] Another aficionado of the floating text was the poet Shelley, who had a passion for making and sailing paper boats, and whenever he came to a pond reputedly made one from whatever book he was carrying. In *Imaginary Homelands* Salman Rushdie recounts how in his home in India it was customary to make apology to an object when it was accidentally dropped by kissing it. Even before he'd kissed a girl he'd laid lips on countless books, little realizing that one day a book would change his life: 'We kissed dictionaries and atlases. We kissed Enid Blyton novels and Superman comics. If ever I'd dropped the telephone directory I'd probably have kissed that too.'[4] Whereas Emperor Menelik II wrapped his lips *around* books, for he believed the Bible had curative powers and would chew a few pages whenever he felt poorly. Following a stroke, he masticated a whole Book of Kings, blocked up his bowels and died.

Books have been made of every conceivable material besides paper. Anselm Kiefer, heavyweight German Neo-Expressionist painter, is building a library of lead books in iron bookcases. In the Italian Dolomites a picket fence of giant pencils surrounds sculptor Livio de

Marchi's 'Book House', built from 2,000 volumes carved in pine beneath the sheltering eaves of an open-book roof. Fluxus artist Alison Knowles made a book, devoted to beans and dreaming, as big as a bedsitter: you could live in it. Books have been bound in fur, cricket pads, soiled bandages (by retired surgeons), and the most primal binding of all, the skin and nipple of a mother's breast. Books are eminently tactile and sensory things. The sexologist Havelock Ellis describes 'a lady entirely normal in other respects who was conscious of a degree of pleasurable excitement in the presence of leather-bound ledgers'.[5]

As well as smell, touch and taste, colour can be the key. Little red books were waved like flags by dragooned millions. We must take Flann O'Brien's word for it that Trellis, the character in *At Swim-Two-Birds*, who only read and collected books with green covers, did so because he considered all other colours to be symbols of evil.[6] A books-by-the-yard rep might see this as a tasteful interior-design decision. Books may be bindings and nothing else, with portentous spine titles to impress the in-laws but blank-paged or polystyrene-slabbed inside.

Ian Breakwell in the book-wallpapered bar of Nolan's, Rosscarbery, Ireland.
Photo: Sean Dillon

Even pubs have taken to using books as decor, yet editor Breakwell, who developed his lifelong hunger for reading after growing up in a household where the only book was *The Parkinson Cookery Book* that came free with the gas cooker, has been threatened more than once with grievous bodily harm by inebriates because he'd ruptured the fragile code of bonhomie by reading over a quiet pint. Co-editor Hammond was once in a bar where the books were to hand, and was tempted to browse until he noticed that they'd been sawn to a depth of two inches to go round a chimney breast and not disturb the straight lines of their ranked spines.

Books and fire don't go well together. From Alexandria to Berlin to Bradford there are always bibliophobes who don't need a book to show them how to strike a match. Books can also conserve heat: in fifties' America there was such an over-production of pulp fiction that builders used remaindered paperbacks as infill for the cavity walls of new suburban homes. If you can't find the volume you want in the wall then look under the ground: more than one poet's corpse has been disinterred to rescue that priceless manuscript. In fact the first paper book in the world, a 1,600-year-old Coptic psalter, was recently found in a grave near Cairo tucked like a pillow beneath the head of a twelve-year-old girl. The logical extension of reading in bed is, it would seem, osmosis through endless sleep.

From the time of that Egyptian bedtime reader, books have been made from materials of animal or vegetable origin which naturally decay, though usually less quickly than the book's owner. The destruction of books is a slow living death accelerated not only through yellowing by oxygen in the air, and by the ravages of fire, flood, mildew and spilt coffee, but also through recycling by a vast array of insects collectively categorized as bookworms.[7]

Silverfish, which have a high carbohydrate diet, feed on the cellulose of paper and the starch paste and size that binds it. The end result: the book falls apart in your hands. Humble booklice feast on bookmould, while up-market firebrats are partial to the paper glaze of coffee table tomes. The recent publishing fad for mimsey illustrated publications about herbs and posies, with lemon grass or violet scented endpapers, merely adds piquancy to the insect banquet. Carpet beetles litter literature with variously coloured turds according to the part of the book they've been chewing on: snow white if blank endpapers have been the meal, but black in the case of printed text, and light brown after swallowing glue. Browsers and spoilers such as the universally loathed cockroach live in the space between books and walls, fouling the page ends with evil-smelling saliva. The brown stains on those fetid pages are the tiny corpses of thrips. Even the bookshelves are subject to determined erosion by woodworms, ticking death-watch beetles and those bibliophagic superbugs, termites, who can desiccate not only books, shelves and floors but the whole library building, foundations and all.

However, all is not lost, for the balance of nature ensures that there also lurks in the library the bibliophile's friend, the book scorpion, which lies in wait to pounce on book pests, then clamp them in its pincers, and though hopelessly outnumbered does its level best to preserve the world's literary heritage.

Ecology aside, the world of books is constantly threatened by the technological passivity of so much contemporary existence. The writer Roger Moss has remarked on the contrast between the look of blank tension on the face of the train traveller wearing Walkman headphones and the relatively attentive, benign expression of the fellow passenger reading a book. When we edited our last anthology together, *Seeing in the Dark*,[8] it was in praise of the interactive pleasures of cinemagoing, so unlike the domestic seclusion of the television viewer. Now, in *Brought to Book* we have switched the terrain from the social obsession of cinema to the private one of books. And what we propose is this: that real world and book world are inextricably linked by revelatory synchronicities that enable us to live our lives more vividly.

If you're with us so far, dear reader, please now turn the page and join our international choir of passionate tongues between the sheets. And be brought to book.

(IAN BREAKWELL AND PAUL HAMMOND)

1 Scot Morris, *The Emperor Who Ate the Bible*, Doubleday, 1991
2 (Library Resources Exhibitions), *The Secret World of Your Local Librarian*, 1993
3 Holbrook Jackson, *The Anatomy of Bibliomania*, Soncino Press, 1932
4 Salman Rushdie, *Imaginary Homelands*, Viking, 1991
5 Havelock Ellis, *The Psychology of Sex*, Pan Books, 1959
6 Flann O'Brien, *At Swim-Two-Birds*, Longmans Green, 1939
7 Norman Hickin, *Bookworms*, Richard Joseph, 1993
8 Ian Breakwell and Paul Hammond (eds), *Seeing in the Dark: A Compendium of Cinemagoing*, Serpent's Tail, 1990

Crackerjack

I have no clear memory of the event, even though I was
already two or three days old when it happened. What I
do remember is my mother narrating her version of it.
Repeated often enough these fables become history. From
an enveloping plain of darkness that absorbed all mere
facts she highlighted a few dramatically staged and
atemporal tableaux.

The ambulance hesitates, breaks down, runs out of
petrol – whichever is not important – on the rim of a hill
overlooking the city of Cardiff. The pregnancy was a
tricky one: another baby, a girl, had been lost. Our
journey through the unlit countryside *was* necessary.
Certain districts, like Larkin's squares of wheat, were
ablaze. The docks had been a target for several nights.

Then, a long and painful parenthesis for both of us, I
was born: out, present, here. Cardiff was not where we
lived, I was estranged from it, would not draw breath.
Despite the warmth of the slaps and buffets that introduce
us to the social world, I was stubborn, blue as lead. It
didn't look good.

My father paid a visit, a small pile of paperback novels
crooked under his arm. A typically oblique but significant
gesture. Entering the heat and nervous closeness of that
private cell, he stumbled. A tall man, stiff bones, he had
dutifully dipped to look into the cot. A single book
dislodged itself, fell through the air and struck the baby
on its undefended skull. Plucked from his dreams the
newborn creature howled, sucked used breath into reluctant lungs. Launched, there was no remission.

My mother held on to that title, where she confused all
others. *Crackerjack*. No author, no publication details.
(Subsequent research would point the finger at W. B. M.
Ferguson, who also penned *Boss of Skeletons, Escape from*

Eternity and *London Lamb*. But this is irrelevant.) The book must have been lightweight, in wrappers. My father wouldn't have invested in a hardback under such an ad hoc set of circumstances. He was Scottish; which is not to say that he didn't feel at home. Scottishness is the condition of feeling comfortable anywhere, as long as it is outside the borders of Scotland.

Crackerjack was my 'Rosebud'. I was stuck with it, my fate twinned with some unimaginably obscure pulp novel. In years of combing through stalls, junkshops and remote provincial warehouses it has never manifested itself.

I searched my father's library, clearing things up after he died. No trace. My mother had no library. Her books were absorbed with his, or they disappeared. I don't want to know. I share the superstition of the orphan who refuses to confront his 'real' parents. *Crackerjack* is my black spot, my plague token. It is waiting for me. One day, when I least expect it, it will arrive. And I will gratefully return to that interrupted dream.

(IAIN SINCLAIR)

Hole Story

Like other objects remembered from childhood, a book is alive, absolute, vague and partial. Dreamlike, memory reassembles (and resembles) the past, a scene or a moment, and always in pieces: a sound, smell, colour, shape. The script I write and cast as Memory is almost intangible and unfailingly incomplete. I turn and look at my bookshelves. There's a snapshot of my mother, my sister and me, I'm the infant in the baby carriage. I keep a memory: I'm little, with my mother, walking over a footbridge; there's another woman and a baby carriage. Something disturbing happens. My mother doesn't re-member the scene. She thinks I dreamed it. Is the picture what I remember?

When I was about five I read a seemingly simple tale

that was impossible for me to grasp. A little girl has a blanket. The blanket gets a hole. The little girl wants to get rid of the hole so she cuts it out. The hole gets bigger, and she cuts that out. She cuts and cuts and finally the blanket disappears.

I read the story over and again, as if it might change, and at its new end explanation would erupt from its pages. But the story's dire conclusion – the blanket disappears – left me trying to understand why it made sense and didn't make sense. Why couldn't she cut out the hole? The mysterious effect of reading, the immense undecidability of meaning, all this was contained in a book whose title, author and illustrator I can't remember. And no one's ever heard of it. The book is like a memory whose status as an object is in question.

But I remember reading it on my bed, and on the floor of the bedroom I shared with one of my sisters, and sitting in a big chair, in a room whose walls were papered brown, with little blue and yellow flowers. I didn't like brown. Was the radio on? Was I aware of girls and holes? What am I making up?

Years later I wrote a novel in which a character reads the blanket story. By incorporating the lost book into 'my' book I found a way to restore it to some kind of existence outside, and yet within, 'me'. Now as I write about it again the blanket story gains significance and structure, becomes a private myth in my scripted childhood, overwhelming everything else, much as the hole consumed the blanket.

(LYNNE TILLMAN)

Childhood Incident

One summer day at noon in our family kitchen
In my twelfth year I watched my mother cooking
The Collected Poems of Elizabeth Barrett Browning.

This was, I must admit it, a dirty book.
I had picked it out from an even dirtier junk-stall
Down in the market, near the church that used the incense.

Mrs Browning, as I remember, cost me sixpence –
Which was all my pocket money, plus a penny borrowed,
But I forked out for her gladly on account of her famous love.

Alas as I took the book from the Pakistani stall-keeper,
Wiping the dirt of the years from it with my shirt sleeve,
This funeral came out of the church that used the incense . . .

Back home, my mother saw red at the sight of Mrs Browning
And when, in my stammering, I blurted out about the Pakistani
And then the purple coffin – well, it was just too much!

My mother took Elizabeth Barrett Browning in a pair of fire-tongs
And deposited her in the oven, turning the gas up high,
Remarking that this was the way to kill all known germs.

I feared then that what I would see would be the burning
Of Elizabeth Barrett Browning in our family kitchen;
But, praise to God, my mother knew her regulos.

I remember the venial smell of the baking
Of Elizabeth Barrett Browning in our family kitchen.
I can still see those pages that curled and cracked,

And the limp green leather cover that peeled away like lichen
From the body of the book, and the edges turning gold,
And the hot glue's hiss and bubble down the spine.

But most clearly I recall as if this was just yesterday
An odd but quite distinct and – yes – *poetic* scent
Which arose from the remains of Mrs Browning's Poems

When they came out baked and browned from my mother's oven
And lay steaming there on the table in the family kitchen.
It was, I swear to God, a whiff of incense.

(ROBERT NYE)

Swaddling Clothes

My father went to the bedroom and rooted out the pillow and the clothes I wore immediately after my birth. We sat for an hour without saying a word. I was afraid to touch the clothes. But I was also happy that my parents had taken them to Holland. This is their story.

I was born in 1947 at Semarang on the Indonesian island of Java. At that time there was a war of independence going on between the people of Indonesia and the Dutch. My mother and father were living in a leper house. It was impossible to find anywhere else. They had lost everything. Because we were Euro-Asian the native people were not allowed to give us food or clothes. Hitherto buffers between the Dutch colonialists and the natives, the Euro-Asians were now considered to be inferior and politically suspect. Even my parents' belief that the Indonesian people had a right to independence did not help us. Nor did it stop the natives from killing everyone in my father's family who lived in Indonesia at the time. My mother no longer had any family.

Initially the Dutch government would not accept us as political refugees because we had no money and nobody to assume responsibility for us in the Netherlands. The German name Obermayer also made things difficult, which was completely hypocritical given that many Dutch soldiers were members of the NSB, the Dutch Nazi Party. Later on they had to accept us. My parents could prove their fathers were part of the colonial army. They became Dutch. In origin one was an Austrian Jew, the other part Cherokee. It was a shock to hear from the Red Cross that we had also lost family on the Jewish side in the concentration camps.

Before my birth my parents had no idea how they were going to dress me. They had nothing. Most of the inmates of the leper house were dead or dying. Using their clothes would not be good for my health. We lived in the only place we could, the library. My father peeled the cloth bindings from the books there and made clothes

My first book at the age of four was *Rupert*. There was a picture of Rupert meeting some snakes. I didn't like the idea and kept *Rupert* at the bottom of a pile of books, to stop the snakes getting out.
(A MASS-OBSERVER)

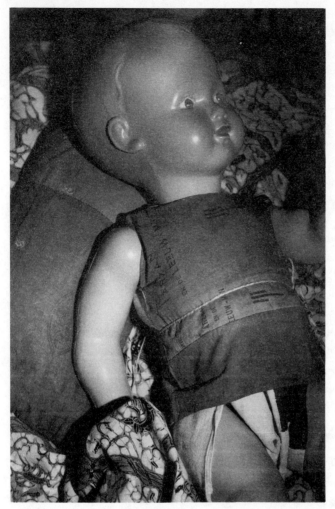

Merapi Obermayer's swaddling clothes.
Photo © John Muller

from them for me. It took ages to obtain a needle. My mother never told me what she had to do to get it. Giving thought to the books, they decided certain titles were good for my spiritual and intellectual health. But they were politically dangerous, especially the one on my pillow: *The Voice of Our Conscience.* My mother took care to have it on the inside. The other titles I wore were *Tarzan and the Lion Man, The Queen and I, Why Do We Believe in God If He Does Not Believe in Us?*

(MERAPI OBERMAYER)

Hold the Word

I was born in a village in a remote province of Iran, a feudal territory where the land, the people on it, their animals and their produce belonged to the landlord. Brides were taken from their beds on their wedding night for the landlord to rape. My father worked on the landlord's land and my mother made carpets which the landlord claimed.

I became blind at the age of three, after smallpox, and a year later my father ran into debt to the landlord. We had to flee the village at dead of night to escape. Had we been discovered my father would have been killed. As we went through the village gate on donkeys the Koran was held over our heads as a symbol of protection for the journey and water was thrown behind us, which meant: 'When the time is right, please return.' But we were not to return.

In every household in Iran there was a Koran, regarded and handled with reverence. It was wrapped in a beautiful embroidered cloth, with three accessories for prayer wrapped separately: the prayer mat on which to kneel, the clay tablet from Mecca on which to press your forehead, and prayer beads. The Koran would, of course, be read by those who could, but in illiterate households such as the one I grew up in it was the only book, unread but a talismanic presence during prayer, a healing force in attendance during illness, and an object on which to make vows and binding oaths: 'I swear on the Koran.' The prayers offered up by people who could not read were the words of the Koran learnt orally. I went blind before I could read it, even had there been the opportunity. The Koran is still the only book I've ever seen.

A bacon slicer at work bears an uncanny re-semblance to a person reading a novel.
(ANTHONY EARNSHAW)

Interestingly, the Braille version of the Koran has recently been published, in fourteen volumes because Braille has big spacing and needs thick paper, which breaks down the image of *the* book, the holy object. Imagine taking fourteen volumes to prayer!

The holy book had blessed us on our journey to Teheran, but my father's plans to earn money there to pay off his debts went badly. He couldn't find work and he put me out on the street at the age of seven, alone, to beg. Our neighbour's daughter became our friend. Sometimes she would read her schoolbooks to me and in turn I would explain to her what she had read. Even though I'd never been to school I understood, and I was afraid that she might get bored and put the book away, then the words would be out of my reach. So I had to concentrate and hold the words before they got away.

Eventually the authorities cleared the streets and I was taken to the Beggars' House. After some months my mother came and took me home. I used a neighbour's phone to ring a radio show which discussed domestic problems. 'I have such problems,' I explained. 'My brother wants me out. He beats me up.' I was looking for a refuge, anywhere to go. The radio announcer asked me to get someone to write all this down and send it to him, which I did. This resulted in a doctor adopting me, but it turned out she was only interested in using me as a receptionist. My chance to learn, to read somehow, was in danger of slipping away. Then a second letter written for me by a neighbour to the prime minister's office gained me a place in the Blind School. There I got tantalizingly closer to books. Each day someone would dictate from a conventionally bound book and I would simultaneously transcribe it, word for word, in Braille. At the end of the day I would have all the book's words on a big pile of loose Braille sheets, but although I had the contents I didn't have the book, the thing.

When I left the school I became the first blind woman to go to the university, where I came into contact with dangerous books. Books which in any way questioned the power of the Shah, such as Marxist texts or libertarian novels, were seen as a threat by the authorities and carried heavy penalties. Under the Shah's regime people were spied on at every level by SAVAK, the secret police. To read any literature that was considered subversive was forbidden. Dawn raids ended with books being

Braille history lesson.
Photo © Camera Press

burned or flushed down the toilet. So reading banned books had to be carefully planned.

In Iran the houses stand at the rear of walled front gardens; the doorbells are on the entrance gates. One person would be in the garden pretending to be busy, another would stand by the front door of the house, and a third in the hallway leading to the room in which a fourth person sat reading the forbidden book. Thus, if a stranger rang the bell a signal could be passed and the book hidden. Books were smuggled in from abroad, then distributed hand to hand. But not to my hand: there were no banned books in Braille, so again I was dependent on being read to, and to read banned literature aloud was even more dangerous.

To know that for me so much literature, and all typography, design and illustration, is a closed book inevitably brings with it a sense of loss. For years I could not bring myself to enter libraries. I'd stand outside and tears would fill my eyes at the thought of all the books inside which were inaccessible to me. Even now when I go into a library or bookshop a heavy sadness settles on me. The smell is so rich, so overpowering, so exclusive. Oh, if I could only browse, it would be the greatest luxury. Just that, to browse.

(GOHAR KORDI)

Waking to Eden

I was infected with the venom of language in early childhood when, sitting in a room flooded with sunlight, I opened an alphabet book. *B* was a Brobdingnagian tiger-striped bee, hovering over a crimson blossom, its sting distinct. This image was of such potency that my entire face – eyes, nose and lips – was seized by a phantom stinging, and my ears by an hallucinatory buzzing. In this way, and in an instant, I was simultaneously initiated into the alphabet and awakened to Eden.

In Eden to see a thing Yahweh had dreamed and to say its name was to bring it surging into the real. The letter *b*, so solid and threatening, *was* the bee; it was the embodiment of all its potencies. Looking at that letter, that blossom and that bee, was like looking into a mirror from which the skin had been peeled away. The page afforded a passage, transcendental and yet altogether tangible.

Much later I learned that for the Cabbalist Beth is female and passive, a little house waiting to be prodded by the thrusting barb of letter *a*. Aleph, knowing that Beth will always be there, her door open in expectancy, boldly confronts the universe: O vigorous, confident, thrusting Aleph! Now I know, too, just how erotic the image was: those engorged petals about to be ravished! Perhaps my sensuous life is here somehow reduced to its essential honey!

Just as once Persian wizards read a sacred text on the bodies of tigers, I had, from that morning, entered into an exulted state from which I was never to recover entirely, expecting, no, demanding enchantment each time I opened a book. That letter *b* convinced me of what I think I already knew, that the world is a ceremonial dialogue to be actively engaged, and life's intention the searching out of the fertile passages and places, a fearless looking for the thorny *a* and *b* in everything.

A wood stretched behind the house. It was a place of wild hives, seed rattles, lost feathers, quartz fragments and occasional arrowheads, and the gods themselves materializing in variable forms: horned beetle, red deer, fox, owl, snake (this was copperhead country), death-head moth, hawk, hummingbird; stinkweed also, and a treacherous mud with a will of its own whose depth, in certain seasons, could not be determined. So many of the games I played there read now like rites of passage. I was very aware of danger, supernatural and actual; every time I penetrated into the wood I crossed a threshold from one cosmic dimension into another.

Each element of the wood implied a magical possibility. Each element was, in fact, a potent letter, and all was contained – or so it seemed – in one vast magic act. I could not see the ladybug without entering into the ritual,

> Ladybug, ladybug, fly away home!
> Your house is on fire! Your children have gone!

It was here that I confronted death for the first time, in the shape of a fox, its inert body animated by a swarm of bees. I stood transfixed beside that vortex and knew transformation defines and rules the world. And because I had, in a room which now seemed worlds away, been myself changed forever by a letter in a book, I crouched and left a votive gift sublimely transitional, before moving on deeper into the world's wood – those gorgeous and terrifying images, like a necromantic alphabet of molten glass – pulsing behind my eyes.

(RIKKI DUCORNET)

Web

Once, rather than just moving my emotions or opinions, certain books had a *physical* effect on me.

I don't mean tears – I never cried over stories – and I don't mean ejaculation. In the days before *Lady Chatterley's Lover* you really had to use your imagination. Eroticism was hard to find on the shelves of the public library in Newport, Isle of Wight. Hank Janson books such as *Torment for Trixy* or *Sweetie Hold Me Tight* were a bit of a joke even to adolescents, though they might contain one or two interesting sentences. And on our pocket money the only dirty magazines I or my friends could afford were either *Health and Efficiency*, which pretended too hard to be serious about nudist camps, or else *Spick* and *Span* with their rotten airbrushed photos of grotty pinups.

No, sometimes it was the smells. Whiffs of tobacco or mould or eau-de-Cologne lingering on in the books handed down from uncles and aunts. The sad pre-war flavour of my father's old adventure stories like *She* or *The Last of the Mohicans* which I read on visits to my grandmother. The terrible musty reek that the only prize I ever won at school, *The Ghost of Gordon Gregory*, gave out from the day it was presented to me. Any of these might make me feel sick in the stomach or kick off long sneezing fits.

Schoolbooks could affect my bladder. They always held menaces which the drawings and jokes added by previous owners never allayed. I wasted many evenings trying, in between frequent trips to the toilet, to memo-

rize for homework some turgid Tennyson poem or Shakespeare speech. Worrying, as I pondered incomprehensible
algebraic equations, about the trouble I'd be in tomorrow.
Nearly shitting myself as I stood up alone in class staring
at blurred pages of French and Latin while the teacher,
impatiently tapping his cane, waited for me to start
translating.

The day my set of
*Arthur Mee's Children's
Encyclopaedia* arrived
my delight was so great
I rushed to stand on
my head in an arm-
chair.

(A MASS-OBSERVER)

Other books sparked off different symptoms. Horror
or mystery stories never stirred me much, but among the
Second World War paperbacks always doing the rounds
at school – tales of Resistance heroism, bombing raids
and prison camp escapes – were the exposés of German
and Japanese war crimes. As I raced through *Scourge of the
Swastika, Knights of the Bushido* or *Camp on Blood Island* I
imagined I was learning some history and sharing in the
outrage at the atrocities whilst shivering excitedly at the
descriptions of torture or sexual sadism and blushing
guiltily at my fascination.

Less complex reactions were caused by the old set of
Pictorial Knowledge encyclopaedias that Uncle Willie gave
me. How Aeroplanes Fly, Galileo's Pendulum, The
Wooden Horse of Troy, The Life of Schubert, Why
They Chopped King Charles's Head Off: I knew every
one of the hundreds of photographs and drawings in the
set. But the big problem every time was the natural
history volume. Every time I leafed through the lions
and monkeys, lizards and sharks, my fingers began to
move slower and slower and my heart to beat faster
because I knew on page 277 the *spiders* were coming.
Page 271, my neck prickled; 272, my stomach tightened;
273, my left hand was clamped over my eyes as I peeped
through my shaking fingers; 274, 275, 276 ... here they
are! And worse yet, drawing me helplessly forward page
by page towards 281, like a fly into the web, the creature
of my sweat-soaked nightmares: the big, furry *Bird Eater.*
278 ... 279 ... 280 ... 280 ... 280 ... aaaargh!

(TONY RICKABY)

Complete Taxonomy of the Kangaroo

And she was standing there
about as close as I am to you.
She was like a cross between a woolly monkey
and a gypsy queen!
I loved her at once.
Then Marion appeared,
and I put my finger to my lips, and smiled . . .
The night before,
the stars were so clear

it was as if they were trying to tell me something.
It made me feel strange,
and I woke up the others.
Only Marion responded.
She had stepped out of her little tent in her nightie
and hit me on the head
with a *Complete Taxonomy of the Kangaroo*
she was holding like a tray
in both hands.

You ask me if I get on with women.
My answer is Yes –
so long as they are dressed in velvet
kangaroo suits
and disappear into the bush
the minute they are told to!
Perth was the nearest town,
but that was a good six hundred miles away
by ute.

(SELIMA HILL)

Bible Story

Last night I went to bed with an old Bible, I imagine
telling you. You would laugh perhaps. I searched my

bookshelves. I hadn't opened one for years. I flicked its gilt-edged pages, flimsy but durable. The smell of age, dim church pews and old stone to comfort me. The crumpled navy ribbon lay nestling between Ecclesiastes and the Song of Solomon. The words sang as I traced the thin print of the Song of Songs. They sounded like Nana. *My beloved is mine, and I am his: he feedeth among the lilies.*

Did I ever tell you my first Bible was red? It slid out of its royal blue slipcase unashamedly, like the Red Hand of Ulster. It was too garish, it embarrassed me. Spindly writing in blue-black fountain pen dedicated it to Margaret Ann on her birthday, with much love from Nana, 1969. Her reading glasses always lay next to the Bible, beyond my reach on the mantelpiece. She would read to me, her voice trained in solemnity, rising and falling like the minister's. I drank meaning from her intonation. The parables were best. Lazarus, Nicodemus, ten lepers cleansed. The countries on the map looked hot. The purple land, yellow land and pink land around the Sea of Galilee. I never knew they were real. One evening Nana had whispered, 'Kneel down Maggie and ask the Lord Jesus into your heart.' A plague of fiery serpents blazed in the hearth. I obeyed. But how could I know if he had come? Would I feel him moving? I felt nothing. Nana pressed me to her chest and rocked me, tears rolling down her plump, veined cheeks. 'Hallelujah!' she cried. 'Saved.' I could smell moth balls and Blue Grass perfume. I felt sick with responsibility.

'Lord above!' Nana looked at the clock as it chimed half past ten. 'I haven't had a cup of tea for goin' on an hour. How's about a nice wee cup of tea?' She was already racing like the hammers in the kitchen. Bedtime slipped magically away. Being a Christian was worth it. She spread out homemade scones, coconut drops and fruit cake on a tiered cake stand and put the teapot on the cooker to brew. Bubbles of steam sizzled and spat on the hotplate. It began to boil. 'For what we are about to receive may the Lord make us truly thankful. Amen.' 'Amen,' I echoed and reached for a wheaten scone with

My 1950 pop-up version of *The Story of Jesus* affords you the rare chance to view the Last Supper from *behind*.

(NEIL HORNICK)

jam. I swirled my teaspoon round, enjoying the chinking sound of metal on thin china. I blew on the surface and tasted the dark sweet liquid. I watched Nana's mouth as she skirted her tongue under her dentures, seeking out a niggling raspberry seed. The air sucked around her gums. When I had drained my cup she picked it up and turned it to the light. Her watery brown eyes glinted. 'I see a journey across the water. And . . . is it a bird or an angel?' 'Where? Where? Show me.' I searched for a shape in the lump of black leaves cluttered at the rim of the cup. Nana said that was enough and made me promise not to tell that she ever read the leaves. I snuggled on her broad lap as she whispered, 'And who's my favourite girl in the whole world?' 'Margaret Ann McIntyre.' My name bloomed with the confidence of unconditional love and I fell asleep.

Last night I went to bed with an old Bible. I wept for Nana. I ached for you. *Thy two breasts are like two young roes that are twins, which feed among the lilies.*

Once you sat up in bed. You couldn't sleep. Although you were silent I sensed your sorrow and woke. I went to the toilet and as I came back I picked up my two bicycle lamps by the door. I switched them on. White and red roses bounced off the ceiling. I danced with the lights, twirling naked in the middle of the room. I made their beams cross, touch you, make you laugh. Lines crinkled at your eyes. I shone a wreath of white light on your breasts just above the sheets. You opened the duvet for me and I climbed into your scent. Your arms around me hooked a deep memory. Your eyes demanded confession and I had to tell you of the game I played as a child, after Nana died and prayers were never enough.

I was in a prisoner of war camp, in a dormitory of children. Each night the Gestapo officers would come round and shine a torch on to the face of every child. If you were found awake you would be taken out of bed and severely punished. I told you how I would lie, imagining the sound of their boots on the wooden floors, the stiff chafing of their thighs, the light pricking my skin. I would practise concentrating every muscle, every thought to make myself appear asleep. My lips must not stir, nor my eyelids flicker. Sometimes a strain of erotic pleasure in the gaze of the officer would arouse me, until being awake with my eyes clammed shut took on a delight of its own. I would squeeze my legs together, press my hands on my pubic bone and hold my breath for as long as possible. The tingling release relaxed my body. I would fall asleep. That night you wept as you told me about your mother. How she had survived the Holocaust. You told me how much the small act of drinking from a glass of water at your bedside in the middle of the night disturbed you. 'It is so simple and necessary and yet they couldn't have done it.' You could barely allow yourself to quench your thirst. It was as if, you told me, you had to undergo a small penance each night for having survived, for having never known the depth of the fear. Instead you recreated it most nights alone, in the dark, since you were a child.

That night we rocked our secrets to sleep and the dread of our betrayal sank like stones.

Let us get up early to the vineyards; let us see if the vine flourish, whether the tender grape appear, and the pomegranates bud forth: there will I give thee my loves. Each morning Nana would get up, God willing, at six, pray, listen to the morning service on the radio and bake. At half past seven she would bring breakfast in bed and get in beside me. She would tell me stories about Molly, Polly and Dodo, three cows who lived in the field down Percy's lane. They would go to the seaside and eat ice cream from Morelli's on the prom. They would take picnics to the burial mound and look out over the Bann.

That morning it was still. I wait for her. There is no clock in my room. I listen for the shuffle of her slippers, the sound of her singing along to hymns, her voice quavering like an opera singer on the high notes. The house is too quiet. I get up slowly and pull on my slippers, dressing gown and matching hairband, pushing my hair off my face. 'Rats' tails,' I think. I go downstairs into the kitchen. It is empty. The tea towel still rests neatly on last night's washed dishes. On the shelf in the pantry I see the breakfast tray set with willow plates. I climb the stairs and study the carpet edges where the burgundy flowers have been rubbed away and bits of string stick out. I push open her bedroom door. It creaks gently. The room smells different. I sense that I must not enter. I think of the Lord in my heart and suddenly feel that he has left hers and come into mine. He is too big. Tears will not come. I close the door and tiptoe down the landing, afraid to disturb the silence which feeds in her room.

I go out into the street. It is a cold, fresh morning. The milkman has been. A pint of milk and a pint of buttermilk stand in the crate. A thin head of frozen cream with a silver cap on pushes out of the bottle. The milk below looks blue. A smiling dial asks for two please on Saturday. I can see Nana's fingers setting it the evening before, the liver spots on the back of her hands. The street is still. Mrs O'Neil next door has not yet taken in her milk, nor has Jimmy Wilson on the other side. I walk up the pavement towards the main road. Then stop. The cold comes through my slippers. Mrs Bacon has a telephone. She could phone Mummy. I walk back down the street, carrying the heavy Lord in my heart. The small terraces are quiet and grey, their curtains closed. I go down Patsie's alley and along the cinder path that smells of cat's piss. Nettles grow up the sides. There are small chips of coal lying on the edges. Bits of broken bottle jag out of the tops of the wall. 'Ten green bottles hanging on the wall, and if one green bottle should ...' The tune runs through my mind. Then I stop it. I shouldn't sing a song, only a hymn. I search for one and hear Nana thud haltingly on the piano. 'Jesus wants me for a sunbeam ...' I shiver as I try to remember the words. I come to Mrs Bacon's yard and knock on her green back door. She opens at once, in her pinny, her hair wrapped up in a scarf, curlers poking out the sides.

'What's the matter child?'

'Nana,' I reply flatly. A sigh comes out like a little white soul and drifts on the air.

'God help us!' She grabs my hand and we run awk-

wardly back to the house where silence dwells. I wonder if Mrs Bacon can tell that I have the Lord in my heart. Rats' tails down my back.

Thou hast ravished my heart, my sister, my spouse; thou hast ravished my heart with one of thine eyes, with one chain of thy neck. Once I wanted you so much I phoned you from work.

'I'm sick.'

'What's wrong, Magg?' you asked, fear in your voice.

'Sick with missing. Can I come round?'

You laughed. Do you remember? I leave at lunchtime. It is five hours since I saw you, held you, kissed you goodbye. I cannot wait till evening. The red double deckers on Essex Road are bright and huge in the sun. Faces catch mine and turn around. I glow with want. My eyes shine. I pedal faster. I pass a flower stall and stop and cycle back. I buy all the blue cornflowers she has. I give her twelve pounds and hold them carefully under one arm. They drip on my bare leg. I balance, sitting high as I cycle. I let myself in. You are in the kitchen.

Although you don't turn round your body is alert to my presence. You pretend to be engrossed in chopping lettuce. I place the flowers on the table and come up behind you, cup my hands over your breasts. Your neck smells of fine white sand. Your throat makes a deep swallowing noise. My heart beats through my body against your shoulder, loud as a drum. My breasts press into your back. I run my hands down your thighs and between your legs. We don't speak. Your hands are poised, knife in one, lettuce leaves in the other. I loosen your grip and lead you to the table. I make you lie down beside the cornflowers, your knees bent up, legs open. I remove your shorts. I run my hand down the edge of your knickers. The wet has come through. I ride my fingers under the white cotton. Your blue eyes are deep and solemn. They don't leave mine. Your hair is tousled on your forehead. I smooth it away with my palm.

'Michael Dineen,' I begin to speak softly. 'You know who that was?'

'No.' Your voice is like a growl. You swallow again and turn your head away as if I am able to draw the desire out through your eyes. I go on.

'He was the first person to put a finger in me. Just a finger, without asking. He was a Catholic. I was thrilled. I was ten, he was maybe thirteen. It was in a darkened room.' You turn your face the other way. The cornflowers swim in your eyes. 'There was a party downstairs. I don't remember why I was upstairs. On the landing. Perhaps I had gone to the toilet. Had he followed? Had I wanted him to? He kissed me and guided me into the bedroom. It was his mother's. It smelt of powder. The satin quilt felt cool against the backs of my legs. He kissed me like I imagine a man would. Have men kissed you?' I hesitate abruptly. 'Have they?'

'Yes.' The word slides out with a great sigh. Your voice has deepened. I love your 'yes'.

'I don't recall the sensation of being wet,' I tell you. 'Perhaps I was still wet from peeing. Did I have pubic hair then? Did he notice or care if I didn't? You are so wet now, my love.' There is a loose sucking at my fingers.

'Mr Dineen had a sweet shop. I spent my pocket money there every weekend you know. I spent it all. Then I sat in a darkened room watching Saturday cinema, eating sweets and thinking of Michael Dineen. He went to America. He never touched me again.'

You make love to me, fuck me hard against the door and I leave, no time for lunch, and cycle back to my office. The saddle is hard against my swollen, full cunt where I carry the soft thump of your love.

I will go up to the palm tree, I will take hold of the boughs thereof: now also thy breasts shall be as clusters of the vine, and the smell of thy nose like apples. Nana had a photograph of all her brothers and sisters standing posed in the rose garden in Coleraine. I took you there once. There are ten of them. The women wear printed frocks, the men summer suits. They are in their thirties and forties. They all smile except for Great Uncle Wesley whose face is blank. When Nana died I knew that she was in a rose garden with her mother and father and she was happy. Then I grew anxious. Nana's parents would not recognize her when she came. She had grown so old. Perhaps as old and white-haired as them. Did God reunite people at the same age as when they last saw each other? That would make Nana a young woman. And so when I went to heaven would *I* recognize her? Would she still smell of Apple Blossom lotion? And would she become old again for me, and I become the little girl with long straggly hair and cold feet?

Set me as a seal upon thine heart, as a seal upon thine arm: for love is strong as death; jealousy is cruel as the grave. You wanted someone else. That was all. I saw you both laughing at the bar. Your face had that open fresh look it once gave mine. 'Don't you trust me?' you asked as we got into the car. 'Yes, of course,' I lied. She was older than me, nearer your age. I felt suddenly inhibited by inexperience. The lines on her face told you different stories. You had heard all mine. Or so you thought. Even my invented ones. I wait for you one afternoon. You are late. You are with her. The Sunday papers are unfolded on the kitchen table. I reread the same page several times, but the small printed matter has no meaning. I wonder if you are still in bed, what she smells like when she comes, how long her fingers are. Then I catch myself and pull strenuously back to the kitchen, the cup of tea which grows cold. I make a fresh cup. I brew the teapot on the cooker till the steam calls out of the spout. The phone rings. It is you. You tell me that her mother is very ill and that you will go with her. I am as calm as a low tide sea. I am reasonable. I set down the receiver. I cry out, no, no, please, no. It is the cry of a seven year old. The cry that was buried on a Saturday morning when Nana went to sleep.

Last night I went to bed with an old Bible. I turned to the Book of Psalms. I read them till six in the morning. Abundance, abide, deliver ... Lost words stroked my brow like her hand, your hand, fine hands.

All the night make I my bed to swim. I water my couch with my tears. Your way was to sleep earlier and longer. Mine was to wake and weep. The pain in my heart was cold to the air, like a fine paper cut which opens easily and stings. It would take night upon night to unravel the hurt that pushed its way through dreams, woke me shaking with fear and memory at dawn, alone.

I stretch forth my hands unto thee: my soul thirsteth after thee, as a thirsty land. My window looks over a small harbour on an estuary. Tonight I am restless. I listen to the tide filling the bay almost imperceptibly beyond the shutters. I hear a low shudder and then the gentle throb of a boat engine. I get up and go to the balcony. Bats twist in the empty street. Moths spin in blue lit pools. I do not let myself think how much you would like it here. I can see a white light with its clear reflection pass by. The boat seems to glide on air as it slips away in the dark. It is almost as if it has known that it must wait there silently for the flow before it can leave. I cannot see the water rise, only hear the lapping of the new tide against the harbour walls and the sighing of ropes on each other. The rhythm of waiting and the quiet passing on the surface of the sea calms me and I sleep deep and still.

(CHERRY SMYTH)

No Big Drop

Cornwall has been a favoured port of call for smugglers. In Polperro's Museum of Smuggling we have an *AA Motorists' Standard Guide Book*, hollowed out so as to form a box of a book to smuggle top-class jewellery, diamonds and loose cut precious stones. Also, a carved block of wood, largish, in the form of a Church of England family Bible. This gave concealment to a decent sized flat tin container filled with brandy. The customer–supplier routine was simple: no deliveries made to the customer's home; instead Sunday at the parish church. Handover as the congregation was leaving. A brief meeting on the churchyard pathway where the Bible, held under the right arm, was given a swift tap which released the tin flask into the waiting pair of hands, thence transferred into the warm comfort of the armpit under the best Sunday overcoat. Popular with the tax-dodge gentry from 1830 to 1910. As in all good smuggles the principle is that little and often is far better than a big drop.

(CECIL H. WILLIAMSON)

The Bible Belt

My maternal grandfather, a Glaswegian, had been married for ten years but, to the dismay of the family, had failed to produce any offspring. At the outbreak of the Great War he enlisted. Serving in the trenches at Passchen-

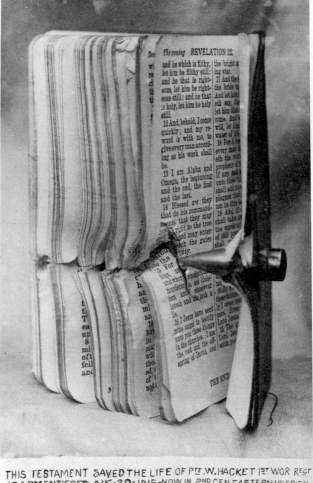

THIS TESTAMENT SAVED THE LIFE OF P͞T͞E .W. HACKET 1ST WOR REGT
AT ARMENTIERES. AUG·20-1915-NOW IN 2ND GEN EASTERN HOSPITAL
DYKE RD BRIGHTON· BULLET PASSING THROUGH OUTER COVER
AND ALL THE LEAVES AND STOPPED AT THE LAST PAGE.

daele, he sustained severe shrapnel injuries to the abdominal region, but was protected from the main body of the blast by a stack of hymnals he'd been carrying for the regimental chaplain. Among the books was a copy of the Bible. This was found, virtually intact, a hundred yards from the explosion.

Later, convalescing back in England, fragments of shrapnel were expelled from his body, the largest being an inch-square piece from his groin. Close examination revealed, fused to the metal, a minuscule portion of text which was eventually traced to chapter two of the First Epistle of Paul the Apostle to the Thessalonians. It read, 'For yourselves, brethren, know our entrance in unto you, that it was not in vain'.

My grandmother attributed her four sons to this miraculous sign and in deference to it named them Matthew, Mark, John and Ivan.

(CHARLIE HOLMES)

Civic Pride

We were walking round Liverpool, just me and my mother. It was one of those good times when we went together instead of just in the same direction. In the vestibule of the old cathedral we discovered a set of huge leather-bound books that listed the city's sons who had died in the Great War. 'I wonder if your grandfather is in here?' she whispered. 'I shouldn't think so, he was R.C.'

Page after page of victims' names we turned, identical calligraphy listing the unknown, unremembered, wasted fodder of that senseless carnage. Then, thousands on, we found H. Then Houghton. Then Thomas. Mother's finger trembled over the yellowed page. She smiled bravely, touched with tragic pride. 'I never thought he'd be in here,' she said.

It was almost as if she felt his paying the ultimate price had been worthwhile.

(CHRIS PROCTOR)

Prophet on the Banks

I've got a little boat on the River Lea. One day I was out in it with my daughter, she'd have been about ten at the time. As we were approaching the locks we saw a man

walking along the towpath reading a big, heavily embossed book. After we'd negotiated the lock we saw the
man again but now he no longer had the book. He called
out to us that it was in the river and would we help him
get it out? Of course we would, a bit of unexpected
excitement to brighten up the day: a book rescue. So we
circled round and found it bobbing along, half-submerged
in the middle of the river. 'How had it got into the
middle?' we thought as we fished it out. Surely if he'd
tripped and it had slipped from his grasp then it would
be by the bank? He explained that he hadn't dropped it,
he'd thrown it. He said, 'Water is a very good way to get
rid of the Holy Book, but it must sink.' He borrowed a
piece of string off us and began to tie the book to a brick,
but he was fumbling with the knots, making a very poor
job of it. Luckily my daughter Katie had just come back
from the dinghy sailing course at Banbury Reservoir; she
knew all about half hitches and reefs so she was able to
help him secure it properly. Then he threw it back in, it
sank, and off he went.

(HENRY PILKE)

The Fire

> *A funeral will be held for them*
> *We will form a procession*
> *And I will tear my coat*
> *And we will bury them*
> *Just as in a funeral for a human,*
says Rabbi Zadle Leshinsky.
The books burnt:
3 sacred scrolls,
a 600 year old Mishnah,
a Torah annotated by Maimonides,
an early cabbalistic text
'damaged beyond use'.
Piled on each other like lovers,

pages thumbed to time worn tissue
light's filtered through.
Fire lights nothing.
It's light below light longed for.

(DAVID MELTZER)

Caveman in Kolberg

I learned to read at the age of four. There's nothing else
to do, really, if most of your childhood is spent in a
hospital bed. I'd started wordsmithing whilst walking
with my mother through the streets of my small home-
town in central Poland. It was irksome having to stop her
at every corner to ask the name of the street. With an
insistent tug of her skirt I'd implore, 'What does it say,
Mum? Tell me.' Letter by letter I'd recite P−u−l−a−s−
k−i or K−i−l−i−n−s−k−i, trying to build the word.
Later, when the books came, brought by my parents to
the hospital together with bars of bitter chocolate and
monkey nuts, I'd struggle to get through the simple
stories printed in big letters and accompanied by faded
but charming illustrations. They were mostly tales of
anthropomorphized animals, Polish or Russian in origin,
and while I was only too happy to give the nuts and
chocolate away to the other children, I wouldn't let them
touch my books. Glued to them I was, from dawn to
dusk.

At seven I was sent to a sanatorium at Kolobrzeg on
the Baltic coast. Today unremarkable, in the Second
World War it was a town of huge importance. First
Polish, then for centuries German, its name was changed
to Kolberg: the Chancellery of the Third Reich decided
its fate as the Russians advanced in 1945. It would
become a symbol of the German will to resist the
barbarian hordes descending from the east. Huge fortifica-
tions had been thrown up around the town. To boost
morale Goebbels had initiated a film project. *Kolberg* was

When I was ten our
house was blasted by a
v2 rocket. Flat on the
floor I pulled myself up
when the dust had set-
tled to see all my books
hanging from bushes in
the garden.

(A MASS-OBSERVER)

shot in colour and, despite an almost total lack of money, resources or qualified personnel, was finished on schedule. The Battle of Kolberg cost hundreds of thousands of lives on both sides and left the town razed to the ground.

Kolberg began its new life in post-war Poland in ruins. Even walking through it at the end of the 1950s, on my way from the train station to the sanatorium on Zlota Street, I felt as though I was in a documentary about Stalingrad, or Warsaw during the uprising. A moon-like landscape with hardly a building intact. Empty, deserted ruins which after a while became an ideal playground for us children. Hawthorns grew everywhere, trees grew out of half demolished walls, creepers dangled from empty windows. School was meant to start in September, but the teachers were slow in inducing us into the classroom. And classroom it was, one room for the whole school, its walls covered in German propaganda about venereal disease, plus a few glass cases containing stuffed birds and a human skeleton: such were the teaching aids. Since there was hardly any school the Zlota Street kids dove through the underbrush and ruins, playing the part of Home Army partisans setting up ambushes against the Germans, fighting on the barricades of Warsaw, or soldiering with the Allies at Monte Cassino, a bazooka made from an old drainpipe as a weapon.

For me, however, the Kolberg jungle came to represent something else. It began after a foray around the sanatorium, a purposeful trawl it has to be said: a quest for books. Books were not plentiful in Zlota Street. To my delight I found a cache thrown on to a heap of coal in the boiler-room, ready for burning. Decrepit, their covers missing, some were in Polish, some in German. I selected a few and smuggled them back to the ward. One book in particular caught my attention, a book not meant for children and thus difficult for me to read. Nevertheless, I devoured it with hungry eyes.

The world I entered had existed long ago, before the war, before even my grandparents were born. The book was about Stone Age men, hunter-gatherers who strug-

gled for survival in a hostile environment. The pages were littered with illustrations depicting the inventions man had come up with in his attempt to master Nature: stone pestles, flint arrowheads and knives, fishing spears made of bone and then, finally, tools in bronze. I saw how he made shelters from branches and leaves or animal skins; how he made fire using two bits of wood, then a bow; how he hunted mammoths or made traps for cave bears. Having no sense of history I telescoped all this in my mind into the lifetime of a single prehistoric man.

The book was a revelation. For me it was a treasure without price, just as the first bronze knife or pinch of salt or tongue of flame must have been for our ancestors. I kept it under my pillow and read it in secret before going to sleep. By day I wandered through the Kolberg

1991 and the books are still burning. Photo: Severin Carrel © Camera Press

forest, high among the branches, leaping from tree to tree, hunting wolves, collecting hazelnuts and fungi for the winter ahead. To my compatriots I became an alien, a renegade Nazi soldier they shot at or tried to take prisoner. I'd escape by climbing to the top of a tree from where I'd shower them with arrows which, because they were real, had a certain advantage over their pretend bullets. Soon some of the partisans, attracted by my Stone Age weaponry, defected to my side. Shelters made of twigs and leaves began to spring up all over the forest and long strings of fungi could be seen hanging between the trees to dry. There were debates as to whether a certain stone was a flint or not, or if a spear with its tip tempered in a fire was admissible, since the fire had been lit with matches. Our clan expanded quickly, to the detriment of the Home Army, whose surviving members kept finding themselves caught in the bear traps we had set in bomb craters covered in twigs and camouflaged with leaves and moss.

And then disaster struck. Alerted by the sight of my bulky, coal-blackened pillow the sanatorium staff searched my bed. The book was found and confiscated and ended up where it was originally destined for: in the flames. I was shattered. For the other kids the book had little interest; for me it was a calamity. Created in a matter of days in the forest of Kolberg, my world lost all legitimacy, as Christianity would if deprived of its Bible. I took to sitting on the beach and watching the waves. A few days later we were sent back to central Poland. The Stone Age was gone for good.

(ANDRZEJ BADZIAK)

The Invisible Suitcase

The search began at dawn. It was conducted by about ten privates and NCOs, with little groups of prisoners queuing up in front of them. It was obvious it was going to be a lengthy operation, and I had the feeling that things wouldn't be as easy as they'd been when I was arrested. Some serious thought was called for. While I waited I began to sort out my books so that only one of my two suitcases would contain the authors classified as most dangerous on Dr Goebbels' index. If the worst came to the worst I would abandon it. I continued giving the matter serious thought; there was nothing else to be done.

The day dragged on interminably, in spite of my supply of reading matter. But I was in no mood to read. I was reluctant to stand up and join the queue for the inspection. And anyway, that didn't help kill the time because after you'd gone through the search you had to wait on the other side of the field. In short, I took so long to make up my mind that once again night fell. Exasperated and exhausted, the Germans stood up. They'd got what they deserved. They signalled to the rest of the group to pass through without further ado, the whole lot of us. And I found myself on the other side, my suitcases intact. That was how I learned from experience that many a knotty problem can be solved by relying on human lassitude. An open secret no doubt, but always and everywhere, however much it may be frowned on, of unfailing efficacy.

The next day we were crammed into a goods train and without due haste dispatched to Nuremberg in a fairly tolerable camp which subsequently turned out to have been a sort of hell-hole. I couldn't wait to get away from it because I knew I wasn't going to stay there, and I was sent farther away, to the Görlitz camp in Upper Silesia. A lot of good it did me, because the men left behind were released and sent back to their own countries. At least that was what happened to the Bretons on the French side, and to the Flemings – and I am half Flemish – on the Belgian side, as the Germans discriminated in their favour.

So that was a good lesson for me to learn, but I wasted no time in forgetting it.

One Sunday morning we were ordered to assemble in the yard with all our luggage. The time had arrived for the dreaded inspection that I had avoided so successfully until then. We took down our suitcases. The dormitories were to be searched simultaneously to examine all our belongings and anything we might have left or hidden there.

In the building opposite, open to all the winds that blew, was a little corridor leading to the kitchen. At meal times we queued up there with our mess tins. And that was where two of our jailers had put the table on which our bags were going to be inspected.

They lined us up in alphabetical order, to make things easier for them. Then the search began. It was so slow and so meticulous that I suffered agonies. I was carrying my two suitcases, the one with the forbidden books and the other containing various objects, my linen, and my more innocuous books.

As I was nearing the search table I suddenly noticed that, due to the obscure yet straightforward composition of the alphabet, Mabe, the navvy I had been talking to the other day, had just gone through the inspection and was about to turn round and come back. There was only one man between us, who was preparing to take his place. My forbidden suitcase was in my left hand. Mabe had only a small bag, which he was carrying in his right. As he turned I moved forward. Without thinking, without even looking at him, I unhesitatingly thrust my suitcase into his free hand which, amazingly, obeyed. Unless someone had been keeping an eye on us, no one could have detected this substitution. The narrow corridor hemmed us in on both sides. In front of us the guards had their noses stuck into the belongings of our brother who, according to the laws of the alphabet, came between us. There was virtually no risk that anyone behind me in the queue could have spotted this sleight of hand, which

was all the more rapid in that I had in no way prepared for it. I realized later that I probably wouldn't even have tried it on if I hadn't broken the ice with Mabe a few days earlier. No doubt it was the modicum of fellow-feeling born of our one conversation that had guided my hand before my brain had had time to weigh up the pros and cons and hold it back. It is also very likely that anyone else would either have refused me his complicity or, out of pure cowardice, denounced me.

I passed the inspection without incident. Mabe, whose dormitory was on the first floor, brought the heavy suitcase of his own accord to the second floor where I slept. He was full of suppressed anger, because nothing could either justify or recompense the risk I had made him run. But all he could do was mutter. In return I mumbled a few apologies and, as needs must, the incident was forgotten and things went back to normal.

At the head of my wooden bunk I had left a haversack containing various odds and ends and also, in an envelope, some small photos of my friend Magritte's paintings, taken by himself, amongst which I had slipped a couple of minuscule erotic photos. They showed a kitchen in which a *maître d'hôtel*, his trousers around his ankles, was disporting himself with a maid who was sitting on the edge of a table, her thighs wide apart. In a prison such treasures are as important as a knife or a cigarette lighter, even though once you have seen an obscene image it immediately loses its spell because it can really only affect you the first time.

I found all the Magritte photos, but not the improper images. My inspector had confiscated them for his own use. Thus it is that images and dreams travel from one head to another.

There were no more searches after that, except on the day of our release. We had been taken back to the Görlitz camp and lined up with our luggage before starting out for the station. In the menacing tones common to soldiers, the German officer in command of the convoy treated us to a harangue which a Belgian sergeant major immediately translated for us – not forgetting the threatening tones – into Flemish. (It was as a Fleming that I was released early, just as the Bretons on the French side were.) All our books and newspapers had to be declared and submitted for inspection. Non-compliance would incur severe penalties, among which would certainly be the deprival of the liberty that had finally been restored to us after nine months of slavery.

It was too late to turn back. Taking an even chance, I put myself in the hands of the sometimes benevolent blindness of fate and didn't turn a hair. Soldiers moved up and down our ranks, here and there getting a man to open his suitcase or bag. A prisoner in the line in front, to my right, was chosen. I was far from being at my ease, with the two suitcases at my feet; their very bulk, I thought, made them look suspicious and was bound to give me away. But the soldiers carried on without seeing me, examining other luggage behind me. I was saved, and so was my mobile library.

Immediately after my arrival at the Görlitz camp I had lent Valéry's *Variété* to an architect from Brussels. That was the only book I didn't bring back. How true it is that even in prison a book lent is a book lost.

(MARCEL MARIëN)

Deutschmarking Time

In September 1981 I was looking after the Circle Press stand at the Frankfurt Book Fair. The Fair is held for five days every autumn in exhibition halls as big as aircraft hangars. Thousands of publishers, large and small, come from around the world, hoping to sell their new titles or the foreign rights to them. Although the halls contain hundreds of thousands, perhaps millions, of books the atmosphere is far from that of a library. The British Museum's famous round reading room is like a quiet brain bursting with the knowledge of the world, whereas the Frankfurt Book Fair is a loud and crowded market and, if you have a publisher's booth, full of strange meetings, moments of expectation, and long periods of boredom.

One such encounter took place when a scientist who worked at the gigantic CERN Atomic Particle Accelerator in Switzerland bought one of my books, a hand-printed limited edition called *Between the Dancers*, with six of my own screen printed images and ten poems by Ken Smith. I asked the scientist hopefully if he was a big collector, but no, he just found these images fascinating because they reminded him of the paths traced by colliding atoms that he'd photographed at CERN. The prints were based, in fact, on the foot patterns for the tango from *Teach Yourself Ballroom Dancing*.

Nineteen eighty-one was my third year at the Fair and as usual our booth was situated in Hall 8, the Art Hall, on the first floor, along with the religious books. Trade was slow and to pass the time people looked at, and bought, each other's books. The stand to my left was Coracle Press, run by my friend Simon Cutts. On my right a stand run by a stranger to me, Helmut Dreyer, who seemed to sell only prints, no books in sight. (The definition of a book is stretched to its limit at Frankfurt, reaching as far in one direction as a 'publisher' selling lampshades covered in reproductions of famous paintings.) In an idle moment I realized that by a quirk of fate and language I was sandwiched between Herr Cutts and Herr Dreyer.

In front of his booth across the gangway stood an odd-looking Bavarian. He wore thick cord dungarees, a bright check shirt, big strong boots and smoked a curved pipe. His round, olive-coloured face was topped by a small skullcap. As the days wore on we became friends. He spoke very good English, having been at one time, he told me, a Lufthansa air steward. Out of curiosity I asked him about the outfit he wore every day.

'These are Dutch dock workers' trousers, I have ten pairs, they'll last me my lifetime.'

'And the shirt?'

'The shirt comes from Canada, I have fifteen of these

shirts, they'll see me out. The boots, they're American, I have ten pairs of these.'

It went without saying that they too would survive him.

As we were looking through his books two Germans walked by dressed in lederhosen, embroidered jackets and hats with a long feather pointing to the roof.

'These fucking Germans,' he said. 'They love uniforms.'

(JOHN CHRISTIE)

Report

The shop window is filled with false noses, ears and teeth, strap-on latex breasts, self-adhesive chest wigs, inflatable skeletons, edible underpants, squirting bow ties, bendy coat hooks, farting cushions, coughing ash trays, jumping bandaged fingers, pools of plastic vomit and rubber turds, in the middle of which is a brown, leather-bound book entitled *Report*, by Doctor Johnson of Hollywood, with a silhouetted man and woman passionately embracing on the cover. Inside the shop the hunched man behind the counter, with a bolt through his neck held by steel nuts, takes the flashing lights out of his ears, shifts the drooping fag to the corner of his mouth, raises a dusty eyebrow and says:

'Yes?'

'What does the book in the window do?'

'It explodes when you open it.'

'Does it do anything else?'

'No. Goes bang that's all. You can't expect much more from a book for £1.50. Do you want one?'

'No thanks, you've given the plot away.' But already he's not listening, the wires are back in his ears as he dusts the fallen ash off a werewolf wig.

(IAN BREAKWELL)

When I pick up a book from the supermarket shelf I instinctively feel as guilty as the people in the next aisle creeping furtively around the cake counter.

(A MASS-OBSERVER)

I have read every
horse book I could get
my manure-stained
hands on.

(A MASS-OBSERVER)

Quiet Day in the Bookshop

The desk scrabbles with
demands for money
red threats reports
on the audacity of patrons
asking for things unavailable
– anywhere it seems.
The principle seems to be
        garbage with bright accoutrements
        like seasonal weeds.
In the bin are 64 surplus
Tom Sharpe with their jackets gone.
The one in demand is reprinting.
With my finger I flatten the edge
of a booktoken successfully
exchanged yesterday for a gross of postcards
depicting the city hall. It is inscribed
'Well done son. Buy yourself something
you've always wanted, love Mam.'
The poetry section curls softly
like a row of sandwiches.
Who listens?
Someone drifts in and buys a pencil
For a moment the till hums.

(PETER FINCH)

Ice Cream for Small Plants

Somewhere in the world there is a book in which each of
our lives is written out, word for word, day by day, in all
its richness and banality. Of this Marcus J. is certain. All
he has to do is seek out his book and then he will gain
complete control of his own destiny. He knows such a
book could never physically be read. But he knows it

exists and is being rewritten as each moment passes. It is a small idea, but it has a liquorice tongue which attracts him on such cold days and sustains him. He doesn't know its name, but he can feel the texture of its spine. He can stroke the velvet rise of its typography, the smooth warmth of its opening. He is hungry for it and he knows it is within reach. Somewhere in the obscure recesses he senses it, a few pages still uncut, the original binding still intact. The only thing he is not aware of is the title: *Ice Cream for Small Plants*.

To all intents and purposes his powers to read, write and talk are no different from the next man's. It is just that Marcus J. always has the feeling that, whatever he does, someone else is doing the intending. There are always plural purposes in other minds, different from the singular purpose in his own. If someone is spoonfeeding him then maybe it is to keep him in his place, and he is looking for a way out. If someone is egging him on he has no option but to keep on the trail.

Marcus J. stood outside the antiquarian bookstore on Martin Buber Street in downtown Tel Aviv. In the half-light his cropped black hair had a silvery tint. With shoulders hunched, his weak chin seemed to merge into the top of his neck. He looked cold yet the heat was oppressive. This particular street had attracted him. There was a small park opposite the store, where a fountain shot jasmine-scented water noiselessly down a sleek black wall. Children splashed and jumped in it. Parents and minders sat on benches nearby, rocking prams. Marcus J. watched as a small plump woman in a Chanel suit stood up from her bench and toiled across the gravel in the direction of the kiosk that sold ice creams, sodas and fizzy drinks. He watched her buy two ice creams and, as she pulled out her purse to pay, Marcus J. noticed she had exceptionally long fingers encrusted with emerald and sapphire rings. She looked up at him and nodded as she turned back to the fountain, calling her little ones to the feast.

Ice Cream for Small Plants. Since sixty per cent of ice cream is water, the texture is governed by the manner in which this water content is converted into crystals. Freezing begins in the freezer and continues in the hardening room.

Marcus J. entertained the sense that someone might have recommended this spot to him. The woman with long fingers fed her grandchildren and shooed unwanted guests away. Her rings scraped against the cardboard of the ice cream tubs. Marcus J. went inside the bookshop. It was heavy with the must of rotting leather, damp paper and mouldering parchment. Books putrefying in the air, the embers of lost cultures, the decaying remains of other people's energies, shelf after shelf filled with undiscovered lives in unassuming bindings. He felt sure this was the place. He was certain his book was here.

Marcus J. browsed the shelves. He squinted through the narrow gap between Numerology and Computers and then he saw her. He thrust one hand defensively into the front pocket of his jeans. The assistant, queen of this mausoleum, was talking on the telephone, bent over the desk, tracing down a page with a long finger, reading out details of catalogue entries. All Marcus J. could see were the dark roots of her hair, belying the fact that her blond tresses were dyed. When she looked up for a moment he saw her eyes, but she turned away quickly and he could not register the colour.

'Yes, I have one, *Ice Cream for Small Plants* by Etta H. Handy, Chicago 1937, never reprinted.' Her low voice sounded faintly disdainful. Marcus J.'s jaw tightened. It was as if someone had unexpectedly put his skull on the chopping block and asked the price. There was a pause. 'No? Not interested? OK, thank you for the request. Please call again soon.' She sighed heavily and replaced the mouthpiece on to its emerald locust handset. It was a weird apparatus, shaped like two creatures frozen into some ecstatic contortion of the sex act. Marcus J. slumped against the shelf.

Ice cream cones split lengthwise are used for decorative treatment, but may also be consumed. The molds of small figures can be added, if desired, for special occasions. The pattern and arrangement is designed by the chef and executed by an assistant under instruction.

'Can I help you at all?' Her voice had a faintly Germanic tone.

'I was looking for a book.'

'And in which book were you interested, sir?'

'Well I'm just looking. You have a fascinating selection. What a mixture!'

'We don't discriminate on any grounds.' Her eyes opened wider. 'If there is some sort of home in the neighbourhood for the poor darlings then this is probably it. Now what kind of subjects do you particularly like, what flavours?'

'No, really, I'm just browsing.'

'Well, when you know what you want I will help you.' Normally this would have driven Marcus J. out of the shop immediately. This time something was holding him back.

The sheets and pillows are made with vanilla ice cream. The hearts are made by laying strawberry in one side of the mold and vanilla in the other side.

Marcus J.'s hand strayed to his mouth, searching around his lips as if he had lost something. The assistant, her chin on her fist, looked past him. He adjusted the shoulders of his sleeveless jacket, the edge of the cold zipper scratching at his arms. On the shelf behind where she sat were a cluster of New Year cards, filled with traditional wishes: 'May You Be Inscribed in the Book of Happy Life', 'May You Be Inscribed in the Book of Merit'. She gazed at him, piteously.

'I have a special reserve section which might be of interest. Are you a collector?'

'No, I'm not a collector, no. But which titles are held in special reserve?'

'All sorts, for all kinds of reasons.' She played with her hair, a little reluctant, a little coy. 'Orders from customers who have yet to collect. Illustrated volumes of explicit content. Personal or emotional collections of individual interest only.' She glanced up at him knowingly. There was a pause while she searched for the right example to convey what she meant.

'One woman came to us and ordered an entire collection of poetical works to be sent to her in Dubrovnik. I think they were her father's. If we could find them she was willing to pay handsomely. Well we did find them. It took us fifteen years, but we found a complete set. They were Morocco bound. Only now I have lost her. There was a telephone number and a fax number. She left them with us, but I can't get any response. I have the father but I've lost the daughter. It's often the way in this country.' She hugged a pale hand around her bare shoulder. 'We find fragments, but as fast as we gather them together so they fall apart in different places. What can you do? I lost my father too. I've put that collection on special reserve. Perhaps one day she'll contact me to collect it.' There was an air of resignation in her voice now, although she seemed to get more familiar the more she spoke, as if she knew better than him why he was there.

The glowing crystal bowl is usually carried to the table with the dining room darkened so that the illuminated ice shows to its full advantage.

'Well, please do show me then,' he said quietly. She stood up from the desk and for the first time he saw her properly. She wore a shiny blue silk skirt, narrow as a pencil, clasped high at the waist with an emerald dragon breathing a fan of gold fire. Her white cotton sleeveless blouse was thin and almost transparent. It opened deep at her neck, which was hung with a glowing string of scarlet amulets. They curved like a wave across her breasts. Her face was oval and her skin had a pale olive sheen. She stepped across the shop and closed the front door. As she quietly turned the old-fashioned latch and it locked Marcus J. noticed she had unusually long fingers adorned with emerald and sapphire rings.

Heat shocks of any kind or sudden changes in temperature during the hardening process are likely to cause sandiness. Such moves should therefore be avoided in order to achieve the best textures.

I'd monkeyed with *Tarzan of the Apes*. By cutting through the pages, barring a narrow outside border, I had removed the text and replaced it with a lead ingot. The book now weighed a ton. I would enquire of an un-suspecting friend, 'Have you read this?' Their knuckles grazed the floor like Cheeta's. No Tarzans they.

(LES COLEMAN)

'Follow me. Come through here.' She led Marcus J. through a small archway into the back of the shop where there was another room like an office. The walls were lined with overflowing shelves and there were several desks piled high with bundles of volumes all tied together. 'Some are waiting to be unpacked, others are waiting to be sent away,' she said, airily waving her bare arm at them. At the back of the room, on a wooden mantel shelf, was a sculpture of a naked woman with a naked child on her lap, both leaning over an open book. The hands of the child merged and became one with the covers of the book. The woman had wings folded over her back, but no halo. To one side of the mantel shelf was another door and the assistant bent slightly to unlock it. Then she beckoned him inside.

Beat the mixture when it is hot and cooking, fold in the flavor or liqueur and add three quarts whipped cream for stiffness.

The only light came from a candle burning in a brass holder moulded in the shape of a fist. The floor was covered in the deep scarlets and vermilions of a Persian carpet and the walls were hung with gold-framed mirrors. Their infinitely receding images reflected back at them at every turn, heightening their awareness of the other's movements. All they could hear was the sound of their breathing. He could feel the warmth of her breath and of her skin. She could see the glow of perspiration on his forehead, the aura of heat that radiated off him. He could see the full form of her breasts, shifting slightly beneath the thin cotton of her blouse. She stood in front of him, facing him, saying nothing. He looked into her eyes and she stretched out her arms to him. As she touched his skin she seemed to become smoother and softer, like silk and cream. He waited for the next movement, trembling slightly. She was not aggressive but she asserted herself over him completely. 'I have been looking for you,' she whispered, 'for a long time. I had an order.'

Line the two halves of a cylindrical mold and cover with a film of cream for bonding. Then put in a layer of cranberry on top of that. Ensure that the adhesion of both parts is complete by stirring a slight ripple between the two layers.

She took a step back, looking disdainfully at him. Then he saw she was holding a book in her hands. She offered it. He lurched forward to take it but she pulled it away and he fell down on the carpet like a drunk.

The mixture should be treated with care at all times and on no account shaken or stirred after forming has begun.

'Be careful, you might lose your balance,' she whispered. She stood in front of him, her blouse open wide, cradling the book between her breasts. He opened his mouth to speak but she put her finger to his lips, stroking her silky skin across his. She opened the book and took him in her arms. They sank down together into the warmth of the stitching, huddled in the tight embrace of the margins. The endpapers closed over him. 'Some are waiting to be unpacked. Others are waiting to be sent away,' she murmured.

In the park on the other side of the street the children were tired of playing in the fountain. Ice creams had melted, sodas had been drunk. The small plump woman in the Chanel suit called in her brood, wiping her long fingers and theirs with a Kleenex. She propelled them along the street, laughing and chuckling with them. The shop assistant smiled as she came back to the door and turned the Open sign to Closed. 'Good night, Etta!' She waved and the old woman turned and waved back. Their emerald and sapphire rings glinted in the evening sun.

Ice Cream Couple Fantasy: a novelty service of ice cream and cake. The male figure is ice cream, chocolate on the top and vanilla for the stem, with a body of red marzipan. The female form is of cake and meringue. The breasts are made of petit fours and glacé cherries, her mouth and nose are outlined in a paler, pink marzipan, the eyes are of fresh mint leaves.

On a fine summer's morning in 1937, in the crowded marble foyer of the Edgewater Beach Hotel, Chicago, Mr Korp, the catering manager, stood chatting to his colleagues Baltera, the chef, and Conrad Springer, the pastry chef. 'Look, there she goes, our patron!' Korp whispered excitedly. A small plump woman in a Chanel suit strode towards the swing doors, wiping her hands with a handkerchief. Her long fingers were encrusted with emerald and sapphire rings that clattered against the glass.

'Who are you talking about?' Baltera was bored.

'Etta Handy, the famous writer! Haven't you seen her latest? We're in it. Our Ice Cream Couple Fantasy is featured. They finally published it. The Hotel Monthly Press.' Korp waved the book excitedly under their noses. 'Yeah?' sniffed Springer, putting a cigarette out under the toe of his boot. 'Let me see that!' Baltera grabbed the book from Korp's hand and read from the title page, '*Ice Cream for Small Plants*, by Etta H. Handy. How it can be made economically in the small plant, as in a self-contained hotel, or a restaurant, tea room, soda fountain, or similar organization, where it can be produced in wide variety under wholesome and hygienic conditions. Plate One: Ice Cream Couple Fantasy as made at the Edge-water Beach Hotel, Chicago.'

'Well, I'll be damned,' Conrad Springer spat defiantly. 'Fame at last.'

(JEREMY SILVER)

Winnowing out the Words

I was born into a numerous family that loved books, kept them about the family rooms and did not bother much who read them. One of my aunts had been a teacher and was familiar with books. She liked to see us reading. We lived in a small village with mangrove trees and a wide sandy beach between the river and the houses on the eastern side. The main road divided the two rows of houses which were the village. The road flaunted its dust and debris like Sunday clothes. There was a lot of coming and going to exchange books and magazines, catalogues and religious tracts. A bookseller visited our village once a month.

My cousin Sydney taught me to read from *The Royal Reader Bk I.* Nobody said Book I. The series was a popular set of colonial readers, featuring all things English. They were 'Mother Country' or 'from home' books. I saw my first picture of a daffodil in *Bk I* and rode my cock horse, whatever that was, to Banbury Cross by way of it. I also met vowel *a*, found in 'hay' and illustrated by what looked like blackened grass. To my three-year-old mind *a* was tucked in a bundle of black grass.

I flew through the books and soon began to scrutinize 'grown-up' books. Whoa! What wonders awaited me! John Galsworthy and *The Forsyte Saga*, *To Let* and *In Chancery*. What did they all mean? Then I recalled the Swagger Boys, or Sagga Boys, of our society, whom all respectable people vilified for being 'rude' and reckless. Perhaps they were related, who knew?

I graduated to the Sir Walter Scott section: *Kenilworth* was first. I remember my shock at discovering that it was a house. Why give a castle a name? And then *The Fortunes of . . .* who? Niggel, Nig-el, *Nigel.* Hard *g*, until I heard the name in Britain. My friends had familiar 'Mother Country' names: Wadsworth after Wordsworth, Rudyard after racist Kipling and Alexander after Pope. My middle name, Agatha, celebrated Agatha Christie.

Some words, though, continued to perplex me: words like 'jousting' 'tournament', 'drawbridge' and 'façade'. I hadn't a clue about the first two aliens, but drawbridge had a familiar ring. I had seen my Gran ironing her drawers, all lacy, cloud white and long-legged. They looked so extraordinary I asked her to spell 'drawers'. It began 'draw', so drawbridge must be related to underwear. My aunt had always said to move from what is known to what is not. Façade – 'fackade' to me – ended like lemonade, so straightaway I knew it was a drink, probably one that hadn't reached us yet in the colonies.

The struggle went on. Words, text, meaning thumped me soundly, and failed to match the idioms, images and metaphors of my own cognitive heritage. One day I read 'her auburn hair flowing out into the winds, roaring behind her.' What did that mean? We all had tight curly hair; and black. What was 'auburn', then? Oh those books! Perhaps the big people knew, but I did not ask them. I settled for Aesop, not knowing he had been an enslaved African in days of yore. I read the moral at the end of 'The Dog and the Bone': 'A greedy dog loses both the shadow and the substance.' I asked what that meant. 'Big yeye mek puppy drop he dinnah,' replied my grandmother. 'Oh,' I beamed, text and insight precisely in place.

I discovered travel books: *Gulliver's Travels* and *Travels in Tartary*. My cousin snatched the former and left me with the latter. The words were strange to a five year old, but I had a go. I read 'From the tatrutted, no, the turited – turret-ed – walls, we looked south-south-east and tow-ards – to-wards – the den-se-ly wounded, wondoed – wooded – mo-untains.' 'Ha, ha, ha,' my cousin laughed. 'We sing about mountains in church and you don't know it. Remember "From Greenland's Icy Mountains"?' 'No I don't,' I barked. He continued to laugh. But it was an interesting book with really long words you could put sounds to. I continued to read it. I used to sneak up behind my lesser cousins and tickle them and yell 'menagerie!' and 'ruminant!' and phrases like 'forestalling lunch' or 'ricocheting across the hills'. Such fun until someone got fed up and silenced me.

All of us loved animals and used to capture small ones and watch them and listen for their sounds. My cousin loved toads and kept a pet one. It sat quite still while we fed it, its tongue so quick it could hardly be seen in motion. But its little throat pulsated as if another patient heart prayed for nightfall. Before uttering its sound it would come alive bit by bit, and then croak, indifferently at first, then with great intensity. I heard other sounds too. The river roared in the distance or sometimes came close enough to splash with its foam the wall separating it from the houses. On occasions logs floated down to the sawmills, clanging and clashing against one another like giant castanets. And I could often hear coconuts falling as the rough winds nudged them to the ground. I wrote, and signed it Anonymous:

Hear de coconut fall down, Gal
Hear de coconut fall.
The palm tree grow so long, so tall
Bup, bup, de coconut fall.

And then someone lent me *Rip Van Winkle and the Legend of Sleepy Hollow*. Somewhere within the dense print I came across two fascinating words, the first being 'malady', which I boldly read as 'Ma-Lady' – easy to understand. Is not 'Ma' a name for one's mother or grandmother? And a 'Lady'? Well, she does no housework and leaves it all to the menials. I was so certain of the meaning of the word that I wrote it in chalk on the hen house in 'mother tongue'. Our priest came to visit and, calling me over, asked me what the word on the fowl coop meant. I was affronted. I looked at him closely. He wore sandals that showed his fat, stubby toes. Like them the hem of his black cassock had an irregular fringe of dust. There were little tears of sweat on his large red nose and his hair lay in broad and narrow lines on his forehead. He looked a sweaty mess from chasing souls in the heat of the day. I told him, 'An old white mother who has servants to cook for her.' 'How did you arrive at that?' he asked incredulously. I told him and he began to laugh. First the laughter came in little gusts; then it grew larger, stronger; and then it took him over, causing him to shiver and shake like a blancmange, bellowing and shrieking in turn. All my family joined in, especially one of my older cousins who saw me as her pet 'peeve'. I had simply gone from the known to the unknown. I was so ashamed I cried.

That same day my grandfather bought me a *Collins Gem Dictionary*. No one showed me how it worked, but by trial and error and sheer determination I prised open its heart. I found out I could not be anonymous to myself. And that 'apparition', my second word, meant a ghost. As for ghosts, I knew them! A whole nation of them frisked about our world: as the common and ubiquitous grave-yard 'jumbies'; and as zombies or walking dead, drugged, buried and resurrected by the spirit mediums. At last I had a source of meanings, and my adoration of diction-aries as founts of knowledge began. I have shelves of dictionaries. I continually update them, and when I write I am surrounded by them as though they are faithful dogs guarding a fragile intellect. Of all the books there are I love my 'dickies' best and wish I could learn all the words in the world by feasting daily upon them, so many words with each mouthful. I've found I must rush out of shops that sell dictionaries while I hang on to my purse.

Only text remained illusive. I heard talk of other known village apparitions, those that lurked in the crev-ices of our atavistic past. The old women told me of

Chick Charnies, sea robbers who dressed in weird bird masks and lured ships to destruction, killing the sailors and keeping the booty; of mermaids who charmed eager suitors with their songs, and of mermen who braved pebbly shores to woo village maidens; of Massa Kruman, who lifted slave ships into the air and threw them on to dry land to the Cane Men who led the wretched slaves to safety among the canes, while Massa Kruman himself grew bigger and stronger by swallowing the strength of friend and foe alike. Then there were apparitions of the high bush: spiteful Bacroos; hot-headed Dopis; Moonlight Babies whom only the blessed could hear, but nimble enough to jump on the backs of the evil ones and to grow heavier with each passing day. The oldest women talked of Cabresses or women of easy virtue; of Ole Higes who became vampires; of Sand Dopis; Spraggots; and Moon Gazers who lived on the sandy beach and played ring-a-roses there when the moon was full. Last of all were the Dream Walkers who led the dying back to Africa, where they became froth and foam and decorated the mighty rollers of the ocean.

During the diaspora language was lost to our forebears. With this loss went the heritage of fantasy, mythology and the folk imagery of a captive people's culture. Only the echoes, dispersed and indistinct, remained, echoes of experiences like dreams, dance and music as the voices of time, art as spacial reorganization and poetry as a song from the heart. Gesture supported illusive language but soon became language in its own right to provide cohesion and kinship. The dream, the dance, the songs of the heart kept our forebears sane in slavery. Today, along with language, they form a core of identity. They say, 'I know'.

(BERYL GILROY)

Muslim Soup

For some traditional West African societies printed memory in the form of records or books is considered unnatural, even abhorrent. The positive and negative powers of living things, including thoughts, memories and historical events, are understood as embodied in words but, transferred in written form, are seen as trapped in an undesirable state of rigidity and permanence, a state contrary to life. The recording of negative experiences is considered particularly unhealthy and potentially dangerous.

In certain instances, though, the powers harnessed in written words may be perceived as beneficial, and a nonliterate people will sometimes borrow a literate society's script for specific purposes. The Nafana of northwestern Ghana, a nonliterate group familiar with the customs of, and in close contact with, their Muslim neighbours, the Mande, are such an example. Part of the cultural exchange between the Nafana and the Mande is the use of Arabic script by the Nafana, in the form of written charms and verses from the Koran. Although the Nafana do not share the Mande's religious beliefs, the power of Islamic magical and holy words is recognized and highly respected. The royal regalia of the Nafana king commonly have a variety of Muslim amulets attached to them, usually cabbalistic signs or Koranic verses written on scraps of paper, which are believed to protect the objects as well as the king or any other member of the court who might come into contact with them. Important ritual and social areas may also be fortified by the placement of similar talismans in strategic spots, such as entrances, corners or other potentially vulnerable boundaries. For especially significant ritual festivals the king will appear in a special white cloth covered with Arabic letters and signs.

The efficacy of these Islamic charms, adopted by the Nafana from the Mande, extends from the public to the private. As a personal preventive and curative, the power contained in written cabbalistic signs and Koranic verses may be transformed and condensed into a more potent liquid form known as *siliama-gue,* or 'Muslim soup'. This 'soup' consists of special roots and herbs steeped in the water used in washing Islamic writing slates or chalkboards. Like the amulets, the tonic made from water used to wash boards with Koranic verses on them is believed to be the strongest, the degree of strength determined by the degree of learning attained by the individual writing the verses. As a kind of holy water 'Muslim soup' may be sprinkled on to an individual for protection but is considered much more effective when drunk. The claimed success of this apotropaic beverage extends even to invulnerability to gunfire.

The transformation and condensation of the power of Islamic and holy writings into liquid form represent, in a sense, the end phase of a cyclic process. If the power of any word may truly be said to lie in its origin in abstract thought, then this power, once transformed into literal form, must necessarily be somewhat diminished. From this point of view the release of a word from a stable written form to an impermanent liquid state may be understood as restorative. 'Muslim soup' is a method of preparation in which the power of the word is physically freed: it is the word returned to thought.

(TINA OLDKNOW)

Aye

Waiting for my turn to come up on the pool table, I'm sitting in the bar reading. The Irishman at the next table says, 'What's the book?' '*Melmoth The Wanderer.*' 'Is it a good book?' 'It's a very good book.' 'What's it about?' I describe the first few chapters wherein young John Melmoth is called from Trinity College, Dublin, to inherit the family seat in County Wicklow and is then haunted by an ancestor, Melmoth The Wanderer, who has sold his soul to the devil in return for prolonged life. My neighbour sinks his Guinness, and after a long pause says, 'Aye, they're all fucking wanderers in Wicklow.'

(IAN BREAKWELL)

Cover to Cover

Next door
Next door but one.
Found in dust
buried in its own history.
Going back fifty years.
Alongside crosses, bicycle pumps, bric-à-brac,
Catholic keepsakes, walking sticks and crutches,
these string-tied rent books, weekly tallies, dues paid
year in, year out, a record, a file, a history,
an account, landlord and tenant.

Nigel Rolfe's 'Cover to Cover'. Photo: Stuart Smyth

Gaoler's terrace, Wicklow granite, three foot thick,
underground, in the shadow of where James Connolly
died, you could hear the shots from here.
Separate houses, secretly joined, bring them in one door
and out the other.
Next door.
Next door but one.

(NIGEL ROLFE)

Dublin

Between teasing the horsehair and beating the flock
that will go into the chairs and mattresses he is uphol-
stering, my grandfather is showing me the smoky black
and white illustrations of the Seven Wonders of the
World in Harmsworth's *History of the World.* The Pyramids of Egypt, the Hanging Gardens of Babylon, the
Colossus of Rhodes, the Pharos Lighthouse at Alexandria, the Statue of Zeus at Olympia, the Temple of
Artemis at Ephesus, the Mausoleum at Halicarnassus:
he says their names and I repeat them, looking at the
pictures.

'Wonderful achievements, son, the highest aims of
civilization,' he tells me as the dust from the horsehair
settles easily around the room and into our lungs.
'Imagine thousands, no, millions of men working day
and night. Slaves they had in those days. Lashed into it
for the most part. Only the pyramids remain to this
day.'

He blows his nose and surveys the unfinished armchair
frames, the empty mattress covers, the heap of teased,
and the bigger block of unteased, horsehair lying around
the room. 'Wonderful achievements, right enough. You
can learn from these things.' He clears his throat. 'Look.
Your grandfather's just going across the road to Doyle's.
I'll be back in no time.'

He leaves me there in the ruins with the book and

the small bow and arrow he had made me for my birthday.

The first book we had in the Grantham Street School for Mixed Infants was the small green catechism which we couldn't read. We rapped out the text in a miniature singalong that was all form and no content.

Q: Who made the world?

A: God made the world.

Don't, won't; neighbour, labour; good, should; lost, cost; hell, fell; callen, fallen; must, just; saviour, behaviour. The rest of the book clipped along in this way until finally we got to die then the sky with the crowds in the clouds. Bliss this. It was not until I got to Synge Street Primary School for Boys that we got the big salmon-coloured catechism, which we could read.

Your man: The sixth precept of the Church? You.

Me: Sixth, not to solemnize marriage at the forbidden times nor to marry persons within the forbidden degrees of kindred nor otherwise prohibited by the Church nor clandestinely.

He sensed that I sensed that the world might indeed be something to look forward to. *Clandestinely.* He hit me because of the way I looked at him after I gave the answer.

Going up to receive the prize I shook the guest's hand as required. He fixed me with a benign gaze and spoke some empty words. I twisted my face into an appropriate expression. As his eyes fell on the title his face flushed. 'Did you ask for this?' 'Yes.' 'Good God,' he muttered, staring perplexedly into the fascinating vacancy of space behind me.

(TIMOTHY EMLYN JONES)

Mr Madison ran the grocery shop at Leonard's Corner. Mr Madison was from the country and he had a brisk, patronizing way with Dubliners. I was on my way to Kevin Street Library to return *Oil!* by Upton Sinclair. As Mr Madison wrapped my pound of butter he noticed the book under my arm.

'What are you reading?' said Mr Madison.

'*Oil!,*' I said.

'What's that about?' asked Mr Madison.

He paused a moment to note my dumb bafflement then pressed on to the next customer. 'A pound of tomatoes? Right, ma'am,' said Mr Madison, brightly closing the subject.

To this day I rethink that moment and I hear myself

saying: 'It says *Oil!* on the cover Mr Madison, it's about fuckin' oil! What did you think it might be about, you stupid fuckin' money-grubbing gombeen man?' Or I seize the moment to give a crystal-clear summary of Sinclair's analysis of capitalism in general and of corporate America in particular. This is so spellbinding and convincing that Mr Madison and the shop full of customers throw away their possessions and follow me to the American embassy in Ballsbridge, which we all set on fire.

In the event I said nothing.

(NOEL SHERIDAN)

American Girl Meets China Boy

Let me tell you a story my grandfather told me – and he told it only once, remarkable enough given the habit of oral historical telling and retelling of family tales – a story concerning his father.

My great-grandfather was a diamond cutter in London, raised in Amsterdam where he married and had three children, my grandfather among them. I know a fair amount of this history – remarkable enough given the habit of Jews to wander – but Napoleon gave nomenclature in the Netherlands a kick in the ass in 1811 and the Dutch are prodigious record keepers anyway. To trace the deepest roots of this tree requires a knowledge of Hebrew or the knowledge of someone with a knowledge of Hebrew so unless I win the lottery, which seems unlikely since I never buy a ticket, it will have to remain another of life's great unknowns. At any rate, here's the story. When my grandfather was a child he would wait outside the diamond factory doors at the end of the day and when they would open he'd scan the group of men emerging, looking for one particular, thin frame, one full, dark moustache, both belonging to his father. Once spotted, he would slip his small, boy's hand – remarkable enough given the habit of small boys to grow into grandfathers – inside the safety of this adult's large, male grip and they would stroll home together over canals and cobblestones, in early evening light or winter darkness, exchanging utterances in the guttural, rough musicality of the Lowlands. That's reminiscence. You recognize it by the uniform patina of its surface, its highly polished warm glow. Memory is different. It's full of dents, holes, scratches, faults.

Childhood is always in the grip of adults, one way or another. Primary experience is merged from the beginning, our memories a collage. My mother, Judith, wanted to be a paediatric nurse but desire collided with the Great Depression and the small-minded, leaving her permanently bruised. She's not much of a fighter. The Dutch aunts and uncles who'd come to the States, as my grandparents had, suggested, 'Judy should be sent to a trade school. People with Ph.D.s are working downstairs in Gimbel's department store.' All those doctoral-wielding human beings in the basement; if you could afford to shop, the service must have been outstanding. Then, my grandmother herself said, 'Judy, you're too good to be emptying bedpans.' Infants don't use bedpans, but logic is often not people's strong suit, transference is. My mother's hopes were robbed in two directions, one an inside job. She ended up wiping shit off my grandmother in later years and no objections were raised. Judy always did as she was told.

My mother won the Theodore Roosevelt Medal for History and was voted Best Dressed in Girl's Commercial High School. It says so in our yearbook. Did I say our? Must have been a slip, but those hardbound pages, only slightly preceded in time and impact by the Brothers Grimm, the Christian, Hans Andersen, the Pooh, Winnie, and the like, revealed themselves to have a more specific and lasting influence. It was the yearbook and its implications which aided in an early rebellion against placing others' decisions about my life above my own, that makes me prickly to live with if I feel the time taken up by either the buoyancy or the encumbrance of love interferes too much with what I wish to do, that is, work, that is, most often. The yearbook whipped me into disciplined shape at a young age. If life stopped at eighteen, as my mother's had, I wanted no part of it. If the life that someone else designed for you led you to feel cheated and angry for the rest of yours, no thank you. If my mother thought I just might mother in turn, or was content to have me hang around and keep her company, and my father pictured me with a law degree, those were too many hearts and fingers in my pie. Never underestimate the power of a yearbook to take hold of the imagination, to make you think about being thwarted, defeated, to keep desire fluid, haemorrhaging, coursing until you don't breathe anymore.

If my mother couldn't be a paediatric nurse she found her own way to remedy the situation. She had four children, a mini-nursery of her own. I was the first. I think one of the reasons I'm aroused by reading and writing was the sensuality of hearing stories in an otherwise noiseless room, the closeness of her physical presence. She married my father because she liked the way his hands looked on the steering wheel of a car and she knew her children would be guaranteed nice noses, read: not large, hooked, awful Semitic noses. Her own was fine. No trace of Shylock there. No trace of the Jew. Whew! So far so good, and this man would do the rest. This successful experiment in hookless, straight-bridged perfection arrived eleven months after they were married, my mother eighteen, my father twenty-one. Not many years after, the yearbook entered my experience. The young women in it, none of whom I ever met, became real to me. There was Iris Jankowitz, beautiful but who, I was told, walked with a terrible limp. Poor Iris. There was Lucie R. De Gennaro, Zoera Velys, Joan Robertson, and Claire Haggerty, Class Beauty, also by vote. I knew them intimately, the way men know women or other men in porn magazines. I knew them through my mother's eyes, eyes that viewed other women distrustfully, eyes in a face which smiled and appeared warm but hid fear, and an eventual martyr's grimace. These were stories at a safe remove, distanced impressions, remnants, judgements of the nice girls, the tramps, the fat ones, the skinny ones, the freckled and acned ones.

The yearbook played a role with men, too. When she would bring it out and see herself as she'd only recently been – single – she'd talk about the young men she'd dated, and her regret at marrying so young was evident in a general way, her disillusionment that it was my father quite specific. The yearbook was the end of dreams and, somehow, so was I. On and on it went, a still young woman living firmly in an only just past, the seduction of a voice in a quiet room drawing me into her story, the closeness, my worship, the comfort, the abundant chestnut hair and soft, brown eyes. On and on. The joy of recounting mixed with distress, as though she had been the victim of an accident or crime in which she had no hand. No one else had listened with so much attention to her desires, taken them so seriously, I'm certain. As her confidante I felt compelled to put it right. The Best Dressed girl in Girl's Commercial deserved better, I tell *From Judith Alexander's* you. Child to the rescue, a double-whammy with a half-*high school yearbook* twisted reversal coming too early to be recognized, her

needs too furtive, like not perceiving the alcoholic in the room because everyone at the party is drunk. Hard to know what anything is, what love is, hard to discern a clear image when it's so near to the bone, pressed, however gently, right up against your face.

Finally, there was the poem:

'China Boy'

You caught my pity from the first,
   Your hands, your helpless stare,
And, 'though you never said a word,
   I read your story there.

Your tangled hair, your dingy rags,
   Your swollen feet that bore
The hungry form, the aged face
   That showed the hurt of war.

And as I bent and saw you near,
   I found your cheeks were wet;
I wanted to replace your loss,
   To help you to forget.

I picked you up and held you close;
   I touched your troubled head;
And as I prayed, I hoped you knew,
   Although I'd found you dead.

Evelyn Fischer

I would say that this execrable piece-a' verse offended my sensibilities as a born aesthete but let's be real. We harbour many dirty secrets, among them an attachment to some painting, piece of writing or music that every critical faculty we now possess admits is pure crap. Call it reminiscence or nostalgia. Call it the demands of your own need to make distinctions, to separate. The last line of this poem from a yearbook was rough stuff for this child at that time. It was also the first instantly memorable verbatim explosion of the written word on an unsuspecting, unsophisticated book-loving intellect, on not yet armoured emotions.

I called Judith to ask her to xerox some pages for me from her yearbook.

'Yearbook?'

'Yes, Mom, your high school yearbook. I need some stuff from it, including the poem.'

'Poem?'

I quoted some lines. Later, she called my sister to say, 'Elena has such an amazing memory. Do you know she remembered my yearbook, and even lines from a poem?'

It only hurts when I rant. Memory, full of faults, dents, scratches, gripes and love. This is for Judy who always did as she was told. At the time when hers was the only voice in a room, her yearbook was only another page in her story and she was happy to have a friend to read to. It wouldn't have occurred to her that when leaves are stuck together the only way to see what's inside is to tear them apart.

(ELENA ALEXANDER)

Only Women Do

I can't bear the silence. Living round here is like being buried alive. Apart from when the schools go past. Noisy of a morning. You couldn't lie in bed. I would be very bored and depressed if I didn't keep busy. I still get lonely, but you can't alter life.

I love reading, but once again it would stop me getting on with things. If I pick something up I *must* read it. There are so many things I would like to have time to do. No one can have it all ways. I just grab bits of what I can. Everyone is too busy or has other reasons for not visiting.

I stopped going to the library because I couldn't get the books. Catherine Cookson. She is ill now too so when her books run out I will have to think of something else. I have to always have a book on the go. Mostly at bedtime. While my husband has that last cigarette. I think it is good for him to have a bit of peace anyway. He is never on his own.

I have always had loads of books. Unfortunately, and I deeply regret it over and over again, I gave most of my books away when we moved here from Liverpool. Never thought I'd have children of my own. When I think of all those lovely stories my family could have read. I still have some very old books of my father's and his old aunt's. Some of which I have not read yet myself. Now the proud owner of a whole shelf of Catherine Cookson. Won't part. You can't get them in the library.

My house is full of things I want to do and can't get round to. Oddtimes I have read until my back aches and I am stiff all over. Sometimes I wonder how I had the time. Usually I read while my nail varnish dries before our one and only night out of the week. It helps me keep my patience with my husband. He is one of those who likes to keep the wife as the underdog. He knows I couldn't possibly go out on my own. I have had to blackmail my husband into taking me out. After eighteen years of not. Still trying to get him to take me out for drives in the country. Haven't made it yet but won't give up. Meanwhile every week he used to upset me pretending we weren't going out. My reading has done the trick.

I read in the dentist's but the doctor's you have to watch your turn. The receptionists are a bit spiteful nowadays. Once they crossed me off. Now they won't get the chance. One book I bought at a Brownie sale was very good. Not easy to read. Very old. If I am stuck I will read anything and everything. Even the most difficult usually end up good in the end. Curiosity usually wins through. Also it is amazing what you learn out of books. Time flies too quick. I should be doing things now. Everyone deserves a rest. Some things are too interesting. We all must do our bit. I must go and catch up. I wouldn't buy books on cars or machinery. I can't abide tools and bits and pieces. Can't type. Hate machinery. Noisy things too.

Since getting married I had to give up reading except for holidays. Until one day. After years and years of trouble with my in-laws. When the final straw came. A few days before my older daughter's wedding. Four and a half years ago. I have not been to my husband's parents' house since. Not after what was said to me in that house. I joined the library. Read all Saturday afternoons. While my husband watched sport in the other room. Now it is just part of everyday life. Among other pleasures I have since made time for.

When I was first at school I could not read. I found it very difficult. As also I did with first learning to knit. A year to make a six-inch-square dishcloth. The others were on to tea cosies. The teacher had me out by her desk all the time. It was very hard. I used to cry a lot. At home my dad used to batter me. Even when I was older he used to shout a lot, and write words which I could not spell on our living room wall in big letters. I remember once feeling very upset and ashamed because he had me write a big long article. In my best handwriting. For a competition in the Sunday paper. I hated every minute and it was all lies you see. Mum always battered us if we told a lie and dad went on for hours. Didn't matter how long we cried or got shut in our rooms for punishment. Dad was suffering from something through not being allowed in the Army. Bad heart. It must have affected his brain. His best friend was a quartermaster. In the Desert Rats. Dad was always reading SS stories and watched police stories of interrogation. He went on at me for hours. What time was it? Where were you? Or whatever the subject was. He just went on. Even mum used to stand crying, too scared to stop him.

This writing, when I was only very young you see, was not just very hard to do. It was all lies. Mum and dad used to belong to a cycling club. The article was all saying it was me. I was in the club and it was all about me cycling.

I noticed my copy of *Vile Bodies* was missing from my room. I made a fuss, until my mother handed it back to me saying she had found it in the drawer of my father's bedside table. It must have sorely disappointed him. Finally at breakfast one day he turned to me with a studiously casual air and said, 'Who *is* this woman, Evelyn Waugh?'

(JOHN GUEST)

Now you think is it any wonder what happened when I was at school? He sent me crying to the second chance of going to grammar school. Verbal exam. I just said very few words. I don't like reading. Didn't answer the Head when sent for. Ended my school days in trouble. Crying all the time. Nearly walked under a bus at fifteen years old. Just saw my mother with my six-year-old brother on the other side of the road. Stopped me. Never could leave my little brother. Being so much younger than me. I had helped look after him a lot. He was always catching one childish ailment or other. Much worse than my other brother.

Both my daughters love reading. The son never touches a book. Then he always did copy his dad. When he could. Perhaps he thinks men don't read. Only women do.

(ELLESMERE PORT HOUSEWIFE)

Tit for Tat

Oh, you get them all round here. Carol singers at Christmas, Famine Relief, Soap for the Blind, sponsored swims, sponsored mini marathons, there was even a lad knocked at the door collecting signatures to do a sponsored free-fall parachute jump from 10,000 feet for the mentally handicapped. I said to him certainly not young man, it must be you who's mentally handicapped, you'll probably break your neck and I want nothing to do with it, I'd have it on my conscience for ever after. And only yesterday the doorbell rang just as I was in the middle of cleaning the oven, a messy job at the best of times. At the door were these two smiling men in suits.

'Good morning. We would like to talk to you about a very important book.'

'And what would that be now?'

'The greatest story ever told. The Bible. We would

The Word of God writ small. Photo: Don Rutledge © Camera Press

like to share your thoughts about this book, if you have any madam.'

'Indeed I do. I think throughout the centuries this particular book has had a significant and predominantly baleful effect on millions of people's thoughts and behaviour, and has been a major cause of bigotry, intolerance and repression, resulting in draconian legal statutes, puritanical moral codes, censorship, sexual misery, hypocrisy, guilt and mental illness, sectarian strife, civil war, colonial invasion, persecution, forcible indoctrination, torture, bloodshed and genocide, all fomented by the same self-righteous missionary zeal which you now display on my doorstep. And now, if you don't mind, I must get on with my housework, and the devil only knows how I'll get it done if I stand here talking all morning, so I'll bid you good day.'

Well, I think 'gobsmacked' is the phrase they use nowadays, isn't it? They backed nervously down the steps and I watched them through the net curtain as they went out the front gate. One crossed himself and the other twisted his finger against his forehead. But I don't care, that's the marvellous thing about book learning, you can answer them back.

(FRIDA STAMP)

Prophet and Loss

To: Compendium Books
    234 Camden High Street
    London NW1 8QS

For when ye were the servants of sin, ye were free from righteousness. What fruit had ye then in those things whereof ye are now ashamed? for the end of those things is death. But now being made free from sin, and become servants to God, ye have your fruit unto holiness, and the end everlasting life. For the wages of sin is death; but the gift of God is eternal life through Jesus Christ our Lord.
Romans 6. 20–23

Ladies and Gentlemen,
    I want to confess to you that, during a stay in Great Britain in 1978–9, I stole paperback books from your shop.
    I was, then, an 'alternative' student who was looking for 'enlightenment' and a meaningful, fulfilled life. I tried to find it in eastern religion and New Age philosophy, even in the occult literature that your bookshop propagates. I was living in the darkness of sin, and I was looking and searching into the darkness of those teachings which seemed, then, to be light to me. I bought quite a few books in your shop, and it didn't seem wrong for me to steal one or two as 'profit compensation'.
    After long years of searching – because all the 'paths' and 'ways' and 'wisdoms' didn't give me salvation or

fulfilment – I realized that Jesus Christ is the one and only way to God and to true life. I gave him my life as my Lord and Saviour, who has taken upon him my guilt and died for me on the cross. He washed away my sins with his holy blood, and gave me a totally new life, joy and peace of the heart in communion with God.

Jesus has shown me that I ought to confess to you my guilt and make a reparation. I regret my theft and I beg your pardon for it. As compensation I shall send you DM80 by postal order within the next few days. If the sum doesn't seem large enough to you – it exceeds the estimated value of the books by about a third – please write to me.

May the Lord give you his grace.

(RUDOLF SCHWARZKOPF)

OAHSPE

'Do not skip around in *OAHSPE* in an effort to secure a "general idea" of the contents. When this is attempted a state of confusion results which is detrimental to a true understanding of the contents.'

It was in Watkins Occult Bookshop some fifty years ago, soon after it had come under the management of old Mr Watkins's son, that one Friday afternoon I came across, by stooping down to inspect a dark lower shelf of miscellanea, a large heavy tome that preliminary inspection at once revealed as an item of unusual and peculiar curiosity. On the dark blue cover and broad spine were stamped in faded gold *OAHSPE: A New Bible*. It did not take me long to decide to purchase this rarity, though it cost all I had in my wallet that day, and I took it home with me to Teddington, there to spend a weekend examining my prodigious find at leisure. 'The most astonishing book in the English language' is how the author, or should one say agent or recorder, Dr John Ballou Newbrough, describes it. This is by no means hyperbolical. However, less than a week later I took it back and asked Mr Watkins Jr to exchange it for something less astonishing, as I couldn't stand having *OAHSPE* in the house. I was revolted above all by its unmitigated gigantism: it contains thirty-five 'books', each an average of thirty pages, divided into many chapters, and every one of these books of revelation swarms with excessive enumerations, with maniacal glossolalia. In spite of the immediate revulsion bordering on indignation that *OAHSPE* provoked in me, it was not long after I had persuaded Mr Watkins, who assured me that the book, though odd, was of perfectly respectable provenance, to take it back that I began to regret having parted with it so hastily. Soon it had begun to haunt me.

It would be true to say that I thought of *OAHSPE* – 'pronounced *o* as in clock, *ah* as in father and *spe* as in speak' – not just from time to time but increasingly often. I had from the first been intrigued and puzzled by the existence since 1882 of a sect or cult made up of people calling themselves Essenes of Kosmon, or Faithists, and that they understood Kosmon to be 'a heavenly kingdom over North Guatama', and that Guatama signified for them America. I began to wonder who these people could be, how many of them there were, where one would be likely to find them, how often they congregated and, if they held ceremonies or services, what these would be like. My curiosity regarding them led me to ask everyone I knew who had any interest in the esoteric whether they had ever heard of *OAHSPE* or Kosmon. Almost invariably the answer was negative. One had to conclude that a group of people had for about sixty years been numerous and affluent enough to produce twelve American and four English editions of a well-produced illustrated book as big as a telephone directory, while remaining so discreet about their creed that only a handful of cranks appeared to have heard of them.

During my first stay in Paris after the end of the war I was introduced by a friend with Quai d'Orsay connections to a number of people in diplomatic circles with

Go ye and survey the ground from Croashivi to the Lakes of Oochiloo, in etherea, and for the length thereof make ye a width in the form of Fete; and the road of the Fete shall be sufficient for the passage of twelve avalanzas abreast; and the depth of Fete shall be as from the surface of the earth unto Chinvat. Within twelve sios of Abarom, and of the height of the circuit of Bilothowitchieun shall ye carry the border flames.

(FROM *OAHSPE*)

literary or artistic interests. One evening during a small drinks party at the apartment of an attaché at the Greek embassy a chance turn in the conversation stimulated me to start describing the special oddity of a cult I'd come across called Kosmon. Whereupon an elegant young Greek I'd never met before told me in fluent English, 'Oh yes, I know what you mean. My nanny was one. I remember her talking about it quite a lot when I was little.' I was reassured to find that I had not imagined the whole thing, since at least one Englishwoman in Greece in the thirties had actually been a practising Faithist.

A few years after this one of my favourite Hitchcocks was released, *The Man Who Knew Too Much*, which begins with Doris Day singing 'Que Sera Sera' in Tunis and ends with Ann Todd being discovered to be mixed up with a distinctly sinister group holding bogus services in a sort of Methodist hall in like as not Bayswater. I came out of the cinema thinking: now that's exactly the sort of locale I've always imagined Kosmon initiates congregating in.

For some years I continued to speculate intermittently about the possible existence of an underground organization concerned with an aberrant fake book of revelations purporting to expound the secrets of the visible and invisible universes and their cosmogonies. A time came when my mental state began to deteriorate to such an extent that eventually I underwent a series of nervous breakdowns. Preoccupation with Kosmon and *OAHSPE* began to weave itself into the web of delusions and obsessions in which my inner life had become enmeshed.

I still have a distinct recollection of an incident characteristic of the way I thought about Kosmon's imaginary devotees in those days. After a night of prolonged excess I found myself on the deserted platform of Bond Street underground station awaiting the first tube train of the day. A haggard middle-aged woman dressed in the crumpled remains of what must once have been a couturier's costume was straggling on a bench, getting up now and again to slouch to the edge of the platform and back. I observed on one of her cheeks a black streak that might have been made by a stick of anthracite and left there deliberately. I thought to myself immediately: that's how they recognize one another, it's a secret sign indicating that they belong to ... I probably did not actually think of Kosmon by name, but that's what I felt. For a time, whenever I saw someone whose face had obviously not been cleaned that day, I believed I had recognized another member of a queer clandestine society.

A few years after having been sent back to England as a result of my first serious breakdown, I began to be obsessed with a combination of conspiratorial and parousial notions in which both Kosmon and Scientology played a large part. The disorder I was suffering from when admitted to a psychiatric establishment near Epsom was accompanied by a number of vehement convictions. I believed myself to be a vessel containing momentous insights that it was my bounden duty to impart. The world, society, civilization was in imminent danger and everyone had to be alerted if it was to be saved. Though normally as politically and socially aware and responsible as the next man, the danger I envisaged in my illuminated state had nothing to do with nuclear holocausts or neo-Nazi *coups d'état*. I believed intensely that there was a world-wide conspiracy going on, the intent of which was to rob us of our essential humanity and acquire domination of our minds and souls. Scientology was allied with the adepts of Kosmon at the heart of this conspiracy. Before being sectioned by the police to the environs of Epsom, I made an appointment with Mr Watkins and someone I believed to be his collaborator in the world of occult propaganda and, much to their bewilderment, delivered them with a most serious warning amounting to an ultimatum. When I had settled into the reception ward of the hospital I realized that I was surrounded by people who would be specially susceptible to my message, and were in fact eagerly awaiting without yet being fully aware of how much they needed it.

What a nasty moment I went through when I discovered that the monosyllabically uncommunicative old man in the bed next to mine was actually a longstanding

Kosmon initiate and official, and even had a copy of *OAHSPE* in a tin box under his bed. I spent a whole night trying to get out of bed when everyone in the ward was asleep and my new neighbour was snoring in order to appropriate the precious but deadly box and somehow dispose of it, but just at the moment when I thought I had secured my quarry a prowling night nurse caught sight of my attempted action, and I soon found myself being forcibly sedated.

(DAVID GASCOYNE)

A Voice from the Other Side

As a legal writer I am often asked, 'Who owns the rantings of a medium in a trance?' You see the problem. The round table knock knock operative is just relaying other people's words, but those others tend to be, corporeally speaking, not of this world. So where does the copyright lie?

In a 1927 case decided by a Chancery Judge, Geraldine Cummins, a medium, went to court to establish her copyright in a series of 'automatic writings' which was eventually published as *The Chronicle of Cleophas*. These were claimed to be the words of one of Christ's followers as conveyed to the medium, who wrote them at extraordinary speed while in a trance. The writings were, conveniently, in seventeenth-century English rather than, as one might have expected, Aramaic or some other ancient tongue. Mr Justice Eve complimented Cleophas on his method of communication with the modern world: 'He is sufficiently considerate not to do so in a language so antiquated as not to be understood. But in order not to appear of too modern an epoch, he selects a medium capable of translating his messages into language appropriate to a period some sixteen or seventeen centuries after his death.' But as to whether Cleophas himself ('the individual who has been dead and buried for some 1,900-

odd years') should be regarded as joint author and copy-right owner with Miss Cummins the judge said: 'I do not feel myself competent to make any declaration in his favour, and recognizing as I do that I have no jurisdiction extending to the sphere in which he moves, I think I ought to confine myself to individuals who were alive when the work first came into existence.' He was not, he said, prepared to rule 'that the authorship and copyright rest with someone already domiciled on the other side of the inevitable river.'

A medium dictates a manu-script from the other side.
Photo: Colin Jones ©
Camera Press

(MARCEL BERLINS, THE *GUARDIAN*, 5 JUNE 1991)

Local Radio

My local librarian, she of the tight lips and iron grey hair coiled in a bun, removes the covers of books which display any trace of eroticism and turns their spines to the back of the shelf, thus inadvertently advertising their salaciousness to eager borrowers.

She also repeatedly refuses my requests to stock *Flash Art*, the reputable journal of international contemporary arts. She is convinced it is an illustrated manual for exhibitionist perverts. My protests that, without informed critical opinion backed up with full colour reproduction, it was difficult in our sleepy outpost of rural England to keep abreast of current artistic developments in the cultural capitals of the world fell on deaf ears. It was the word 'abreast' that triggered the narrowing of the eyes and the tapping of the date stamp on the counter top. With hindsight I don't suppose 'full colour reproduction' helped much either.

She is reputed to have had sexual intercourse twenty-eight times in her life, and to have kept a record of scores out of ten for performance. My guess is that a succession of scoreless draws has soured her attitude to us male book borrowers. I think she regards us all as vermin, on a par with mice, termites and other book pests, an opinion reinforced, I'm sure, when on the same day both the King James Bible and the Koran were stolen off her shelves. Not by me, but I suppose we're all tarred with the same brush in her eyes.

Like all censors she takes her orders from above, though curiously in her case not from God. Some years back she picked up a random radio signal on her micro-wave oven. Well, in my youth I recall hearing Radio

Cartoon by
Maurice Henry
© ADAGP, Paris and
DACS, London 1994

Caroline loud and clear on the crystalline glass front of my bedsit gas fire, and twenty years later my son tells me that he gets the occasional burst of Radio One through his wah-wah pedal, but whereas he and I are mildly intrigued by the phenomenon she interpreted it as a message of great significance. This led her to listen for hidden instructions by linking up every fifth word uttered by Radio Four announcers. The ultimate cut-up text. I think I'll give up on *Flash Art* and start to give her request cards for the complete works of William Burroughs. Perhaps I would begin with *Junkie, Queer* and *The Naked Lunch*. Whether I'll get them Radio Four only knows.

(DAVE MARSHALL)

Wikkyd Spiryt

In the early fifteenth century in the town of Lynn in Norfolk lived a self-avowed and half crazy mystic called Margery Kempe, a difficult and morbid religious enthusiast. She was married and had a son. She also made pilgrimages to Jerusalem, Rome and St James of Compostella and was given to wailing and 'wept & sobbyd so plentyvowsly' in churches that she upset the other worshippers. Long spells of chastity upset her husband. According to her she was tempted continuously by the devil, who, for instance, thought nothing of arranging for several priests to stand in line and bare their members, which excited her considerably but still she resisted. Her contemporaries were divided as to whether she was a saint or a hypocrite. Eventually, out of a wish to improve people's morals, Margery dictated her strange life to a priest who could write and, unusually for the time when Latin was more common, wrote down her memoirs in English. They lay undiscovered for five hundred years and were presumed lost, until 1934. Unassuming, unimportant-looking and unpublished, they were very

One step ahead of the Ghostbusters the anarchic poltergeist wreaks havoc in the New York Public Library amidst a blizzard of index cards and collapsing bookshelves, while from the deep shadow of the recessed bookcase beneath the television set two disembodied eyes stare unblinkingly back at me.

(IAN BREAKWELL)

nearly accidentally thrown away by my grandfather, who, having made the necessary consultations and recovered his composure, set about translating them into modern English. *The Book of Margery Kempe* is the first extant autobiography in the English language. Several copies of the translation, first editions and so on, sat accusingly on my father's bookshelf but they looked dull to me. What burned deep into my young imagination was what he now kept hidden in our local village bank, in a black tin box. It was occasionally referred to. It was evidently small. It was also in its archaic form quite unreadable, but perfectly *original.*

(HUMPHREY OCEAN)

Cyril

Cyril was complaining about the hospital library again. 'There's not a bloody book I haven't read from cover to cover,' he moaned as we sat by the cricket pitch sunning ourselves. 'I'm familiar with every word in every volume.' I shook my head in disbelief. He took offence immediately. 'The trouble with you is you're ignorant,' he snarled menacingly. I apologized. It doesn't do to cross a former police sergeant.

The next day we were on cleaning duty. 'What do you reckon to the Brontës?' I inquired boldly, slopping my mop around with gusto. 'Do you believe their genius was genetic?' Cyril stopped dead, thought. '*Wuthering Heights* has its good points,' he mumbled, 'but Hopalong Cassidy could have solved the problem in five minutes.'

I have a friendly relationship with Cyril's girlfriend. 'My man's a real brainbox,' she confided at the weekend over tea and fairy cakes in the hospital lounge. 'Do you know he's read every book in the world?' I smiled politely.

I've started testing Cyril in the evenings. 'Who wrote *The Maltese Falcon?*' I asked last night, just before bed.

'The King of Malta,' he answered, quick as a flash. 'Anybody knows that.' I didn't correct him. I hadn't got the heart. The sight of him clutching a ragged teddy bear and settling down for the night moved me deeply.

They say I can go home soon. It's a relief. I've left a lot of important business unattended since I've been in here. The wife's been good though. I've had regular visits.

And Cyril? God only knows. His girlfriend says he isn't ready yet. 'He'll only be running round the back garden spouting Byron again if they let him out now,' she says when the subject's brought up.

Poor Cyril. Last night I asked him how he found the time to do so much reading. 'Bloody simple,' he said, looking at me as if I'd just arrived from another planet. 'It's all done with lasers and television technology. I've got equipment in my head that can photograph a page of text even before it's written.'

I confess bewilderment. Mind you, it could explain why I haven't seen him pick up so much as a newspaper in the last six months.

(KEVIN COYNE)

Interruption

Seven p.m. On the beach. The calm of the day drawing to its close. Blistering heat replaced by a cool evening breeze. The tourists gone, leaving black-headed gulls hopping across warm pebbles, picking at leftovers, whilst a retreating tide reveals mud-coloured sand flats. Slabs of shiny brown reflect children, tiny and dotted about like crabs. The calm of the evening and me, also calm. It has taken all of the above, a ton of sky and an easy book to get me here. The sun sinks lazily behind pink fluff, shunting through air flecked with turquoise.

As I breathe in the close of the day I am jolted from my reverie by a madman somewhere in the distance behind me, screaming 'Bastards! Bastards!' at the top of his voice. I lift my head from my book and there he is. On the road below him spandex-clad cyclists, bronzed and serious, race in parallel to the pier. Perhaps I misheard, perhaps it was 'Faster! Faster!' But no, once more the cry 'Bastards! Bastards!' He ascends the diagonal climb from high road to higher. He leans on railings painted eau-de-Nil and pours forth his wisdom. 'You fucking bastards. You fucking *bastards*!' He chops the air with flat hands and addresses all that moves. I consider the prospect of getting to my feet and delivering up to the flailing maniac a suggestion, a proposal: 'Do you mind, idiot? I am trying to read!' Yet, no. Gravity has its way and my head lolls back.

Back into the pages of my book:

There was a man from Calcutta, who lived his life in a gutter.

'You bastards!'

'*Leave me to this wretched hole.*'

'You fucking bastards!' His breath now shorter, his rant becoming a wheeze.

'*Can't you see I'm sorry? Can't you see anything?*'

'*I can't see a goddamn thing. I'm mad and I'm blind. I'm mad.*'

'Bastards!' With desperation he addresses the skies. 'Bastards!' But the book calls me back.

'*Good evening, sir.*'

'*Good evening.*'

'*Fine evening. Looks as if it will hold.*'

'*Yes.*'

'*Blow over. Best you can expect.*'

'*Best you can expect.*'

'*Could you give me two ounces of butter?*'

'*Two ounces did you say?*'

More shouting now. Two yobs, shirtless with Union Jack shorts, have stopped a good two hundred feet below the Master of Ceremonies and engage with him. ''Ere, why don't you shut your fuckin' mouth?' Quite. And then, as though blessed with a sudden grace, he bows, arcing his right hand from head to toe and offers down

Auntie Evelyn, all attempts at drawing off having failed, as a last resort lifted up a *Chamber's Encyclopaedia* (Vol VIII: PEAS to ROUM) and slammed it down with tremendous force on the angry red boil on the back of Uncle Harold's neck. Like a sledge-hammer hitting a tomato.

(FRIDA STAMP)

to England's finest: 'Verily, gentlemen, I beg your pardon. Do forgive my little outburst.' They chuckle to themselves and move on.

I return to my book. I turn the page. It's no use. I am supine and it is the end of the day. I leave the pebbles and gulls and the children scampering over wet sands and make my way up to the high road. Up the incline and west of the man with a bassoon for a voice. As I reach the top I hear him scream at the world:

'You bastards! You killed the stars, you bastards. You killed the stars!'

I look back down but he has gone. A flock of disturbed gulls returns his call and wheels away across beach and waves and out into the black sky.

(GREG DAVILLE)

Tirion and Tritium

Above the city there are no stars. Yet as a child I yearned for an atlas to the skies. While grown-ups tussled with the pettiness of domestic life and friends talked of football teams I stayed indoors, buying no comics, seeing no films. Today I can no more save money than I can see my life a year from now. But the child assumes a long-term future.

From the twentieth floor of a London tower block I made out few celestial objects, even when the moon was new: the streetlight glimmer cloaked all but the brightest stars. And because of the year of my birth another factor played with the star maps of the time: precession caused an intergalactic smudge mark across the century, objects moving slowly across the ecliptic. As atlases for the year 1950 lost accuracy those for the year 2000 gained.

The atlas I bought was by a man called Wil Tirion. (There was even something suitably futuristic about his name.) It was not for the era of bobbysocks and Profumo but for a new epoch. Larger than A3, the book, spiral-bound in black with letters of a *fin de millenium* typeface, beckoned the future. Yet the watermarked gatefold pages, each one mapped out by the author, confirmed an ancient truth: that among so many galaxies the Earth is small and insignificant. With needle-point accuracy the stars were plotted as black circles, with the Milky Way crossing some of the pages as a shower of cyan. The skies, divided into hours, minutes and seconds instead of degrees, did not lend themselves well to the Greek myths taught in school. In astronomy magnitude censors the sky, allowing only so much of it to be seen. The naked eye can make out objects to magnitude three or four. Wil Tirion's black circles were for telescopes, the smallest circles representing magnitudes up to eight or nine. To our eyes no amount of squinting could make a hunter appear in the constellation of Orion. There was too much clutter for that, too many stars the Greeks were unable to see.

Later, when trysting with girls was becoming more important than scuffles with boys, I could no more quote a Greek love poem than I could kiss. Girls would laugh when I invited them to come into the park in the dark and see my telescope. No use protesting that my azimuth-mounted tube was for searching out comets! On those summer evenings in the pub, talking with friends whose words commonly began with *f*, I would be carrying my refractor. There were *s* words too: stars were the movie kind; then there was sex, and school.

Eventually a girl did accompany me to the park. Stella's short fringe and overly angular features did not make her the prettiest of star-gazing companions. She was not the one I'd dreamed of. But Stella was sweet, bringing a simple child's atlas with her on our first date. It took some time for her parents to believe she was out so late because she wanted to look at the sky. By then weeks of carrier bags and thermos flasks had begun. She thought it was exciting and different, us breaking into the park, climbing the iron railings before dropping to the turf. In silence the telescope would be erected. Like our friends we ignored the city centre, unable to afford it and secretly insecure before its glamour. But we could see its glow in the sky. The city killed stars. The yellow shimmer rendered the atlas for the year 2000 dispensable. We could barely see any of the objects in Stella's little pocket guide let alone Tirion's red marks. Then the nights began to shorten, the summer to wane. We had to sit closer on the picnic chairs; soon we were kissing under the cloudy starless sky. Dew clung to our jeans as we sniffled. It was too cold to undress and when Stella fell asleep I'd look at the sunrise, a brightening wash of grey, knowing that my book and the skies would outlast her. She stopped coming to the park on Saturday nights. Winter found me alone.

Things improved when I was eligible to claim. Except for the one before my fortnightly visit to the social security office, I could stay up every night, even travelling away from the city to escape its lights. Then my atlas began to tell stories. The pages were now frayed, a couple torn, but at last a shiny mirror-like clarity emerged from the glowing dust above me. My hands became older, my face more worn as the weather of a thousand nights consumed my skin. My hearing became too sensitive, my sight too adapted to low light. Light had become a scourge. Even a full moon made me downhearted, and when children would use the streetlights as target practice I'd laugh as their coke cans destroyed the tritium bulbs.

My secret night life ended abruptly. I went apprehensively to my compulsory job interview, to a mercury-lit office, to a seat with a view of more seats and more desks. I got the job. But it wasn't the fluorescent light that stopped me seeing stars on dark wintry afternoons. As my years at the firm piled up my senses became blunted. I would arrive home tired out, with barely the energy to eat. My star atlas metamorphosed into a drinks mat, a coffee mug coaster, a TV-dinner table. The transparent sheet used to cover pages and measure the distances between stars became grubby and stained. The pages began to fall apart. The spine broke. Back in the office there were no windows.

(AFSHIN RATTANSI)

Quality Control

The game was to close my eyes, stick a pin in the index of an atlas, then look up that place in *The Story of the World*. This work divided the world into Lower, Middle and Upper Savages; Lower, Middle and Upper Barbarians; and the Civilized. I think only the British and the Americans qualified as civilized. It was published in 1934. The year I was nine I was rushed to hospital on Christmas Day with appendicitis. I refused to go without the books, but was eventually persuaded to restrict myself to the atlas, my key to the world. It was removed from my grasp under anaesthetic.

A book so treasured that one could only be parted from it by being forcibly rendered unconscious. For years I thought that everyone had such passion. Then I met a man on a course for the unemployed. He didn't mix with the others during the lunch and coffee breaks, just sat writing in an old notebook. Eventually I asked him what he was doing. He was cataloguing his book collection, he said. He had over three thousand of them.

'What kind of books do you collect?' I asked.

'Eight and a half inches by five and a half inches.'

'But on what subjects?'

'Oh, it doesn't matter about the subjects. I've never read any of them. The important thing is they should all be the same size. I can't stand to see books looking untidy on the shelves.'

(DEIRDRE CLARK)

Twitcher

When I was nine came books I've not seen for decades, can't now name, slim introductions to natural history, each variety of fern or wader beautifully depicted alongside summary but curiously inspirational information.

You could recycle this information. I made out my own comprehensive list of all the warblers of the British Isles, not that I'd seen more than one or two of them. These and other creatures were so fully named in Latin as well as English that a *haecceitas* (Hopkins's term, from Duns Scotus) resided sufficiently in the words and the picture.

In Zimbabwe recently a safari guide said as we drove through the bush, 'That is a lilac-breasted roller.' The bird itself is very beautiful. But you could say that it merely lived up to its name, like the oystercatcher, like the skua, the coal tit.

Why not produce books like these for myself? In little reporters' notebooks I illustrated what I called 'pretend animals' and 'pretend birds'. Wordsworth's 'solitary reaper' existed only in a book. I could write vividly of lilac-breasted rollers with nothing to go on but a field guide and my own imagination. And these books, which I can't now name, also provided the pleasures of classification: it is important that a coal tit is not a blue tit. And pedantry: skuas are rarely seen south of Scotland, where hoopoes never even by chance occur.

Too many textbooks for children and handbooks for adults make counter-productive concessions to ignorance. I say let the uninstructed mind plunge at once into a range of well-ordered information. Let children have real atlases to play with, not simplified globes. The pages are flat but the Earth is not, nor is the imagination. David Attenborough can show you the world's wildlife in action and yet neutralize or destroy imagination because what seems to be the real thing is flickering out of reach on the screen, then gone. But the arctic wastelands of the atlas, the fish eagles of the field guide, are on hand at any time to be created in imagination, like the empires of the Medes and Hittites in that atlas of the Bible which came my way in early childhood.

Flying over Baffin Island *en route* to western Canada a few years ago I was thrilled not as if by a shock but by recognizing something long known from atlases: yes, there's the very emptiness, shores fretted just so. And when I was divebombed on Orkney once by skuas into whose colony I had carelessly strayed didn't I delight that they were living up to their names while they flew lower and lower as I crouched almost on my knees, hurtling towards my forehead, then veering up before the last impact which would have killed us both? Skewers: I always knew you were. Great northern divers, I've still to see you dive.

(ANGUS CALDER)

Pluck

Years ago I was given the job of being editor to one of our best known and biggest selling authors. It was a daunting assignment. He was well known for being difficult, touchy and fierce. I have to admit that I was frightened of him. Well, not exactly of *him*, but of not getting on well with him. The relationship of Author and Editor is a matter of mutual respect and trust. If an author doesn't take to his editor it can lead to big trouble. At the worst to an author transferring himself and his books to some other firm.

In order to get to know one another better he had summoned me to stay the weekend at his house by the sea. As he was a keen ornithologist he suggested on the Saturday morning that we might go for a walk along the cliffs: 'We might see some good birds,' he said. I agreed with sham enthusiasm. 'I've just got to write a couple of letters first,' he added, 'then we'll be off.' Left to myself I picked up a book from the sofa. It was called *Birds of the Coast*, and I began idly to read it. My eye fell on a passage describing the purple sandpiper, a bird which I'd never heard of.

Half an hour later he returned and we set off with walking sticks and binoculars along the cliffs. In due course he stopped, raised his binoculars and focused on a group of birds below us at the water's edge. He looked puzzled.

'What do you make of those?' he asked. I looked.

'I should say they're purple sandpipers,' I said.

'Unheard of!' he exclaimed. 'Whatever makes you think that?'

'Well,' I said, 'there's the rather plump shape and the speckled breast, and particularly that long yellow beak which darkens at the tip.'

He was concentrating furiously through his binoculars.

'And, *as you know*,' I added placatingly, 'they love to stand in the spray just above the waterline.'

'By Jove!' he exclaimed. 'I believe you're right!'

We continued happily with our walk. By the grace of God he didn't ask me to identify any more birds; it was the only page I'd looked at. But as we returned to the house he put a hand on my shoulder. 'Guest,' he said warmly, 'those purple sandpipers, that was a very fine piece of identification!'

Very fine indeed I thought, in fact unique.

(JOHN GUEST)

A Good Novel

My twin sister Mary
didn't even look up
when the Fluchthorn could be seen
right outside the window.
By the time we reached the chalet,
War and Peace was finished,
and then she complained
of having nothing to do.

She sat under her duvet
like a pope,
asking for 'a good novel',
and ignoring the Sunne-Blüme Tee
we offered her instead.
My mother got more and more gloomy,

and gave up her plan of yodelling
across the Inn at night.

My poor mother – she was trying
to get over her affair with H.
Novels made her feel worse.
Her favourite book was
London's Countryside
By Green-Line Bus and, recently,
that great mountaineering classic,
Pilgrimage to Nanga Parbat.

She liked the way the climber
talks about the Clear Voice
that he hears; and when he sits,
high above a nullah,
eating the last of his sausage,
he feels the mountain
watching every mouthful, like a dog.
My mother could just imagine it.

(SELIMA HILL)

Food for Thought

My 'edible publishing' career began in 1967. My first
productions consisted of cochineal on rice paper using
lino blocks and hand lettering. The content was poetry
with abstract illustration. Rice paper printing had been
used during the Second World War by HQs issuing
information to pilots who would eat the messages after
the words had been mentally digested. Wartime frugality
was, after all, concerned with the best use of limited
resources. The government press was 'somewhere in
Penge'. The ink used was poisonous, but not poisonous
enough to worry anyone in those urgent times. The
messages sometimes produced the need for a chalk
tablet.
    I had found diagrams of the printing methods in an

Exeter junk shop and started to print using an iodine dye. I published biographical film star verse by Pearl White, concrete word poems in the post-Lettrist style of the period and a political tract on the need to reintroduce food into thought. By the time the Association of Little Presses had their book fair in 1970 I was producing rice paper books with pastry covers and shortcake broadsheets, all served in sandwich bags containing poisonous paper supplements. A reviewer from the *Daily Telegraph* complained that the supplement had got caught in his teeth.

(ALLEN FISHER)

Bookworm

I was in an unfamiliar room, thick carpets, heavy curtains and floor-to-ceiling, wall-to-wall bookshelves. I felt numb. Stunned. I didn't know which book to attack first. I stepped forward and pulled one from the shelf. The title and author were a blur. From back to front I flicked the pages by thumb. I found nothing but evidence. I held the book by its spine and shook it. Fire ash, burned paper and dust fell from it. I knew the worm had moved on. It was devouring books page by page and book by book. I pulled another book from the shelf and it crumbled in my hand. Each book I handled disintegrated before my nauseated eyes. The worm was too quick for me. I didn't see it and yet I knew it was a cross between an earthworm and the worm from the film *Dune*. The carpet was covered in heaps of paper dust, grey and musty. I knew the worm had tricked me.

I woke and turned on the light. I wrote the dream down in a notebook.

About a month later Lesley called. She was a friend of my sister. She was moving house. Did I want to go over and look through her books? She was having a sort out. I had nothing better to do. I rang the bell and she opened

A velvet-bound copy of a Dictionary of Symbolism and Historicity *translated from the Spanish into English and devoured by subterranean termites in* Greece. Photo: Rentokil

the door. She directed me to a room. 'I thought you'd be interested. Do have a look. I've got a dealer coming tomorrow.' She went to make some tea.

The room was instantly familiar. It was the room from the dream. Books lined the walls from floor to ceiling and wall to wall. I hadn't realized she had such a collection. Here was my chance to find a real worm. I reached for a book and started to flick rapidly through the pages. I abandoned it for another and then another. I was obsessed with the idea of catching a worm; a glimpse would have satisfied me. The books were in good condition. There was nothing wrong with them. A mottled endpaper floated to the floor. I kept dropping the books at my feet. They piled up randomly.

Lesley came in with the tea. 'Have you found what you're looking for?'

'No,' I said, 'I haven't.'

'I'm getting rid of the lot,' she explained. 'I've decided not to be a bookworm any longer.'

(RALPH HAWKINS)

Wavelength

I once knew a man who sold his entire book collection only to replace it with books identical to those he had sold. It was his wife's fault. If she left the blinds closed as he had instructed then no one could admire the pristine daily dusted, twice daily hoovered room. But if she opened the blinds then dust collected on the slats. She preferred to disregard his instructions and, as soon as he had gone to work, she would open the blinds allowing the watery northern sunshine to filter in.

D., her husband, was an obsessive book collector. One front room wall in the semi in the seaside town was lined with books. Unfortunately the books were of different heights and, as he came to realize, the sun bleached the dust jackets of books that projected above those adjacent. Hence the instruction to keep the blinds closed at all times.

She was eventually found out. Most of the books on the upper shelves were ruined, and even some on the lower shelves had been damaged by the sun. His solution was both ingenious and logical. With carefully shaped fillets of wood he was able to make wave-form bookshelves, thus raising each book to the same height as its neighbour.

(DAVE MARSHALL)

His Craft Ebbing

Psychopathia Sexualis, in English, by Krafft-Ebing, was in the public library in Hull, east Yorkshire, in 1954. I was a fourteen-year-old schoolboy who wanted to be a psycho-analyst. In those days the public library always chucked the dust jackets away, as I still do, cheap and nasty, uncomfortable lures that they are. Silver paper around chocolate is thrown away before eating; only twerps have car seat covers; packaging is puerile. The binding of the book reminds me of the library and its devotion, while the jacket reminds me of the huge sadness of the remainder shops, home to failure in tatterdemalion covers. In Hull Library there was a monolithic canvas and leathery look to the shelves. I found the *Psychopathia Sexualis* embossed on the spine, pulled it out to find it was a book-shaped piece of wood. You took this token for a book to the issuing desk and the librarian, having looked you over, swapped it for the real thing. Now I would rather read the wooden book.

(PATRICK HUGHES)

Communing with Culture

The library was on the other side of the park. Pocketing your tickets, two pair of stiff card pouches with clipped corners, you strode with resolute tread the path leading from one institution, the junior school, to another, the children's library. Most days of the week when school was out you were sucked into the vortex of the park to scale trees, vault the brook, spin on the playground 'top hat' or lob clods into the muck swamping the foundations of the razed hall whose grounds now formed this selfsame parkland. The library nestled in a remote corner behind some yews spilling over from the parish church next door. Oft-times this modest box clad in tongue-and-groove pine, with swivelling plate glass windows, loomed large in the child's mind. Thus it was that the zigzagging physicality of play gave way to the tunnel vision of a calm and purposeful intellectuality. Now you did not stray from the pathway. Winter was best. And worst. The lights of the library beckoned in the gloaming, like an ember in a cindery hearth. And the race to beat the curfew of darkness descending, when all about became sprinkled in the soot of night, drained of colour, muffled and disquieting, gave a sense of urgency to your browsing. The library's blazing bulbs contradicted and enhanced the sombreness of its situation. You'd be anxious and not a little frightened when you put those lights behind you, ears straining to catch any noise louder than your footfall. You were primed to pelt in panic as you recrossed the eerie and empty park alone. The books you clasped to your puny pumping chest afforded little protection against the alarums of shadow and sound. Was that man in black the parkie, the local bobby, or ...? This was the witching hour when gypsies, sinister old women and tramps were abroad. A madman called 'Ginger Beard', a wild-eyed Celtic double of Howard Keel in *Kismet*, was reported to be prowling the district, lurking in copses, eager to pounce, although neither you nor anyone you knew had actually seen him.

The gentle arabesque of tarmac that ushered you to the library door passed through a zone of cedars and yews whose inky, morbid canopies shrouded all beneath in a claustral light. It was always chill here. The library itself had been built in the post-Festival of Britain fifties of angular prefabricated parts, but the buildings around it were older, each one bearing the patina of another time. To one side was a Norman church and graveyard, one of whose incumbents was a deceased horse, first cousin in your imagination to Tam O'Shanter's ghastly mare. To the other was a cricket pavilion, a spectral presence by night. Close by was a gents' toilet. A road lined with thirties' mock-Tudor semis, the 'English sunrise' motif prominent on their garages and gates, abutted on the library and this flank of the park. An alleyway linked the library and the lane. The rawness of the council estate was clearly something 'other'. It was the well-heeled middle-class citizens of the parish who'd annexed this seat of learning. The park separated them definitively from the *hoi polloi* of council rent-payers. On their side the lush, well-tended, sacral turf of the cricket pitch and bowling green over which swallows, swifts and martins wheeled in summer; on yours a brace of bumpy and sparsely grassed football pitches, shot through with lacerating gravel, their flimsy goalposts leaning at crazy angles, perches for rooks and jackdaws, the odd windswept seagull. The stream neatly bisected these two worlds.

But you, crossing the bridge over the brook, perhaps stopping to let a stone plummet into the swirling waters, sensed you were on the up and up as you ascended the slight slope towards the library. Books were a way forward, a way out, an entrée into a reality whose class values you dimly perceived were different. Years later you would furnish the eyrie of your council house bedroom with the now comical signifiers of bourgeoisdom: a roll-top desk, a packet of Earl Grey tea, some VP sherry in a chipped decanter, a box of Sobranie Black Russian cigarettes. Books were the finishing touch, a door opening on to your future, a door you could slam in the face of your prole family, vegetating downstairs behind closed curtains, winter and summer, in front of the telly. On a trip to London you had bought your first 'serious' book, the first brick in the edifice. With the self-aggrandizing miserabilism of the typical late adolescent you had chosen a scholarly study of suicide. Books as kicks in the teeth of those you love. Obliterate them from your eyespan by obliterating yourself. Soon you had a dozen or so Pelicans arranged atop the desk, one more element in the still life of self-improvement. Each volume was read without cracking the spine. Forever *un*read, it would seem. You fawned and fussed over them all with an eraser, cleaning off the dust, sellotaping corner and spine, almost sobbing if they succumbed to soiling. Twelve ambiguous badges of pride, twelve demanding custodians of your anxiety, your lonely and masturbatory self-absorption, your forever pristine unease.

One crepuscular winter's day a timid and deferential kid found himself on the threshold of the branch library. Hefting open the door he passed by the foyer posters about road safety, Post Office savings stamps, joyous doings at the Girl Guide hut, and padded across the herringbone parquet to the desk where a bored, clock-watching librarian sternly relieved him of the books he bore. It wasn't long till closing and the building was deserted, just him and the civil servant, as he made off into the kiddies' section. There was a pleasure in registering the books he'd read and the ones he hadn't. Yet a double dose of paranoia haunted him, eroding his pleasure. It was getting late. Best be off before night really fell, before the librarian wanted to shut up shop. Can't risk her displeasure, mustn't irk her, make her notice him, single him out. Furthermore the lad felt an excruciating pressure in his loins: he needed to relieve himself. Walking stiff-legged, holding back his water, he frog marched around the shelves, making a quick mental note of tomes to take out. Ever the self-conscious interloper in the palace of culture, the boy lacked the strength of will to do the practical thing – he was his mother's son,

after all – to go outside and take a leak. (There were no lavvies in the building.) Surely it would look funny if he were to leave and then re-enter a few minutes later? Perhaps the librarian, who was certain to notice him, would think he was stealing a book? Or worse, that her library held no mystery for this young upstart. And then, once outside, where to pee? He didn't dare do it against the library wall, it would drum on the tongue-and-groove. The public convenience nearby was in a sinister copse of hawthorns, very inconvenient, and didn't have a light. Anyway, who knew what was lurking in its dank, stinking interior? No, he'd have to hold on. By now, though, his ruminations had landed him in a bit of a pickle. He was ready to piss his pants. No time left to even make it to the door. His cogitations about social etiquette had wasted valuable seconds. He should have run the gauntlet of the librarian's gaze minutes ago. He needn't have come back in, even if he would have had to explain at home why he'd returned empty-handed. Yet he *did* want some books to read. The kid stood stock still. Quivering like a guitar string he listened to the vibrato resonances of his urethra. He braced his body taut as a mint ten bob note, uttered a silent prayer to a merciful god and urgently took stock of the lie of the land. Several stacks shielded him from the desk and its occupant. Nothing else for it, he had to let go. Consumed with a heady mixture of anguish and release he felt a stream of hot piss run down his leg, soaking his short pants and long socks. He watched in fascination as it slowly formed a saffron pond on the waxed parquet. He wiped his leg with his hanky, hoped that the odour of the urine hadn't reached the nostrils of the librarian. All that remained was to conceal his crime and make a run for it. As chance would have it he was right by the outsize books. Making a mental calculation he selected the biggest of them and laid it gingerly on top of the puddle, praying its weight wouldn't spread or splash the stinkwater. A job well done, the subterfuge was perfect. Rolling down his socks to hide their telltale stain and smell, belting his gabardine mac over his saturated shorts, he strode briskly to the exit. He sensed a pair of suspicious eyes boring into the back of his neck as he struggled with the heavy door. A few more steps and he was out in the sharp night air. A wave of guilt assailed him as he pictured the weary librarian making her last rounds, finding the book on the floor and innocently picking it up. He pictured the piss running down the glassine wrapper, dripping into the puddle, getting on the woman's hands. What a dog's life, hers and his. He was sorry for her, sorry for himself. Would she remember him? Would his forehead blaze next time with the invisible brand of his culpability? He couldn't chance her baleful glare, her accusing finger. He wouldn't be able to go back to the branch library for months.

(PAUL HAMMOND)

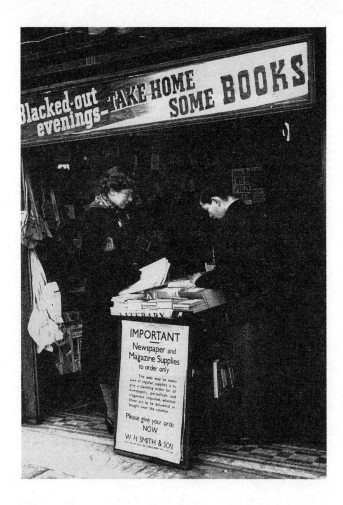

The Laundry Library

One of the ideas behind doing-it-yourself is that you thereby do it better. So it was that my brother and I decided to run our own lending library at home in the first celebratory days after the Second World War had officially begun. Our model was the local library in Timperley, Cheshire: a plain brick villa set back from the road with a drive full of prams and bicycles. It was a reassuring place with a good children's section and firm middle-aged ladies who flicked expertly through nested tickets like card sharpers. The drawback was half-day closing and rules that forbade chatting with friends, to say nothing of the occasional fine.

My brother reasoned that our library would be extensive and, above all, liberal, a more relaxed place run by children for friends. Money would not come into the picture and great goodwill would be generated. Our parents, both serious readers, applauded the notion in principle, though my mother had doubts about the location. A stock of books was no problem: truck loads of hardbacks and paperbacks were piled in our bedrooms with titles like *Essays of Love and Virtue* and *Kangaroo*, from my father's pre-war reading. These jostled with *Rupert Bear* and *William*.

The site options were: one, the garage; two, a slit trench dug at the far end of our garden; three, my mother's wash-house. The latter seemed to us the answer since there was a door to our side drive and just enough room for wall shelves to be erected opposite where my mother kept her boiler and mangle. Any steam, we thought, would escape through the transom window. The pleasure was all in the preparation: our card index system, jam-pot stickers on the inside covers; filling the shelves with our novels and my mother's teacher training manuals. Mother watched with customary indulgence and wondered when her wash-house would revert to her own keeping.

She waited for about four months. Unread books became soggy from steam and one or two of our best hardbacks – annuals in the main – failed to reappear, often from the more respectable of our friends' houses. In the end we decided that the space taken up by the library was best given over to curing rabbit skins.

And no one borrowed *Kangaroo*.

(J. K. ROBERTSON)

Bás Beatha

By the 1960s my mother finally had a washing machine. A top-loading Bendix, it was *hers*, the only piece of machinery she owned. It symbolized a degree of freedom from household drudgery and was a big, impressive thing. In fact too big to fit in the lean-to kitchen of our house on the west coast of Ireland, so it was kept under the stairs where it gleamed white in the darkness: the shrine of Our Precious Bendix.

Alongside the washer, tied to a six inch nail with knotted pink thread, was a booklet. *Bás Beatha* (Life Death) told you what to do when The Bomb went off. It was distributed to every house in the country by the Department of Civil Defence. We had no idea there was such a thing. Department of Agriculture and Fisheries, yes, but Defence? Never heard of it.

More mysterious still was 'Radioactive Fallout', especially since the book confided that 'it cannot be seen or felt'. But happily for us the Civil Defence people 'have instruments to tell us when it is about'. The booklet claimed, 'Protection is not too difficult for the householder to provide for himself and his family.' Being a child I took this to mean that I could safely leave it all to my parents, symbolized in the book's pictures by Mr and Mrs Average. Mr A. wore a white shirt and neatly knotted tie as he reinforced the refuge room with drawers filled with earth, and Mrs A. wore high heels and a floral pinafore as she filled the bath with water and collected the necessary items to take into the shelter. I was pleased to note these included a toy train and a teddy bear with two eyes (whereas mine had only one).

If the atom bomb went off when I was on my way home from school I should take 'instant action' by lying face down on the ground and turning up my coat collar. If I had to go out later into the invisible fallout I should wear a scarf and gloves and when I came back take off my shoes on the front step. I thought it would be best to stay at home, particularly as it seemed there'd be a school holiday.

Bás Beatha was white, black and red. White for the pages, black for the words and red for the radioactive spots, which looked like measles and were crudely printed on top of the diagrams as if they could just be brushed or washed off, no need to worry. So the obvious place to keep the book was alongside the washing machine, especially as it was under the stairs, which was where the book told you to go when the fallout came over. How exciting! That was where we were all going to live: mum, dad, us kids, the dogs, the cats and the donkey, huddled round the Bendix. The cleanest nuclear family in Ireland.

Spotless.

(GERALDINE O'SULLIVAN)

Joyless Format

Our Liverpudlian great-aunt had a cupboard at the top of the stairs and we were allowed to search through it when we stayed with her. In the cupboard were children's books. There was an assortment of Richmal Crompton, *Jennings*, and the *Mary Mouse* series by Enid Blyton. The latter came in a peculiar format: three drawings to a page, the page being around 18 by 9 cm, with the spine on the short side. Mary Mouse looked dried up, tired and strict. The air of joyless moralism scared me stiff.

Years later I saw other Lilliputian books in the window of a Christian bookshop. They were the work of the great Dudley Watkins, whose comic strips included 'The Broons' and 'Oor Wullie' for the *Sunday Post*, and 'Lord Snooty' and 'Desperate Dan' for the *Dandy* and *Beano*. I bought copies under the impression they were Watkins's versions of my favourite *William* books. They *were* about a boy called William, but he was known to his chums in the Bible study class as 'William the Warrior'. The lads did a lot of kneeling and praying to the deity for forgiveness. The books were in the same format as *Mary Mouse* and crudely drawn. Here again was the pinch-mouthed puritanism I associated with Mistress Mouse's adventures. The usually ebullient and creative Watkins seemed depressed and out of sorts. I assume he did the books out of some sort of religious conviction.

Recently a friend brought back from the States a volume called *Life's Little Instruction Book: 511 Suggestions, Observations and Reminders on How to Live a Happy and Rewarding Life* by Jackson Brown Jr, published in Nashville, Tennessee. (The last time I'd seen a book like that was in Oslo: a big hardback entitled *What Is The Meaning?*, with photos of a baby, a football match and a brain on the cover. Halfway through you found a whole list of meanings, at least twelve of them.) H. Jackson Brown is in the now familiar format of *Mary Mouse* and *William the Warrior*, and it is instructive to read a book that is so sanctimonious and smug.

The 369th suggestion is 'Read *Leadership Is An Art* by Max De Pree.' I am now in search of this book and I am sure what it will look like when I find it.

(STEVE BERESFORD)

Laminated Caine

After I'd ploughed my way through James Bond I decided to move on to the Len Deighton spy books. I'd clocked they were being made into films starring Michael Caine: *Horse Under Water, Funeral in Berlin, Billion Dollar Brain.* For some reason *The Ipcress File* was put out by another publisher, but I bought the Penguins and was hooked immediately, by the look of them more than anything else. In the top third of the cover there was a dot matrix picture of Michael Caine with specs and a machine gun. Well, just a portion of his face really, which added a cinematic feel to the whole thing. Below that, title and author. Further down, taking up the bottom third of the front, bold lines slanted at a forty-five degree angle, conjuring up images of checkpoints between East and West. *Horse Under Water* was yellow, *Funeral in Berlin* was orange and *Billion Dollar Brain* a metallic silver, which associated it in my mind with rockets, Daleks and military hardware. The photo of Len Deighton on the back, in dark shades and standing in front of a whirling helicopter, made him look a bit like Michael Caine.

The dynamic image the jackets conveyed extended to the inside front covers, which carried the sort of reviews you usually got on the back: '"Never were shadows more dazzling" – *L'Express*.' The type was thick and blotchy, implying I'd been given access to a hastily photocopied secret file. Also the device of using lengthy appendices about things like telephone tapping and virus growths added to the impression of authenticity. The footnotes, Secret Service internal memos and – in *Billion Dollar Brain* – chapter numbers that looked like they'd been done on a computer convinced me that these were the most real books ever written. And I hadn't even started reading them yet!

When I did I took them at a chapter a day. The plots were complicated and the dialogue quirky, but it didn't matter, the style of the covers and the *look* of the books had told me what to expect. I'd go through a ritual of holding the books in my hand, just staring at them and feeling them for a minute or two before reading them, as if I could soak up extra meaning through the object itself. Unlike the James Bond novels, where I only saw Sean Connery's features when I read the text, Michael Caine didn't spring to mind at all, despite his grainy face on the covers. It was as if the books were too real for a mere actor to be speaking the lines. If it was anybody going through the motions it was me. *This was what I wanted to be.* That's why I wanted to consume all of it, not just the words but also the typeface, the pictures, the paper it was printed on.

Over the years the books got lost and when I wanted to reread them later I bought the new editions. To my disappointment the covers now had illustrations on them, colourful little pictures of the characters that looked nothing like I'd imagined them. Also they'd enlarged the typeface, robbing the reader of the illusion that they were dipping into a densely typed secret dossier. And because the print was larger the books were fatter. Not only did they not look right, they didn't *feel* right either. There were no splodgy reviews inside and the chapter headings were less stylized. Everything about the books was wrong and I couldn't bring myself to read them. Luckily I found a complete set of the old Penguins in a second-hand bookshop down the Holloway Road. Now I had them in the way culture had intended, I read them all again straight through.

(ROGER MILLS)

Anthony Earnshaw's 'Ex Libris' design for public library books

All is Calm, All is Bright

I fell in love with the dark blue cover of a reading book called *The Radiant Way*. My father, a restaurant manager in the centre of Glasgow, had bought it there as there were no 'free' books in those days for primary school children. He'd brought it home to the new housing estate in Stamperland while the blackout was on. I was five years old. While thudding, whumping bombs were destroying the Clydebank factories and sugar refineries I slept safely with my parents in the big bed–settee pulled out in front of the sitting-room fire.

Dad was not called up. He was disappointed about this. His father before him had been a reluctant stretcher bearer whose only comment about his experiences in the First World War was, 'It was terrible.' Our dad had tried to enlist more than once but he failed the medical: he had no sense of smell and was totally deaf in one ear. As a young man he'd served an apprenticeship in those Clyde shipyards that were being bombed while I gazed at *The Radiant Way*. The girl on the cover of this, my first very own reading book, smiling in a flower-filled landscape, was my ideal. My father's future with the Mercantile Marine had been scuppered by the Depression. He was pushed against a three-door wall. Above the doors was written: Bread, Beer, Burial. He chose the first and went westwards to America, where he got work in Baltimore as a short-order cook. He voyaged home in time to miss the Wall Street Crash and he met my mother, a chambermaid in the Hotel Metropole on the Isle of Man.

I remember listening to her, no trace of Scouse in her voice, reading aloud 'Rumpelstiltskin', 'Snow White and Rose Red', 'Hansel and Gretel'. The ominous power of evil challenging good was echoed by the atmosphere of wartime, when Fear the genie is out of his bottle. Just the two of us by the coal fire: enchantment ruled. Dad would get home hours after my bedtime. It must have been the excitement that kept me awake the night he came back with *The Radiant Way*. *The Radiant Way* contained very short stories and small exquisite drawings in colour. Interspersed with these were neat lists of similarly spelt and similar sounding words. The child beginner was encouraged to note patterns, visual and aural. But it was the pictures that beguiled. René Cloke painted and drew them. There was Red Riding Hood; Aladdin and his lamp; Tom Thumb, bedraggled and stunned next to the pudding bag from which he'd escaped being boiled alive in. Men put on red coats and galloped upstairs on horseback. Other men sent cheeses off to market, instructing the rolling round ones as to their destination. There was the tale of a toothbrush; instructions on flying kites and finding a bird's nest containing eggs; a passage on the seasonal plight of shell-less crabs hiding in rock pools.

The precious *Radiant Way* rubbed against the snap in my satchel as I walked beside the tram tracks to school. Like the tombstones arranged to face the parson's in a church graveyard, so that on the Day of Resurrection his flock will be looking towards God, our desks faced the blackboards and the formidable misses, remnants of an army of unmarried women denied husbands by the war to end wars. Atop my desk my radiant reading primer. I remember the moment in class when I cracked the code in true gestalt fashion. It was a revelation. Yet I still had to work out how grown-ups like my father read silently, as he did on Sundays when he wasn't playing golf with his left-handed clubs or participating in Home Guard manoeuvres. He'd shown us how his rifle would work were his platoon ever to receive ammunition. The highlight of our dad's army career was the day they captured Rudolph Hess on Eaglesham Golf Course.

It was dad who brought my first Enid Blyton book. I was in bed. The light was put on for just long enough to remove the wrapping and flick through the illustrations. A family was pictured on the dust jacket of *The Enid Blyton Christmas Book*. There were six of them and, being middle class, they had a maid and a cook. The children come home from boarding school and discover Santa Claus relaxing by the fire after filling their stockings. Before departing with the reindeer he explains his origins in myth and legend. And he tells the Christmas story: the Nativity, the shepherds, the Wise Men, the flight to Egypt, the Christmas tree and card, the yule log, the holly and the mistletoe, the gargantuan spread. The chronology of time was drawn as a queue of ambulant people on the endpapers, era by era. From pre-Christian Romans and Vikings to gift-carrying, car-, plane- and train-using moderns. The child interpreted the picture from the top down and reading left to right. It symbolized progress, that life goes on and gets better. I was entranced. *The Enid Blyton Christmas Book* was so precious I kept it in a special hiding place in a wall cupboard behind the dressing table.

I hear that the politically correct movement has caught up with Miss Blyton, and also threatens to remove sexism and racism from the Famous Five books that also shared that secret space in the wall. What then will become of *The Enid Blyton Christmas Book*? Would a revised edition work? What would be missing, different, would be the heightening of the book's power in the minds of children affected by war and pictures of the Final Solution. Those people in the trucks being transported to their deaths were related to each other, had homes and books and significant dates in their calendars. The panic in an English child's breast could be eased by identifying with a fictional white middle-class family gathered around a Christmas tree, by identifying with those who were not victims. A dream of a world made safe from the world outside. Sentimental? Yes. Politically incorrect? Of course. But the fearful are never rational. They clutch at straws.

(SYLVIA AYLING)

Legacy

Radical politics, dark sexuality, premature death: these three things are for me forever connected and intertwined with images of books. And images of books themselves are forever connected and intertwined with images of my father.

I grew up in the fifties, the youngest child of three, in a lower-middle-class housing project in the north-east

Bronx, in a predominantly Italian Catholic, working-class, politically conservative neighbourhood. My parents were Jews, atheists and leftists, marginalized even within this community that was itself marginalized from most of the rest of the United States, and from much of the rest of New York City as well.

My father, the dominant figure in our family, was a large man with bright blue eyes and dark hair, both of which I alone of the children inherited. He was also a rage-filled man, frequently irrational and violent. When I was a small child I drew a picture of a scowling, fierce-looking man entering a room as three frail females cling in terror to the walls. The females in the picture, an adult and two children, represented my mother, my sister and me. For some reason I left out my brother, although he was in fact also frequently the victim of my father's rage. I titled the drawing 'The Tyrant Comes Home'.

My mother was never violent. She was passive around my volatile father, as well as given to frequent debilitating migraines. She drilled into me from an early age that my father was 'a big baby', and that in order for me to survive in their household it was my responsibility to learn how to please him, and never, obviously, to displease him. It was very difficult though for me to get it quite right, what pleased or displeased him at any given moment.

Luckily for me however there was one thing I learned to do that never failed to please him. And that was to take down from the shelves of the many bookcases in our two-bedroom apartment, most of which he'd designed and built himself, his beautiful, dusty, hardback books. He loved books of all sorts: non-fiction, poetry, plays, short stories, novels, even cartoon collections. He loved the very idea of writing itself, of taking the raw material of language, of manipulating and controlling it until something original, complete and beautiful on its own terms emerged.

He also loved to own books. Although we were always short of money he never minded spending what little money we did have on books. So it pleased him enormously when I memorized passages and poems from these books, from *his* books, and recited them aloud to him. And, since pleasing my father was so intertwined with my own survival, I was deeply grateful to books and grew to love them.

Among my father's books were the collected works of Edgar Allan Poe. I fell in love with Poe, whose poems in particular seemed to please my father. And so I learned to recite them by heart: 'Annabel Lee', 'Lenore', 'The Raven' and 'The Bells'. While my father sat in his easy chair in the living room I stood before him and recited, my childish, high-pitched voice throbbing with emotion, my face turned heavenward and my eyelids fluttering dramatically. I identified strongly with the heroines of Poe's poems, those frail young girls who died so young and so romantically. I sometimes longed for a similar escape.

My father also took great pleasure in telling me tales of Poe's own wanton life and premature death. When my teacher took my class on a trip to Poe's Cottage in Poe Park in the West Bronx I eagerly let her know that I knew all about Poe's alcohol and drug addiction, as well as his emotional problems. She was shocked and quickly changed the subject. Before the trip my father, always mischievous and eager to subvert the authority of others, had urged me to demand that my teacher show us Poe's liquor bottles and opium pipes, but luckily I had stopped short of that.

Books pleased my father in another way too. My brother, sister and I would sit on the rug before him while he read aloud to us sections of his political books, educating us about race and class issues. A great favourite was *The Atheist Manifesto*. He would read from it so beautifully, with so much passion and force, that I was completely won over to the book's argument. I felt especially united with him at those moments because I too understood, even if I was only five years old, that religion was the opiate of the masses. And I also knew that it pleased him greatly that I'd taken his side against the oppressors.

Another favourite book of his was *The Green Pastures*
by Mark Connolly, a play which, for liberals of my
parents' generation, was innovative and ground-breaking.
It takes place in a sunny outdoor heaven located in the
deep South where a festive fish fry is in progress and
where God and the angels are all poor and black. My
father would have us perform it with him and, naturally,
during these performances, and despite his atheism, he
always assigned himself the role of the powerful but
benign God. My brother, sister and I were the angels.
We would sit at God's feet, rapt and adoring, as he read
his lines. And then in unison we would happily sing out
our scripted angelic praise of his wise and mighty
proclamations.

My father was a pharmacist. He'd gone to college on the
GI Bill after he'd fought in the Second World War. He'd
gone into pharmacy because it was one of the fields then
open to Jewish men without money or connections. He had
written short stories and poems in college, however, and he
frequently lamented not having gone on to write professionally. For a while he'd thought about teaching English in the

public school system, in order, I suppose, to instil his own love of books into the hearts of countless worshipful pupils. My mother told me years later how happy she'd been that he decided not to go into teaching, since with his temper, she said, 'He would have killed someone'. And after all he had me, his most worshipful pupil.

My father frequently regaled me with anecdotes about his own childhood. To me they simply sounded like tales from another of his wonderful, dramatic books, not much different than Poe's tales, or the tragic narratives of 'The Highwayman', 'The Rhyme of The Ancient Mariner' and 'The Solitude of Alexander Selkirk', the other poems I loved to recite to him. He told me about his violent mother and father who had fist fights in front of him, and how he would run away from home, sleeping on park benches until his father found him and hit him over the head with a violin – his father was a vaudeville violinist – and then dragged him home by his hair. My mother frequently said that I was like the members of *his* family, hot-tempered and stubborn; whereas my sister and brother, she would say, were like the members of her own, much calmer, nicer family. Whatever my mother's intentions, I felt flattered to be included among my father's family, among those colourful, fictional-seeming characters, none of whom, with the exception of my father's older brother who lived in a nearby suburb, I had ever met. It was only as I grew up that I began to hear the subtext, the pain in my father's stories, and came to understand what a sad book it was that his life would have made.

When I was very small my father worked at a pharmacy in the South Bronx, a rough, drug-filled, Latino neighbourhood. His dream, however, was to own his own pharmacy. Despite his leftist politics he had a fervent desire to become a capitalist, to own something, just as he loved to own books, to see great numbers of them displayed in his bookcases. But even more than that I think he needed always to be the boss, to give orders and not to take them, to be the one, the only one, in control.

In order to make my father's dream come true he and his brother decided to go into partnership together, starting up a pharmacy in the West Bronx near Yankee Stadium. His brother, also a volatile man, was an affluent lawyer, much shrewder and far more socially at ease than my father. My uncle was the moneyed partner, while my father worked in the store with a third partner, also a pharmacist. Eventually of course, given their violent personalities and the legacy of their parents, my father and my uncle had an explosive falling-out and never spoke to each other again. Years after that my father and his other partner too had a huge dispute and also never spoke again. And eventually the pharmacy went bankrupt.

But what had fascinated me most about my father's pharmacy when I was a child was the pharmacy's paperback book rack. Again, he seemed especially proud that he sold not merely pharmaceuticals and cosmetics but books too. From age ten or eleven I would go over and pick books off the shelves, as many as I could load up in my arms. They were less beautiful, true, than my father's big dusty tomes, but they were so much lighter, and in a way they were still *his*. My father was too busy working around the clock, trying to make his store into a success, to take any notice of which books I was grabbing. He never knew that among my new books were a group of soft porn novels: my favourite was *Awake, Monique*, about a woman who learns true sexual happiness after a number of false starts. He also never knew that I was discovering formalist and experimental novels like *The Floating Opera* and *The End of the Road* by John Barth, books that were a far cry from his own favourites, the politicized social realists: Steinbeck, Hemingway, Odets, Sinclair Lewis. Since he never did find out, though, he remained genuinely pleased by my continued interest in *his* books, from *his* very own store.

Only once do I remember a book displeasing my father. I was about fourteen or fifteen. I was in my room lying in bed, reading *Another Country* by James Baldwin. I was about a third of the way through it. My father came

'Books!'
snarled my
  grandfather
'are a bloodless substi-
  tute for life'
the thick blue ink of
  his veins
clotting happily
into commas, semi-
  colons
and colons
towards a sudden and
  glorious
full stop
  (GERRY MURPHY)

into my room, saw what I was reading, and flew into a rage. He didn't strike me although I waited for it. But he did yell at me, insisting that I not read 'that trash'. I was shocked. He had always been irrational, true, but never before about books. Books were our great bond. 'Garbage, trash, I forbid you to read this!' he kept shouting. It was inexplicable, but I didn't question him or try to defend myself since I had learned by then that such things were to no avail. Instead I agreed not to finish reading it, although I didn't have a clue what had so enraged my father. I knew it couldn't be because Baldwin was black: my father, the leftist, had more black friends than white friends. And it certainly couldn't be Baldwin's own non-mainstream politics. I figured I would understand soon enough though, since I intended to finish it in secret anyway, despite my promise. I had learned too by then that secrecy within my family was a great help to survival.

But still, even after I'd finished reading *Another Country*, I couldn't see what had so enraged my father. It was a profoundly moving book about marginalized people and it dealt boldly with issues of class and race. In other words it was exactly the kind of book that, as a leftist Jew in a Bronx housing project, my father had brought me up to love. It was only years later that I understood. It was after I'd left home when, as an adult, I would casually mention things to my father about my gay friends, male and female. Because only then did I learn that my father, despite his liberalism, was homophobic. And I realized that back when I was a teenager he'd been frightened that Baldwin's powerfully rendered scenes of homosexual sex would win me over to 'the love that dare not speak its name'; as perhaps my father himself had once won me over through the power of a book to his atheism.

Still, despite that disappointment the majority of my happy childhood memories *are* about books. And I like to think that this holds true for my brother as well, who grew up to be a labour organizer and who's as passionate and fierce about politics as my father. Like my father my brother is always deeply immersed in some book, some political piece of literature, in his quest to educate himself and others. My sister, who died young of a rare, particularly brutal form of cancer, with nothing at all romantic or Poe-like about her premature death, also loved books, earning a Master's degree in English literature at night while working full-time during the day as an editor.

And for me writing has come to be synonymous with my very survival. When I'm not writing, creating my own stories and books, I don't feel alive. It's clear to me that like my father I must have something I can claim ownership of, something I can control fully. When I'm writing I feel always as though I've entered a very safe place, a place of 'green pastures', a place where, through the power of even just one book, three frightened little children can be transformed into angels, and an angry father into a most benign and loving God.

(JANICE EIDUS)

Homeboys

The day my mother threw my brother's books out of the bedroom window, I was sitting on the back garden step counting my meagre collection of records. 'What's she doing?' inquired a startled friend, covering his head with his hands to repel a cascade of Pans and Penguins. 'Spring cleaning,' I replied, drawing his attention to a rare Chuck Berry in my hoard, struggling to divert his attention from the embarrassing goings on. 'A bit bloody much isn't it?' he grumbled, taking his hands from his head and gazing warily up at the bedroom window. 'She could injure somebody.' There was a brief pause, then another avalanche. My friend was struck twice. 'I've never read this,' he said, bending to pick up the first volume of *War and Peace*, 'is it hard?' I smiled, relieved he'd taken the second assault in such good spirit. 'No, not really,' I lied, 'I got through it in a week.'

'Where's Derek?' asked my mother over tea later, mildly concerned. 'He left without saying cheerio.' I muttered something about the books, suggesting he might be intimidated a little. She laughed. 'I've told your brother time and time again about the dust. I think he must be daft or deaf or something. Books invite dust. I've not time for them.'

The books lay amidst the daffodils and tulips until my brother came home from work. 'Oh no!' he exclaimed as he arrived, catching sight of me lurking by the open kitchen window. 'Why didn't you pick them up for me? They could have been rained on.'

'She forced me to have a bath,' I explained. 'There wasn't any time.' It wasn't true, but I was too ashamed to admit to my laziness. I was an unhelpful little swine in those days.

My brother took his books back upstairs, stacking them in neat piles by the bedroom window. I assisted, reluctantly. While we worked our mother took her evening nap on the living-room settee. 'When's Dad coming home?' my brother asked after we'd finished. 'Have we got to wake Mother up before he gets in? Will he be wanting his tea?' I wasn't sure. 'Perhaps it's in the oven,' I said, trying to be helpful. As we went into the kitchen to investigate I espied a muddied copy of *David Copperfield* lying on the table. 'We must have forgotten this,' I said, picking it up, leafing through. 'It's a big book. Have you read it?' 'Of course! Dickens is an old friend of mine!' snapped my brother haughtily, opening the oven door, thrusting his head in, staring at the darkness inside.

(KEVIN COYNE)

Iron

I discovered books. I went to London to buy them. Poetry from Betterbooks and Indica Bookshop. Books were my ticket out. They led me away from the factory.

My mother wouldn't let me have them on view in the house in case her friends picked one up. Degenerate material. I had to put them in a cupboard where she kept her iron.

One day she put the hot iron on a brand new, unread book by Michael McClure. It burned a hole right through the cover and scorched the pages. I was very upset.

I still have the book. Still unread. It's in a large cardboard box in my mother's flat in Wales. The box is kept on a shelf in a cupboard where she keeps her ironing board and iron. A different iron.

(RALPH HAWKINS)

The Book My Mother Can't Read

Between 1988 and 1992 I worked on my third book, *Where Does Kissing End?* A novel about sex and obsessiveness, it is also a vampire novel. In most vampire books the vampirism is explicit – you always know exactly who the vampire is – while the sex remains coded, hidden, under the surface, although sometimes only just. I decided to write a book where the vampirism is coded and hidden while the sex is explicit.

From the moment I came up with the idea for this book I had a problem. After I'd finished it the new managing director of my old publisher said he wouldn't publish it because it was pornographic. He said he didn't like the way I used the word 'cunt'. But this wasn't the real problem; my new publisher isn't faint-hearted about language. A problem, The Problem, remains: my mother. What will she think of it?

When I was a little kid a book circulated amongst my parents and their friends; it was called *Forever Amber*, and in the British Columbia of the 1960s it was thought of as very *risqué*. This book was famous in my family because my father took it when he went off with the guys on his week-long fishing trips. I never managed to get my hands on the book. I've no idea what Amber had to be forever about.

When I was slightly older – by now dad had his own fishing boat – I discovered he kept a copy of *The Happy Hooker* by Xaviera Hollander in the drawer of his bedside table. This I did manage to get my hands on, to get my hands all over in fact. It is a lavish account by an ex-prostitute of expensive call girl sex in hotel rooms. I was always shocked, and still am, that my father had read this book. Even more shocking was the fact that my mother allowed him to read it. It has only just occurred to me *at this very moment* that my mother might have read it herself.

When I was trying to figure out how to write about sex I wrote to all my friends and asked them to tell me the title of the most erotic book they had ever read. Their answers trickled back: 'I never like sex in books'; *Wuthering Heights*; the *Yellow Pages*. Uninspired by their lack of enthusiasm, I decided to dive in at the deep end. I'd have to tell it like it really is, raw language, four letter words. From the first time I saw those words flickering on my computer screen, those naughty words describing my characters doing terrible things to each other, those words about *it*, I knew that this was going to be the book my mother could never read.

If I had a fan club my mother would be president of it. When my first book came out she flew to Britain for publication carrying with her another book, a scrapbook for all my publicity. She had made it herself, transforming an ordinary photo album into an extravaganza of puffy pink gingham with white lace, white and pink ribbons, and a sampler inset into the middle, embroidered with the words 'Follow Your Dreams' and a small pink heart. My mother loves the fact that I am a writer. With her copies of my first two books she functions as a lending library for all of western Canada.

I have a friend in New York who is also a writer. Her second book was the one her mother couldn't read. My friend, always pragmatic, said to her mother, 'Ma, you won't like it, don't read it.' So her mother didn't. I thought I would try this tactic. I wrote a long letter. I made jokes. Every writer writes a book she wouldn't want her mother to read.

A letter came back to me. When is the book coming out? Is it going to be published in Canada? Nothing beyond that. I breathed a little sigh of relief and thought, how good to have such obedient parents.

A second letter arrived. Family news, et cetera. At the bottom, a postscript: 'PS Aren't I old enough to read it?' A bit further down the page: 'Is it as bad as *Lady Chatterley's Lover*?'

The book was published and I didn't send any copies home. My mother doesn't come for publication any more, it's not such big news for me write a book, and my father has been unwell for a long time and she doesn't like to leave him. I included my siblings in my blacklist just in case. Occasionally my mother asks how the book is doing, what the reviews were like. I tell her. I make jokes.

Last week I got some good news. An American publisher has bought *Where Does Kissing End?* They'll publish it next year. They've also purchased Canadian rights and, yes, they will publish it there too. I toyed with the idea of imposing a publishing embargo in Canada but I couldn't figure out how to explain this to the Americans. 'My book is offensive to British Columbians.' It wouldn't work. So, the novel will be available in bookshops near my mother. Is it feasible to ask her not to buy it when it is there, right there, the family name adorning the cover? What will happen if she reads it? Who cares what the North American reading public thinks of my book? The real question is what will my *mother* say?

(KATE PULLINGER)

Blokes

End of terrace. On a corner. John's cafe. Blue signboard with white letters: 'John's Cafe'.

Bacon, egg, bubble and toms. Tinned tomatoes rather than fresh, because of the juice. Thick slices of white proper bakery bread with two inch seedy crusts. I'm having the works for an early lunch. This cafe is one of dad's favourites.

We are out on business. Me and dad. On a mission to buy stationery for his office. To buy some Day-Glo sign cards and magic markers, so I can draw up a Special Offer sign (dad says I'm a bit of an artist). Some staples for his staple gun.

The cafe is full of blokes. These blokes have big appetites, so they tend to scoff their food. Dad is at ease in cafes. What dad doesn't particularly like about artists and such is their tendency to nibble at things. They are generally a bit quiet and a bit unsure of themselves. Whereas manual workers bite out big chunks. Spread their legs wide. Burp, naturally, in the middle of telling jokes. Screw up the *Daily Mail* when they've read it. There's nothing sly about them.

Our meals are plonked on the table and we start tucking in. We make sure to go the full whack with the condiments. Plenty of salt on the eggs (dad says you can't have too much salt). Brown sauce on the bacon and a dusting of white pepper over everything.

Dad loves the healthy efficiency of the place. 'John' working away with his frying pans. Wife on the till, taking orders and passing bits of paper with cafe code on them. The waitress moving around the tables like a robot.

'They've got it down to a tee in here,' dad says.

A bloke is dipping a cheese roll into his mug of tea. This is to soften it because he hasn't got his false teeth in. The waitress has blank, heavily made-up eyes. She is fully employed with the back and forth and notices nothing. She is about twenty or younger. Lank brown hair. Shapeless face. She has a short skirt that shows off her black stockings.

'Alright I s'pose, if you put a paper bag over her head,' some bloke mutters. All the others laugh. The waitress smiles, not knowing why. I recognize her face. And the blank white paintwork of this place. These pictureless walls. Familiar. I bet it's the same upstairs.

I eat my lunch quickly now. Faster than dad (who normally bolts his grub). I keep my eyes fixed on the street outside.

Home. A little white and yellow painted house with a single bay window. In a quiet terrace. In East London.

No one's at home. I've got the place to myself. I can walk around without any clothes on if I want to. What I want to do is go upstairs. To the spare room. The room dad says he's going to make into my bedroom. But it's empty at the moment. There's some junk in there. No carpet. Bare boards. I double lock the front door. Just in case.

In the spare room there's a book. It's under the floorboards. I found it two days ago. Every time the coast is clear, like now, I check that it's still there. I look at it thoroughly, because I think it will disappear soon.

I know it's not old, because I've hidden things under the same floorboard before now, and it's not covered in dust. I can't remember the exact reason for looking under there. It's enough to say that I'm always looking under things. I love secret places. This is like a dream come true. So now I lever up the board with a screwdriver.

The book is still there. I see it in the darkness, a couple of feet in from the opening. I put my hand in. Careful not to disturb anything else. The electric cables. The pieces of plaster and sawdust. The hard, grey, dead mouse's body. Careful not to let anyone suspect I've been here. I note the book's exact position before I remove it.

The book is handmade. It is a collection of typewritten sheets, with every other page a stiff, curling photograph.

In the carriage seven young businessmen recount the day's conquests in the office while consuming vast amounts of tinned lager. Self-conscious in their midst is a young girl. She is reading. One of the drunken commuters offers her a drink from his can. She ignores him. The men fall about in hysterics. To hide her face she holds up her book, *How To Be Assertive in Large Groups*.

(GREG DAVILLE)

It is bound together with staples. These are covered with a strip of black carpet tape to form the spine. The cover, or front page, is actually a photograph. Which means it bends out and will not lie flat. There is no picture, just white letters stencilled on to a black rectangle: *And Mother Came Too.* It's a 'dirty' book. My brother is not at school yet. Only one person I can think of could have hidden it here.

The story starts with a bloke who is fucking a woman. She is a mother of two. He goes round to her house one day and catches the two daughters playing at lesbian games. They are virgins. With the mother's consent he 'breaks them in'. Mother joins in and is fucked by his 'bloody cock'. Hence the title.

The words are a story, but the pictures are real. Seeing is believing. The story smells of the bloke who wrote it. It's full of daft stuff, but it's also familiar. It's like the lines of limericks I've heard, or rugby songs: 'He was pumping enough spunk in her to float an entire navy'.

The blood pumps in my head. My stomach turns over. I put the book back down the hole. Put the board back. Visit the toilet. Return to the hole. Get it out and start thumbing through it again.

The photographs show a girl's body and two older men's bodies. The main interest is where the blokes' pricks go into the girl's cunt. The men have hairy bellies. Their heads are not shown. The girl's head is shown when they are sticking their pricks into her mouth. Like dark sausages. There are big black shadows everywhere, like you get when you take flash photographs. The fucking torsos are pictured against the white walls of a pictureless room. There is a sofa, which is used for propping up some of the activity, but apart from that there are no other details.

I stroke my stiff willy and the white stuff runs down over my fingers. I imagine blood or that my willy is not white but dark and shiny like the ones in the photographs. The book is real, in the fingers of my other hand. Touching where my father's fingerprints must be.

So close I feel sick. Close to him. Close to real sex. He never uses swear-words but really he's as naughty as I am.

(IAN BOURN)

The Librarian's Fault

I am an attorney practising law in the Tennessee town where I was born and raised. I am thirty-five years old and unmarried. Folks often ask me why I haven't married; it's a favoured question of matchmaking blue-haired old ladies with much time on their hands and a quest to meddle. I have always loved libraries. When I was a small child my mother would take me and my sister to the local public library and leave us there for a couple of hours while she shopped the downtown stores. I can still smell the leather of the gigantic chairs I'd curl up in and, following the rule to treat the books with kindness, lose myself in a world more interesting than my own.

When I was thirteen I began to attend Brainerd Junior High School, and I recall my fear when I first walked into its mammoth halls. By the second semester I'd only been to the school library once, and that for an orientation lesson that did little to orient me. The place was forbidding and did not embrace me like the loving leather chairs of the only other library I'd ever known. I was afraid that I would forget and inadvertently violate one of the ten thousand rules that were posted everywhere.

Like most boys my age I was prone towards infatuation, and at the start of the second semester a girl transferred to our school from someplace else. She was very pretty and I fell madly in love with her, but I could not summon the courage to talk to her. I was quite convinced this was the girl I was meant to marry. All I had to do was get past this not-being-able-to-talk-to-her thing. She was in my art class and one day fate opened a window of opportunity for me. Several of us, including her, were sent to the library to look up some information.

As we searched the card catalogue my courage grew and I resolved to walk up and speak to her. Although I was scared I might violate a rule I was prepared to cast caution to the wind. As I moved closer I could hear her whispering to her girlfriend that her father had been transferred again and she would be moving soon. A jagged piece of broken glass gouged its way into my heart. I thought I would throw up. She and her girlfriend got up to go back to class. I knew I'd have to strike quickly or lose it all. She checked out her book and walked slowly towards the door. I thought if I could talk to her alone in the hallway I could convince her that my love for her was so great that her family would not have to move and we could spend the rest of our days together. It was essential that I make my move, now!

One of the ten thousand rules was that you had to check out a book before you return to class. Thinking quickly, as the door closed behind her, I grabbed a magazine and dashed to the librarians' desk. In as polite a tone as I could muster under the circumstances – fate hanging in the balance as it were – I said to the librarian, 'Can I take this magazine up to Mr Houston's class?' 'I do not know if you can or if you cannot,' she responded. Not realizing that I was being given a grammar lesson, and that I should be saying '*May* I', I asked in sublime, yet panicky, innocence, 'Well, could you check with someone about it, please?'

As the door to the principal's office closed behind me I glimpsed the girl starting up the steps. When I returned from my suspension for having too smart a mouth she had transferred to another school.

So now I live alone, with books to keep me company, and it's the librarian's fault.

(EDWARD THOMAS LANDIS)

The Last Days of Pompeii

'The story of explosive human passions in the
shadow of an awakening volcano . . . 391 pages.'

I ought to read it, having been
brought up in Bulwer Street.

Edward Bulwer-Lytton, afterwards
Lord Lytton (1803–73), that
'hummiest of bugs' – the Book Club
can't know that he,
in my father's gross codologies,
my boyhood's weekend dandyism
of gaudy tie and cultured quiff,
is family too.

I ought to show more loyalty.

And there's another link to make
this dusty grammar of disaster mine:
flattened, burnt by bombs, our street
has claims on dignity. I too
heard rumblings in the night.

Now after all these years of poetry
I sit with books in Boundary Drive,
weighing up Sir Walter Scott's cold words
on Bulwer's 'slang tone of morality'
and Queenie's labelling him the first
of modern best-sellers.

Remembering too
how in his final landlocked weeks
my dying father asked
for 'reading books' and I had said
I'd nothing that he'd like.

(MATT SIMPSON)

Tongue Twister

Aged eight I was engaged on yet another exploration of my grandmother's house. Two thirds of it sat above Aspinall's sweet shop and one third was submerged behind Aspinall's and the high walls of the back yard. It was in this dark lower portion of the house that I discovered *The Joy of Sex* in a sideboard drawer, two down from cutlery.

Alone and undisturbed I opened the book at a page containing a line drawing of a man and a woman, both of them naked, the man with his head between the woman's legs. Barely a graduate of *Janet and John*, I remember trying to pronounce the caption with uncertain success.

Some years later I opened a copy of *The Reader's Digest Home Medical Dictionary* to find a polaroid photograph of my mother reclining in the nude.

To this day I always approach a book with a certain apprehension and still find myself muttering 'cunninglingus'.

(WAYNE BALMER)

My mother hated to see anyone absorbed in a book and could tolerate it only for a few minutes, then she would slap it out of our hands and hurl it across the room. So my brothers and I did most of our reading in bed. (A MASS-OBSERVER)

Confirmation

I'd read but a page and a half of the book and that confirmed my greatest fear. I was impotent. And I was only thirteen. The book, *Making Babies*, had two halves, one for boys to see and one for girls. It was produced by the Catholic Truth Society and shown to me by one of the Irish Brothers whose calling it was to take working-class Liverpool Catholics and educate them into middle-class Liverpool Catholics.

We were walking together to the Brother's house. He slipped the small paperback to me, indicating the passages I should read. He stared ahead, stony silent as he laid waste my nascent manhood. I read that making babies

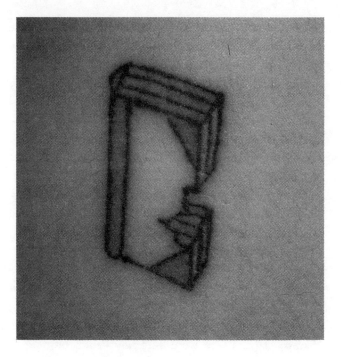

Dick Miller's logo for Aloes Books tattooed on publisher Jim Pennington's left buttock

was done by putting the part where a man's water came out next to the part where a woman's water came out. Then, and this was the tough part, the man passed water.

I turned away weak, and Brother Dee apologized if he had shocked me. He had done more than that. He had devastated me. I knew for a fact that if I got that near to a girl's drawers sure as eggs I'd go hard as nails and there'd be *no* chance of pissing. That was a fact.

I was impotent.

(CHRIS PROCTOR)

Nipped in the Bud

I sat in the vasectomy clinic wearing only a shirt and waiting for my cut. My mind was really on other things and the book I held was rather to take my mind off the future than to be enlightened by more of John Cowper Powys's philosophizing. I'd read plenty of Powys's works.

He was a deep and mystic man who tended to dwell on the nature of the First Cause, the impact of legend on place, the life of the inanimate, the power of religion, things like that. My unsettled gaze flitted over the pages, only half attentive. Then suddenly stopped. I stared in horror at the page balanced on my naked knee.

Hundreds of pages of mysticism I had toiled through in my interest in this strange writer. And now, what had happened in the middle of *Weymouth Sands*? Sex, that's what. Suddenly, instead of musings on things cosmological, the book was full of black stockings, Perdita's legs, long bare tits, even – oh, no! – ragged knickerbockers.

I looked away, hoping I had been misled. Hoping it would go away. Hoping that the tinkering in my groin was a quiet twitch rather than anything ongoing. Oncoming. Urgently, I skipped on a page or two. I glanced down, furtively now. She was in the hay loft where Skippy slept. There were fluttering hands, burning fingers and – Jesus – curves on her flanks and – shit! – two of the whitest, softest, roundest breasts that the world had seen. Any other time I wouldn't have minded. I stared desperately at the ceiling, trying not to notice the raising of my shirt.

'Would you like to come through, Mr Proctor?'

Pathetically, apologetically, I followed myself into the operating room.

(CHRIS PROCTOR)

Bibliofile

It was my parents' dearest wish that both their sons should become priests. My elder brother went into the seminary at the age of eleven, and pending the moment when I too could enrol I practised at home for my future vocation. With the waistband of my mother's velveteen flounced skirt fastened around my neck I had a sumptuous vestment which reached to the floor. The sideboard was the altar and an encyclopaedia propped up on it was the missal. But then my brother abandoned the seminary and went to work in Ford's car factory. My father never spoke to him for the next three years and my mother developed a psychosomatic lump in her groin. To make matters worse my pre-ordained plans were also derailed when I failed the eleven-plus exam. So I made a pact with God. I dug a pit in the garden and filled it with broken glass on which I vowed to walk every day if God would grant me one of the unclaimed eleven-plus places. But God chose to ignore my bloodied feet, and my plea. The priesthood was, for me as well, not to be. So after leaving school I went to work for Mother Teresa, then having paid my dues I changed tack in my mid-thirties and became an artist.

But roots run deep, and on enrolment day at the Royal College of Art I was reassured to note several fellow students carrying what I took to be Bibles, only to discover later that they were Filofaxes. Not too different as it turned out: secular breviaries authoritatively signposting a straight and sure path through the baffling maze of daily life. Now I hear that a new generation of students, children of Mammon standing confused at the crossroads, are seeking spiritual values. Ring-binder Bibles could be just the thing.

(JOHN KIRBY)

Our Edna

In the priest-ridden Irish Republic of the sixties, where the index of banned authors looked like a list of recommended reading for any student of modern literature, Edna O'Brien took pride of place. Somehow Edna was viewed as being more perfidious than Steinbeck, Faulkner, Mann, Sartre, Dos Passos, Salinger, Muriel Spark, Truman Capote, Tennessee Williams, Samuel Beckett, Norman Mailer, Graham Greene, Joseph Heller and all those other writers who were banned. A reader in the Ireland of those days was left with the indelible impression that he or she had drawn the short straw. Ignorance of real life was carefully nurtured, jealously guarded, and it flourished.

We adolescents listened to the Beatles and the Rolling Stones, yet there were girls in Ireland who worried that a kiss might make them pregnant, or that they were bleeding to death. The priests railed against French kissing when what we needed was a manual of the art. Edna O'Brien's books highlighted this unspeakable, un-mentionable need, one which a cosy national conspiracy of elder churchmen and elderly politicians legislated to keep at bay. They were published at a time of huge national denial, when there was an outright refusal to face facts or consequences considered to be unwhole-some. Human sexuality was in the extremely unwhole-some category.

Other writers wrote about faraway places like America or England. Not so Edna. Edna ratted. Her themes were local, much too close to home. A society like this had, and still has, its unfair share of victims. Women fared worse. Sex education was curt to the point of disappear-ance. When it did take place it was of the 'don't ever do it' or 'all men are wild beasts' variety. I never met anyone of my own generation in Ireland who was taught that sex is healthy, natural, necessary and enjoyable.

Contraception was unavailable and abortion was a word that could not be uttered, yet the conception of a child out of wedlock was considered to be an appalling scandal, a fate worse than death. Girls who became pregnant were sent away to homes run by nuns where they were not treated gently. There was no sympathy for such a plight: hadn't they brought it on themselves? Even when confused, guilt-ridden, and abandoned in their hour of greatest need, the all-important Eleventh Com-mandment – Thou shalt not be found out – was nearly always observed. Young women emigrated or went to otherwise extreme lengths to conceal a pregnancy, even from their own family. Adoption was widespread and a 'premature' arrival, post-marriage, was cruelly gossiped about in our much too parochial society.

In this atmosphere of reactionary purity Edna O'Brien's books caused immense offence, and not only because she was Irish and a woman. The strength of reaction to a writer with the barefaced cheek to suggest that Holy Ireland was a pagan place was staggering. A double standard abhors a spotlight and Edna O'Brien beamed a strong one on Ireland's Manichean morality where the woman was always in the wrong, especially if she was young, ignorant and inexperienced, even though the man might be neither. A woman's place was in the home with children, not out writing dirty books, unless of course she was a whore.

In the minds of the teachers – and in those days most teachers were priests, nuns and religious brothers – Edna belonged in a special category all her own: a seat in the hottest part of Hell was surely reserved for her. All us schoolboys and schoolgirls in those strange days were given to understand that we would certainly share that damnation if we even opened her books. *The Country Girls* and *Girl With Green Eyes*, titles intoned in awed whispers whenever authoritarian adults were out of ear-shot, had an exotic and magnetic fascination for an emerging generation. These books were, for many, their first experience of a literature about real life, an amazing alternative to approved titles like *Christian Courtesy for Catholic Girls*.

One of the problems facing would-be readers was where to get a copy and how to smuggle it around. For banning her stimulated interest and ensured the clandestine circulation of her writings. The books quickly became dog-eared because so many individuals read the one copy, passing it from desk to desk in the schoolroom. And while it might mean eternal damnation to read Edna, it was social suicide not to.

(DES O'SULLIVAN)

Leabhar Mór na Héireann

The Great Book of Ireland is a contemporary illuminated
manuscript in the tradition of the great medieval illuminated books of Ireland. But if it follows in that
tradition it also subverts it. Where the early books are
recensions of the Gospels, *The Great Book* is agnostic,
doubting, polyvalent. Where the early books are products
of a monolithic and insular culture, *The Great Book* is
pluralist, self-questioning, cosmopolitan. Where scribes
laboured in a scriptorium *ad majorem Dei gloriam*, the poets,
artists and composers who made *The Great Book* contributed their work not only from all corners of Ireland,
North and South, but also from the Caribbean, from
Moscow, from Paris and from the Arctic Circle.

This huge volume is made in vellum, with endboards
planed from an elm planted by W. B. Yeats at Thoor
Ballylee, his tower retreat in the west of Ireland. The
box which protects the book and the display case in
which it is shown to the public are of the same elm, with
decorative inlays of 7,000-year-old bog oak, fashioned by
craftsman Eric Pearse. The book is bound in white
leather, with a spiralling sun pattern worked by hand
into the front cover by the book's maker, A. G. Cains,
Head of Conservation at Trinity College, Dublin.

Inside the front and back covers, circling around the
edges of the binding, there is a verse of a poem by Eaven
Boland, which ends with the words 'The blackbird puts
out her wing, the whole full flirtatious span of it'. This
simple device signals a number of *The Great Book*'s themes.
The early manuscripts are famous for their marginalia,
especially for the haiku-like recurrent image of the blackbird, the intrusion of a kind of nature mysticism into the
gravid Gospels of the monks. In itself an iconoclastic
image, the early note sounds on and on through the
centuries into Irish poetry of the present day, where the
great theme of the self-sufficient world resounds in the
work of generations of poets. That the verse is by a
woman poet is also significant. For centuries Irish women

were confined to the margins of writing, but in the present day they have emerged in strength and in numbers to challenge their exclusion from the canon, to claim their poetry, their voices and their rights. And the idea has a certain poetic aptness, too, that the book is folded in a blackbird's wing, that the bird's pure note sounds whenever the book is opened.

Two hundred and seventy people worked on the book: one hundred and forty poets, one hundred and twenty artists, nine composers and a calligrapher. The idea was born of a conversation between Theo Dorgan of Poetry Ireland (*Éigse Éireann*), the national poetry organization, and Gene Lambert and Eamonn Martin of Clashganna Mills Trust, a charity for people with disabilities. Lambert, a painter, and Dorgan, a poet, became the editors of *The Great Book*, with Martin as general manager and Trevor Scott as design consultant.

Each page in the book represents a collaboration between a poet or poets, an artist and the calligrapher who worked on the whole book, Denis Brown. Working directly on the large vellum sheets, poets would write and artists would make the images which were then unified by the calligraphy, a different design solution being necessary for each page. Usually the poem came first, and then the artist's work; but not always. In any case the artists were never asked to *illustrate* a poem. The work on each page is a dialogue, poem underpinning image, image challenging or commenting on poem, the fluid calligraphy weaving itself and the other elements into a satisfying whole.

Naturally, in the course of making the book nerves stretched to breaking point as, one after another, the problems emerged: often they were as mundane as the vellum cockling and buckling when wet, alarming the artist. Sometimes they were of a logistic nature: how exactly, for instance, to get Danny Osborne his pages when he was on trek in the Arctic Circle (by air mail as it happened, though a parachute drop was considered). The younger poets had never used dip pens before and the older ones had an alarming tendency to break into cold sweat as long-buried schoolhouse traumas came to the surface. And behind it all the recurring nightmare of finance, finding loans and small grants to enable the work to proceed, a page at a time.

On 25 June 1991 two thousand people joined the book's contributors in the Irish Museum of Modern Art to hear Taoiseach Charles J. Haughey hail *The Great Book* as 'an icon for the new Ireland'. Sixty thousand people came to see the book over the following eight weeks as it began its passage into legend, and the stories started to go into circulation. About Samuel Beckett's last poem, for instance. Beckett, terminally ill, had initially and gracefully signalled his regrets when asked to participate. But when poet John Montague was visiting him near the end Beckett drew out a letter from the book's editors and rasped, 'What's this fellow Dorgan like?' 'Ah,' replied Montague cagily, 'he's not too bad.' Beckett drew from a drawer the vellum, pen and ink which had been sent to him and, with Montague holding down the curling vellum, began to write. He made five attempts to get started before he found his stride and wrote:

> *da tagte es*
> redeem the surrogate goodbyes
> who have no more for the land
> the sheet astream in your hand
> and the glass unmisted above your eyes.

The poem is a variant of an elegy to his father written in 1932. When he had finished Beckett put the cap back on the ink bottle and then, in a gesture of finality, swept ink and pen across the tabletop and into the basket, saying, 'That's done.' It's the last thing he ever wrote.

Through the mysterious serendipity which accompanied the book through all its stages, friends of friends put Gene Lambert in touch with Yehuda Bacon, a Jewish survivor of Auschwitz and Theresienstadt now living in Israel. The page was ferried out to him, and returned. One day soon after, the editors brought the page to Joe Katz in Celbridge, to a factory established by Jewish immigrants long ago for the making of vellum. Katz, himself a Czech immigrant to Ireland following the fall of Dubček, looked at the page for a long time, then pointed to a number in the top left-hand corner of the work. 'My mother had a number like that, and my uncle . . .' and his voice trailed off. Bacon had signed his work with his camp number. The silence that followed on that cold spring morning went on for a long, long time.

Not all the memories are solemn and sombre. Artist Charlie Harper and poet Gerry Murphy travelled together to one working session, perfect strangers seated opposite each other on the Cork–Dublin train. Arriving in Dublin, each hailed a taxi, each arrived separately at his destination and only when greeted at the door of the Arts Council by the session's host for the day, Lar Cassidy, did they realize they were both travelling for the same purpose. That was an easy editorial decision, and now their work sits on the same page for as long as the book endures.

Buried in palimpsest here and there are poems painted over mischievously or accidentally by nervous artists, misspellings to embarrass the poets in the afterlife, complex jokes at the expense of scribes twelve centuries dead, ironic references to persons and events which will have faded from history long before the book fades. The editors particularly treasure a story told by one contributing artist, Martin Gale. After some early pages had been shown on the hugely popular television programme 'The Late Late Show' Gale was in a local shop in the Wicklow mountains where he lives. Some sheep farmers were discussing the programme, 'Tell ya one thing,' an old farmer observed, 'the shaggin' monks wouldn't be up to that now. 'Tis only the poets and th'artists would be up for that class of thing nowadays! Here Martin, are you in this book?' 'No,' said Martin, but the letter of invitation was waiting for him when he got home.

When *The Great Book of Ireland* is closed at night one can fancy the murmuring growing to a roar as the voices of so many artists and poets harmonize and clash, singing the song of what Ireland is, was once, and yet might be.

That it is a book, no more and no less, will be enough for all who made it.

(THEO DORGAN)

Petrification

At home there was a long wide corridor where the books were, impinging on the space we played in. Three sisters, three prams, their dolls and many, many books were obliged to share this corridor. Aside from the usual games there was another that consisted in gently poking the meticulously ranged volumes on the shelves. I can still sense the attraction of the forbidden because this game was guaranteed to displease my father, who expected from us the same respect he had himself for books. The power my minor misdemeanour of prodding his books had over him fascinated me. I found it crazy that the books *had* to be aligned to the millimetre. Why? Without knowing it I already understood that the content of a book didn't depend on its condition, positioning or binding. But my father liked books not just for their content but as almost sacred objects. The book had to remain as pristine as possible, as if it hadn't been read. This respect even drove him one day to change coloured wrappers he'd put on them for transparent plastic ones. A titanic labour, because there were five thousand books in the house.

I detested such veneration because it gave the books a superhuman power. I loathed the place they occupied in the home. The psychological place. My father talked *through* books. Whatever the conversation it would end in the opening of a book to support, or rather substitute for, the paternal discourse. I hated this theorizing, always above my head. I hated the repressive power of books. I hated the absence of my father, how he evaporated in the midst of the pages. The books that filled the shelves were closed to me. And my father preferred them to playing with me or to taking me out. The words trans-fixed him, transformed him into a statue on a rocking chair, a standard lamp to his left, a pile of books to his right. I retained the image of this congealed man right into my adolescence. Always in his place, that place. I have never seen my father dance or laugh with friends.

Books distanced him from the world. I burned to tell him how sick it all made me. Even, on occasion, physically sick.

I just had to escape. I would confront the statue for a few seconds, mutter something about getting out of the house, get his reproving acquiescence, then finally reach the street, its cafés, gardens, the houses of friends, anywhere. Just out of there, away from the books, closer to real life.

I was twelve. Despite the large number of encyclopaedias in the house not one discussed sex. One day one of my sisters remarked to me that volumes eleven and thirteen of the encyclopaedia were missing. Looking through the general index we discovered that these two volumes were about things sexual. A few years later, after a number of sarcastic comments from us, they miraculously reappeared. It was with some sadness that I realized they didn't tell me anything new, so technical and aseptic were they. Even at this tender age I already knew a lot of things through experience. Experiences triggered by a book, *The Little Red Book for Schoolkids*. I'd read it in the evenings in my bedroom, hidden inside another book in case somebody might come in and find me out. There are no erotic memories before the night I first opened it. Not one dream. I had friends who'd discovered masturbation by themselves, very young. Not me. Genitals were only for pissing with and for making babies born of an ethereal, sublime and asexual love.

The image of my father sitting in his chair isn't only that of a hated or feared figure. It's more ambiguous than that. It's well known that children admire their parents and take them for gods. If at home this man/book/armchair inspired contempt in me, at school I was proud of him because he *knew*, he knew about everything. Always an author on his lips, a book in his hand. Sometimes the names I'd heard were of use to me in my short skirts because I could assume an air of erudition. It's a pity this belated defence of my reader–father didn't consciously feed my desire for book learning. The fear of authentic experience I detected in him had dissuaded me

Ruth and Eddie Frow,
Labour historians, in their
Manchester bedroom with
some of their 10,000 books.
Photo: Terry Dennett
Photography Workshop

from following his example. How could books be better
than real life?

As a young adult, having abruptly decided to put
miles between me and the libraries of my childhood, I
fled abroad. It's a strange thing, but I took most of my
own books with me, schoolbooks, novels and tales bought
on the recommendation of my teachers. Soon after a new
symptom of my malaise began to manifest itself. My lack
of attraction for books evolved into soporific aversion.
For ten years books sent me to sleep. If I happened to
decide to read, no matter the book, after less than a page
the result was inevitable, physiological, more potent than
a tube of tranquillizers. Wherever I might be sitting my
head would grow heavy and off to dreamland I'd go. The
experience was repeated time and again. I began to feel
like an invalid. Yet even though I was incapable of
maintaining interest in a book I continued to buy them
all the same, and to feel drawn to people who liked
them.

A house without books seems strange and empty to me. And it's perhaps to recreate the lost ambience of my childhood that I've chosen, now, to live with a biblio-maniac. Frightened at first by this repetition of the landscape, but reassured by the wise words of one of my sisters: 'Yes, surrounded by books again, but not the same ones.' An obvious truth that has helped me reconcile myself to this new alignment with knowledge. To the point even of understanding the solitary pleasure my father took in escaping to his imaginary worlds; to even feeling the need myself not to be disturbed when reading. And even to preferring a solitude surrounded by words on a page to the bustle of life outside.

(ANOUK MORTIMER)

Abandoned Boots

My aunt first led me into the world of books when, during the Second World War, she drove a library van round prisoner of war camps in the Home Counties. She often used to take me, aged six or seven, on these exciting expeditions to our enemies. I remember wonder-ing whether they ever escaped. They never did, I was given to understand, because my aunt's choice of thrillers, romances and detective fiction held them rooted.

Though I never actually saw my aunt reading – she read in bed at night, she claimed, and seldom slept – she was one of those people who are said never to be without a book. Her bedroom was her library; even the bed itself rested on books. They were part of the furniture of our house. We propped doors open with them, sup-ported windows, raised tables, and lined the air-raid shelter under the vegetables.

In my teens I joined the new public library, where I lived like a lord, with heating, lighting, chairs and tables, a trained staff, a supply of up-to-the-minute newspapers and magazines, and a sumptuous range of books from the classics to the avant-garde. This was my university, and the authors lined up alphabetically before me became my professors.

My aunt soon grew curious about this place. She herself patronized the private lending library at Boots the Chemist, where she could pick up a bestseller with her toothpaste and soap. Eventually she followed me, somewhat suspiciously, to the public library. What she saw amazed her. Abandoning Boots she became an instant convert, though she never lost the habit of lightly roasting the books she borrowed in a medium oven for the sake of the germs. You could tell the most popular volumes not by public lending statistics but by the residual heat from Aga and Raeburn stoves throughout the land.

(MICHAEL HOLROYD)

The Electrician

The new cooker was installed and working and we had long since finished our cups of coffee, but our conversation rambled on and on, through subject after subject, until the electrician was slumped, naked by now, on the floor in the corner, his voice a fading mumble. My eyes were still on him, but my mind was wandering as he became quietly unconscious.

Some time later I looked back at his still body. I guessed at his weight, his volume, I considered the varying angles of the surface of his skin, and imagined the internal architecture that must support this. He was still in the same position in the corner. I moved over to him. A close examination showed me that he was still breathing, but no other signs of life were coming from him.

I dragged him into the centre of the room and laid him face down on the floor. Cutting through the skin over the backbone with my fishing knife, I worked down over the ribcage, easing the meat away with my hands,

and then up over the shoulders, exposing the bones whilst leaving the flesh intact. Then I cut around the top of the thighs, working down to the feet, first one leg then the other. Pushing my hands into these various apertures and down underneath him, around his front, I loosened the flesh all around, which allowed me to pull the bones and innards out fairly easily. These I flung to one side, and I was left with a limp pile of meat and skin.

A volume describing the dissection of British murderer John Horwood bound in the hanged man's own skin.
Photo: Bristol Record Office, ref 35893/36(v)

He was a pathetic sight, resembling a collapsed pillow or a discarded woolly jumper. I refilled his fleshy enve-ope with the first things that came to hand: my set of encyclopaedias (Arthur Mee's in twelve volumes), three dictionaries (*The Shorter Oxford English* in two volumes, a French–English and a small Latin), and a handful of novels. For the smaller spaces I used screwed-up newspapers.

Pulling the flesh and skin together over its new skel-eton, I stitched up the wounds and turned him over to face me.

'I am ready,' he said wearily, and we continued.

(D. K. NIELSEN)

Carnal Knowledge

When I come home from a hard day's conveyancing my books await me. The stuff I collect is the stuff I want to read: sex, murder, medical aberration and all forms of excessive behaviour, some of it literature, some of it not. I like the idea of having hundreds of mad people on the shelves of my living room, all saying, Hello, Chas, back from work? Take me out, Squire, you're guaranteed a good time.

I've always been aware of my own mortality. I don't just collect books about death, I dream about it all the time. I'm always thinking about what might happen. I may walk out of the door tomorrow and get clipped by a bus. And even if I'm wearing clean underpants, when the police come into my book-lined rooms, well ... I left my last flat at just the right time. Two weeks after I moved out this girl went to a Christmas party and never came back. They found her body in the electricity cupboard next door. The police did a house-to-house. Imagine if they'd come in and seen all my stuff. It would have been down the cop shop, a wet blanket over the head and a few smackings until I owned up.

The only book I ever regret selling came from a man in the States who answered my want ad in a swap magazine. He wrote to me saying, I'm going to send you some paperbacks gratis. I got the stuff and I said to myself, this guy's got real taste. I began a correspondence with him and his letters started getting madder and madder, he was an absolute fucking fruitcake. He ended up being incarcerated in a madhouse. I tried contacting him, and I got a letter from his doctor saying, Do not write to my patient, you're having an adverse effect on him. One of the books he sent me was called *Screwing Bloody Dead Bodies*. It was a porno paperback, but a real

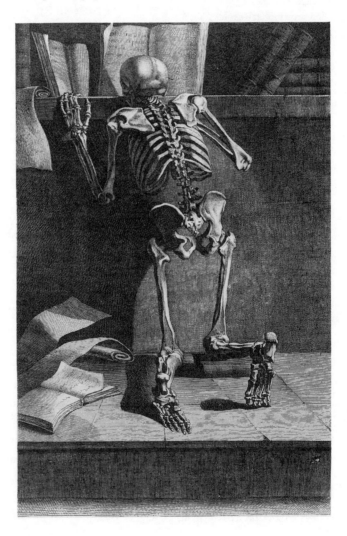

Reading beyond the grave.
An etching from Jacques
Gamelin, Nouveau receu-
il d'ostéologie et de my-
ologie, dessiné après
nature, *1779*

high class production. I didn't know what to do with it. I was living with my parents at the time. I had so many books hidden at the back of my shelves and this one was just one too many. So I sold it for some ridiculous small amount, a few quid. It's a book you'll never see again.

During my schooldays I fucked a book. Me and my mates were pissed one evening and we squirted baby lotion down the backs of our textbooks. I was doing physics for O level and I could never understand anything about the sciences so I thought the best thing to do with a physics book was to try and fuck it. It had a nice spine that bellied out invitingly when you splayed the covers, so I greased it and put it on my dick. It wasn't very good actually. The jute backing on the page signatures was too abrasive.

(CHARLES HILLDROP)

Tip of the Tongue

A video of socks and stockinged feet, made by foot fetishists? Can such a thing be called pornography? If so, are mail order clothing catalogues – apparently of great interest to cross dressers, underwear fanciers and, presumably, sock aficionados – a hidden tributary of the sex industry?

Books: the smell of them, mmmm. So much more refined than the synthetic deodorizer reek of glossy magazines. That feel, like a solid block of chocolate or a chunk of fine wood. A squirting riffle of pages, suggesting the butler's view of a naked woman and the structural origins of cinema. The tick and whisper of turned paper; the creak of a spine.

Many years ago I worked in the record department of a London bookshop. We were adjacent to the economics department (or was it theology? The distinction hardly seems to matter, given that both classifications refer to belief systems which bring misery to millions). One after-

MISS EDNA STILT
of Papua
HAS NEVER READ A BOOK
IN HER LIFE, YET SHE
HAS LICKED EVERY PAGE
OF *Shakespeare's Complete* © Glen Baxter
Works

noon my attention was drawn to a middle-aged man who was moving along the shelves, taking down books, studying them for a moment and then, with a swift animal dart of his tongue, licking the pages.

The floor manager was called to restore order. Luckily for her, fetishists seem to be mild sorts. With the grave demeanour of authority in peril, she spoke to the book licker and he scurried away. But what phrase did she use?

'Excuse me sir, a book is a receptacle for ideas which must be held at a suitable distance from the body and ingested via the eyes rather than the organ of taste. Please revert to customary procedures.' Or, 'In my office, now, for a severe spanking'?

(DAVID TOOP)

Reading on the Beach

The Buxom Lady, physically cushioned by nature, spreads her blanket on the beach, adjusts her sun visor, and settles comfortably on her stomach to read her paperback thriller. A hundred yards away the Chestless Weakling gingerly lowers his bony ribcage on to his rough towel and props his hardback volume of Flaubert's *Letters* against his rolled-up aertex shirt. Nearby, the Hunk lies on his back on the gritty sand, his face shaded from the sun by an open copy of *The Sun Crossword Book*. On either side of the covers stick out his hairy ears, plugged by Walkman headphones from which leaks a sound like hedgehogs scurrying through steel pipes. The Hunk is bored, and placing the Walkman and headphones on the sand beside the crossword book he swaggers off down the beach. Blotting out the sun, his shadow falls across the back of the Buxom Lady as he stands with feet apart, hands on hips, and says, 'Hello, darling, how about joining me for a dip?' The Lady looks up slowly from her book, and perfectly cued by the line she is reading, replies, 'Get lost you goddamn chicken crap square before I kick your motherfuckin' teeth down your throat.' Taken aback, the Hunk thinks slowly to himself, 'This could be more trouble than it's worth. Probably one of them karate teachers.' He shrugs and saunters back along the beach, but with every step he's getting madder, and when he passes the Chestless Weakling he kicks sand on to his head and book. Without turning, the Weakling bites his lip, tears welling in his eyes as he brushes the sand off the page and reads on, 'Through small apertures we glimpse abysses whose sombre depths turn us faint. And yet over the whole there hovers an extraordinary tenderness. It is like the brilliance of light, the smile of the sun, and it is calm, calm and strong.'

Strong, but not calm, the angry Hunk strides back to his crossword book, which lies open as sand fleas hop from blank square to square. Grimly he stamps them to pulp. Meanwhile Patch, the little black and white dog who had, not long since, pissed on the crossword and in the headphones, sniffs his way along the weed-covered timbers beneath the pier, but never loses sight nor sound of his mistress, until she finally closes the book, takes off her sun visor, whistles and calls, 'Here, Patch! Time to go.'

(IAN BREAKWELL)

Her Territory

She was heading for the big bookshop to buy some writing paper and some envelopes. She hated going there these days because she knew her books would be sitting there somewhere, probably in a dark corner where nobody would ever find them. She was sure if she plucked up enough courage to check she would discover that the pile had not moved, that her books had remained untouched. She found that oppressive. It prevented her from enjoying the place. Of course she still browsed, still picked up books to read the back cover, still wanted to buy some. But the knowledge of her novels lying there getting dusty spoiled everything. It was a cold place she thought, the brand new imported hardcovers taking over the whole space on the display table. She felt out of it, and she always left wondering why on earth she kept on writing. She had never really understood why they built such a big bookshop in this area of town. Didn't they know people were struggling to make a living? Didn't they know most of them were more worried about their health bill than about the next novel they were going to read? Didn't they know that for the vast majority litera-ture only meant schoolbooks?

Then she remembered the conference she'd attended a while ago. She had been invited to take part in a debate. The theme was: 'Is African literature a luxury or a necessity?' It quickly got very heated. 'Who are you writing for?' yelled a member of the audience. 'Your books are in a foreign language and only available to the tiny minority of the educated élite, and in any case they are far too expensive!' She remembered the man's face. It was distorted with rage. She had not known what to say right away and somebody else took the microphone to reply to the angry man. She had forgotten exactly what was said, but she still remembered the aggressiveness contained in the question. So, she was heading for the bookshop to buy writing paper and envelopes. She liked nothing more than to walk in the neighbourhood. She called it her territory. The same scene usually presented itself: children playing around the market, looking for leftover fruit or trying to make a few coins carrying some woman's heavy bag of groceries; flower sellers making big bunches and spraying them with water; groups of young people chatting under shady trees. She knew all the beggars and all the hawkers. She was always stopped by somebody who wanted to tell her something. She always smiled to some familiar faces.

But that day, as she was heading for the bookshop to buy some writing paper and some envelopes, her eyes caught a little stall that had been set up on the pavement between the stand of the grilled-meat seller and the small bakery. The smell from the meat was pervading the atmosphere and it was probably that which had first attracted her. The stall was a big wooden box covered with second-hand books. The man behind it had laid them out in some sort of order. She went straight to the stall and looked at the titles. They were mainly old schoolbooks which had been used year after year until nobody wanted them any more. They had done their job. Perhaps they had given some kid a brighter future or perhaps they had witnessed yet another failure, another boy or girl dropping out, another student in the streets betraying the hope that sometimes a whole village back home had placed in him.

She looked at the novels that were there and held a few in her hands. She felt reassured. She felt happy. She knew that whichever one she found would have a story, a past, a life. They were not like those new books full of expectations with their spotlessly clean pages. And then she saw it. The book. The novel. The moment she laid her hands on it and felt its pulse she was convinced she had made an encounter. She quickly read a few lines just to make sure, but she already knew the author and had no doubt in her mind that it was the very book she needed at that moment. She had a short bargaining session with the man and before she realized it she was reading the preface and walking back home lost to everybody and everything, but entering another world.

(VÉRONIQUE TADJO)

Nor a Lender Be

'May you itch where you cannot reach!' came his curse.

I had lost a valuable book he lent me the week before and my feeble excuse about a carelessness for which I was notorious in my own circle only aroused his contempt. I was always losing things and generally displaying a negligence that marked me as an outcast when it came to the normal intercourse of borrowing and lending.

Since the curse was uttered, any itch that afflicts me is located in an inaccessible area of my body. *My* body cooperates with a stranger, not with me! In my view, if I have to itch it should be on a leg or the back of my neck or somewhere that my hand can rub fondly, lovingly. I remember the blissful sensation of stroking two toes in which chigoes had laid their eggs when I was careless enough to walk on the warm Essequibo sand unshod. I wanted to impress the ladies with my brand of bravado and ignored forecasts of unbearable suffering. The itch that woke me up that night was indescribably seductive, so much so that I cared little for sleep lest it interrupt the attention I lavished on my twitching extremity. But the experience occurred before the curse which condemned me to itch thereafter just below the shoulder blade. A conscientious policeman, determined to arrest me for conduct likely to lead to a breach of the peace, could only be dissuaded from doing so when his colleague explained that his own father was also marched to a suburban station for performing the same up and down motion against a private wall and in full view of mystified passers-by. I was itching where I could not reach.

My tendency to lose things did not improve with age, and my mother, driven to desperation, stopped buying me hats, hoping that exposure to the midday sun would achieve what her lectures on the effects of sunstroke could not. Alas! There followed a period of rampant negligence as a result of which everything that disappeared in the house was attributed to my lack of concentration. After all I misplaced at least one book a week and even managed to lose my left shoe on the way home from school one afternoon.

The last straw was a Latin set book by Tacitus. Latin was never a favourite subject, even among pupils who were capable of achieving an *A* in any discipline while standing on their heads. This negative attitude was entirely the fault of our first Latin teacher, Corky. His real name was Mr Knight, but his penchant for wearing a cork hat several sizes too small for his head earned him the fond nickname. A brilliant scholar who knew everything about periphrastic constructions and nothing about teaching, Corky spent half the lesson writing on the blackboard, offering to inveterate delinquents like myself the irresistible temptation to hurl missiles at his back. But paper darts, aeroplanes, bullets and all manner of missiles rebounded off his back and posterior with no effect on his concentration whatsoever. The serious business came in the fifth form when success in Latin involved committing to memory the whole of Mr Tacitus' tedious book. Since no one understood what he was writing about we all enquired at the bookshop after what was popularly known as a 'key', a word for word translation from the Latin into English. As bad luck would have it, however, that was the only set book for which no key existed. Clearly, no Latin scholar in England understood Tacitus either. The headmaster turned to Corky who, taking full advantage of his moment of literary glory, produced a translation which was cyclostyled by the school and sold for a price my mother could not afford.

When I borrowed Moee's key – she was the daughter of an optician, and being new to the school knew nothing of my reputation for losing things – I took it home and placed it carefully on the shelf above my bed. The next morning, mindful of the agreement that I should return Tacitus by the weekend, I read the first chapter and then worked hard at committing it to memory; and that same evening I made the ultimate sacrifice and gave up my three hours of table tennis practice. Well, you guessed, the shelf was bare. Tacitus had vanished.

Just the recollection of that fateful afternoon makes me sweat. Everyone in the house helped me search for him, even my Aunt Josephine with whom I had been having a long-standing feud. I could not even offer to pay for another copy of the lost text for I had no money of my own, and my mother made it quite clear that she had nothing, being up to her ears in debt. So I had to face Moee the following morning and confess. She, however, appeared to take my confession of negligence with good grace and never even mentioned the matter during the school day. But that same night, on returning from the YMCA at 10.30, I noticed that the gallery was brightly lit, an indication that we were entertaining strangers. As late as 10.30? No one except myself remained up at such an ungodly hour.

I put my bicycle away and went up the back stairs to avoid a formal introduction to someone I would probably never see again. But no sooner had I stepped inside than I heard, 'It's him?' I heard my mother's soft spoken voice, 'It must be.' I stepped into the drawing room and was received with a torrent of abuse from a corpulent lady standing with arms akimbo. 'The book! Where's the book?' she shrieked. Oh life! What is the point of describing how I felt? Moee's mother ranted and raved under the glare of lights we could ill afford to burn. She spoke of friends in high places, of prison sentences that blight one's life and of hell-fire stoked by cannibal spirits with a taste for young delinquent flesh. 'Mrs Lee,' my mother interrupted her calmly, 'if you buy your daughter another copy of the translation I'll pay you at month end.' And with that promise of sacrifice the torrent was dammed. Mrs Lee was led to the door, and I detected, I think, a look of embarrassment in her mannish features.

Two years passed before I renewed my membership of the public library, even though I had previously enjoyed an unblemished record. I simply could not take the risk of borrowing their books. Nor would I enter a bookstore or even read the newspapers in my barber shop. I warrant that, had I been born and bred in one of those countries where neuroses grow on trees, I would be a full-blown bibliophobic case.

Still, my thing now is pens. No one lends me a pen. But ball-point pens are cheap. No sleepless nights over Biros. No curse. No itch.

(ROY HEATH)

Public Domain

Books may furnish a room but people make libraries, yet most library users do not necessarily borrow books. They read newspapers, study the form for the 3.45 at Chepstow, write poems, do homework, seek housing advice, fill in job application forms, photocopy immigration papers, keep warm, bring their kids to storytelling sessions, go quietly mad, borrow language tapes and meet friends. Birmingham Central Library even offers a 'hum line' whereby people driven to distraction by an unknown tune running through their heads can whistle or sing it into an answerphone where the music staff will try to identify it. The public library has always been more than the books. There are libraries with theatres attached, libraries with film projection rooms, libraries with meeting rooms, libraries with galleries, libraries which lend pictures, invite writers to read and discuss their work, libraries which run cafés, sell business information, store and annotate local archives, publish works of local history, lend records, videos and children's toys, provide free newspapers, comfort the bereaved, tell people the time of the next bus, advertise local events, provide chess sets and informally supervise and look after those who have been suffering most from the policy of closing down mental hospitals in the name of 'care in the community'.

Libraries have succeeded where most other public and commercial cultural institutions — arts centres, opera houses, theatres, sports centres, theme parks, youth clubs, bingo halls — have signally failed, that is in being used by a majority of the population as a matter of course. Fifty-eight per cent of the British people have a library ticket,

Joe Orton and Kenneth Halliwell's amended cover of a library book. Photo: Islington Local History Collection

a higher percentage than those who vote in local elections, pay poll tax, watch 'Neighbours', read the *Sun* or have a driving licence. Over 1.6 million library books are issued each day. Here is a 'product' and a 'market' that most commercial entrepreneurs would kill for, yet we take it for granted. Perhaps that's why it works.

The town centre library is the public space where you will find the widest cross-section of the community at any one time: young and old, black and white, women and men, rich and poor. In an era of shopping malls, where not to have a credit card is to be disenfranchised, where many shopping centres, public buildings and railway stations are designed to a brief that explicitly bans the provision of seating or waiting space, and in towns in which the needs of the motorist are invariably given preference over the needs of the pedestrian, a clean, well-lit place where one can meet, wait or browse without harassment is a genuine urban haven.

The public library in contemporary Britain now fulfils many of the traditional functions of the church: a place of relative calm and order, a place for contemplation, enlightenment and renewal. I was meeting a friend recently in Coventry. It was a scorching hot Friday lunchtime and the pedestrian precinct was packed with people shopping for the weekend. There were buskers playing and stallholders barking. Tempers were frayed. Children staged sit-down protests against walking further. The Closing Down posters in many shop windows gave the place a Last Days' feel. Yet in the central library, just a glass door away from all this, there was an air of quiet, involved pleasure and absorption. And this was not a rarefied air or a glimpse into privileged cloisters. These were the same people as were outside – families, punks, widowers, silver-rinsed pensioners, overseas students, mental patients out for the day – but the nature of the space had transformed them, as they in turn transformed it. In Northern Ireland the public library is almost the only neutral territory left, bridging the sectarian divide that runs through nearly all public and private institutions.

Not only do public libraries share with churches a more contemplative atmosphere, they also both share something of the same kind of popular trust. When a sniper ran amok in Hungerford killing sixteen people in August 1987 it was the library that provided a gathering place for the citizens, a source of information about the victims, together with counselling for their families. Many of the same functions were provided by Bradford library services after the stadium fire there in May 1985, and by Clwyd libraries in Kinmel Bay, Towyn and Pensarn in 1990 when the sea wall collapsed. People prefer to ask a librarian to photocopy their marriage licences, immigration papers and other personal docu-

Immortalized in bronze by sculptor Kevin Atherton, Dot Winterbridge takes out a copy of Art Within Reach *from Cobbett Road Library, Southampton.*
Photo: Garrick Palmer

Episode in a small-town library. Ian Breakwell, 1970

ments rather than the commercial copy shop because of the respect and trust the librarian enjoys.

This is why crude economic liberalism is such a danger to the public library and the notion of the public realm, as it reduces everything to commodities and discrete function that can be stripped out, separately costed and put to tender. When the Adam Smith Institute turned its cold and calculating gaze on libraries in 1986 it simply looked at the statistics of running costs against the number of book issues and reasoned with the mind of a six year old that it would be cheaper to give out paperbacks for free. Which is like saying it would be more economic to do away with the legal system and the police force by building a gallows in every town centre.

Closed some years ago, to considerable and bitter resentment, my own local reference library in Stoke Newington was always crowded with adult students, many of them from West Africa, studying for law and accountancy exams. Often they would take a break from poring over their set books and gather outside on the steps to smoke cigarettes, talk politics and tell jokes. The library was for many of them, living in bedsits, a social gathering place, a kind of expatriate café society, as well as a source of books, reading desks and study carrels. I've even been told that more people meet their future partners in the library than on the dance floor. But librarians would say that, wouldn't they?

(KEN WORPOLE)

Yobbo Pensioners Cause Mayhem in Library

The peace of a sleepy library was shattered when two old-age pensioners launched into a pitched battle over whose book should be stamped first. Thirty bookworms looked up in astonishment as the respectable-looking pair shouted obscenities and traded insults. Then the row flared into violence as the two eighty year olds charged at each other, aiming punches 'like football hooligans'. Afterwards one stunned witness said, 'It was very nasty. Peacehaven Public Library has never seen anything like it before.' Library staff are remaining hush-hush over the incident. 'We would rather not comment,' said a spokeswoman.

(*BRIGHTON AND HOVE LEADER*, 19 APRIL 1990)

Rare Books 'Set Free' by Thief

A demented library thief with an aversion to washing has been found guilty in Washington of stealing more than twenty thousand rare books worth millions of pounds. Stephen Blumberg, 42, apparently believed that books were held prisoner by libraries.

His main method was to replace the books' library identifying labels with fakes, after licking off the originals, and then simply to take the volumes away, claiming if challenged that they came from another library.

On one occasion he was caught breaking into a library at night with burglary tools, but no charges were pressed. Aware that the FBI was on his trail, he was preparing to ship his hoard to Mexico when he was arrested last year at his home in Ottumwa, Iowa.

Blumberg stole from more than three hundred institutions in the United States and Canada. One of his most valuable catches was a copy of the last world history not to mention Christopher Columbus, published in 1493. He had pleaded not guilty by reason of insanity. His defence lawyer said that he lived in a time warp and had fought mental illness for twenty-five years.

The prosecutor, Linda Reade, argued that his bizarre behaviour did not constitute insanity. 'Mr Blumberg doesn't like to take baths and wears his underwear a long time, but that doesn't make him mentally disturbed.'

Blumberg faces a maximum sentence of thirty-five years' jail and a $1,000,000 fine.

(EDWARD LUCAS, THE *INDEPENDENT*,
2 FEBRUARY 1991)

The Greek dish *kleftico* means 'stolen meat', meat that is felt to have more flavour. Similarly biblioklepts believe that the words in stolen books have added piquancy and zest.

(IVOR DAVIES)

Booklifter

In the corner History becomes Poetry
Ashbery great-coated, Atwood pocketed

Artaud's Anthology slipped into the chest
All property is theft. I approach.
I do not look like a free spirit.
Sullen Ginsberg, heavy at £20,
slid ridiculously inside a double-breast.
Visions. Mescaline. Marijuana. Freedom.
The best minds of my generation
continue not to care a shit.

He turns distractingly to the top shelf
magnificently dismantling the entire display
in a showering wave.
It is over so quickly I am stunned.
Lamantia bent
Kerouac unglued
Ormond, Ferlinghetti and Cobbing
in a democratic heap.

Do you wish to pay for this surrealism?
A pointless question. He's out the door.

(PETER FINCH)

Block Chimes

I'd worked through Biggles by age eleven and was now
on to thrillers. As usual at night my mum and dad had
gone to the pub and I was sitting in the back room,
reading. The tension had been building and building,
when I came to the sentence: 'At that precise moment
the front door bell rang.' As I read this, so it did! There
was certainly no possibility of my answering it since my
heart had leapt from its moorings with awe and fear.
Could words really do this? It still wants to thump – and
I certainly want it to – whenever I recall that moment.

There is another ring at the bell. This time I'm an
adult and working in Vancouver. Answering it I find a
policeman. He's in plain clothes, a detective with the
RCMP, a Mountie, no less. He asks me if I'd worked in

Newcastle upon Tyne as a Fine Art librarian. Yes, I answer. Then he asks me if I'd known an Australian named Barton and had I sold him some rare books and woodblocks. No, I say, and off he goes. A fortnight later he is back. He had the wrong name, the correct name is B—, and wrong nationality. B— is American and black. This I do remember, but tell the Mountie I still know nothing about selling woodblocks.

B— was not easily forgotten. Indeed he was conspicuous in Newcastle not only for being black but also for always being attired in a three-piece suit, with watch-chain on the waistcoat, bowler-hatted, and with his corpulent weight held upright by a corset. Now he'd come a cropper.

He'd tried to sell a Bewick woodblock in London and been rumbled. Maybe he should have chosen a less classy bookseller. Maybe he shouldn't have taken the woodblock all the way from Newcastle to London by taxi after conning it from my successor. He told her I'd agreed he should have it, and here he was to collect; indeed a taxi was waiting outside with its meter running. Maybe he should have been content with what he had already acquired by way of rare books: a large proportion from the libraries of Newcastle and its environs. His collection was mainly literary manuscripts and rare books on architecture and the arts: the ideal 'country house library' in fact.

He could be the sole reader in an empty cubicle with one rare item and somehow manage to leave with it. I was told many librarians were destroyed by this, broken in body and spirit. How on earth could it have happened to them? When their property was returned to them by the law they found it emblazoned with a new 'ancestral' bookplate: an emblematic 'B—'. I was flown back to England as a witness, and did my two minute piece. I don't think he went down: there was an air of scholarship and class about the whole thing that did not require such an eventuality. For me perhaps the real significance of the affair came from meeting old friends in Newcastle.

One of them suggested she return with me to my hotel (paid for, like the flight, by the police). Twenty years later she still doesn't have to ring the bell to come in.

(RON HUNT)

Limbo

In Birmingham during the 1940s Hurst Street was well known for its eccentric second-hand booksellers. One would open his shop, then put a table across the entrance behind which he would sit and vet anyone who wished to enter. Another would set up scales outside and sell books by the pound weight. In one of the shops I noticed an old copy of *The Monk* by Matthew Gregory Lewis, a canon text within Surrealism and a volume I'd long desired. Objective chance? For written on the fly leaf in faded ink was the name 'Maddox', as if, year after year, gathering dust, the book had been waiting in monastic silence, reserved for me.

(CONROY MADDOX)

On the Case

I am a professional book hunter. I can find any book in the world you ask me for. My minimum charge is £75 per hour for paperbacks, then it escalates from there, plus the price of the book according to its rarity or the difficulty in finding it. No obligation to pay until I find it. If you haggle I double the price, and because I provide a unique service the original quote itself is high. In fact if you're over fifty you need to have a medical certificate before I will personally give you the bill. Ever since I had a customer collapse with a heart attack when

I told him what it was going to cost I've always done it in writing, at least then if they croak I'm not there to see it.

You must give me the author, title and approximate date of publication, then I find it in whatever edition I can lay my hands on. I don't do firsts. My service is primarily for readers and a few collectors, not dealers.

I will find *any* book, even if its subject matter nauseates me. I never question the customer's motives. *The Protocols of the Elders of Zion*, radical arguments for paedophilia, the history of the Conservative Party, you name it I'll find it. I once scared off a vegan customer by querying how her search for all the available books on clogs squared ethically with the fact that some clogs have leather straps. That taught me not to make moral judgements. Another customer collected erotic Victorian line engravings and I sold him for £800 a suitcase full that had cost me next to nothing. He never queried the price, signed the cheque instantly. I said, 'Do you realize that for £800 you could pay a lady to dress up in Victorian clothes and do all these things with you?' He said 'Really?', his eyes lit up and he never came back. Dreadful mistake. Since then I've tried to keep my mouth shut and never deviate from the service I offer, which is providing books.

If people annoy or pester me and I don't like them then I add Aggravation Tax. Because although I work fast people get impatient. They think there are about a thousand books in the world and that I have a warehouse out the back with them all in. They have no conception that there are roughly 700 billion books in existence, including the one they want.

I operate like a private detective. Most book-finding services just place adverts in *The Bookdealer*, which is a lazy cop out. Even then they often get the name of the author or the title wrong. There have been ads for T. E. Lawrence's *The Seven Pillars of Willesden*, Harold Acton's *Memoirs of an Aztec* and *The Pie That Came In From the Cold*. No wonder they can't find books.

The people I like to find books for are obsessive

In a world of workaholics and hyperactive achievers I feel a warm allegiance to the person who can lose himself in a book, as my father did while walking down the street, straight into a lamp post. Six stitches. I was so proud of him.

(REBEKAH WOOD)

researchers of specialist topics. One of my customers seeks books about toilets, a subject that also interests me. She says the world's worst toilet is in the Great Wall of China. It's just a concrete box. The person outside gives you two pieces of damp cotton wool to stick up your nose while you crouch in the midden. Didn't put her off though, she can't get enough books on the subject.

You have to *want* to find a book. Some people are never ever going to ring me up. Like today I was sitting on the bus with an armful of hardbacks and one of the two beetle-browed men opposite me said to the other, 'I had a book once.' 'Yer, what happened to it?' 'Dunno.' Definitely not potential customers.

Many collectors won't employ me because I find books quickly. They prefer to spend a long time searching, that's what they enjoy; it gives them something to do, like a big jigsaw; it's occupational therapy.

Often collectors have the strange behaviour that goes with obsession. A favourite of mine is Rodney, who fixes the rings at book auctions, a brilliant expert yet he doesn't even notice he's got his jumper on back to front.

He lives in two flats, one above the other. In the top one are the books and down below his ever-shrinking living quarters, in which are five thousand mouldering pots of unopened yoghurt because he can never remember to cancel the order with the milkman.

One day Rodney and I missed out on a top-notch collection of children's books because it took us three and a half hours to drive from Clapham to King's Cross. Rodney will only drive down side streets, he thinks you get cancer on main roads. And on diesel trains. So it took Rodney three days to hotfoot it from London to Cheltenham with £50,000 in a suitcase to buy a shop, in the basement of which he'd discovered was an uncatalogued collection including original Shakespeare folios. Any other dealer who wasn't bedridden could have beaten him to it, but only Rodney knew they were there. And of course Rodney's assistant, whose real name is Peregrine but who changed it to Patrick. Well, wouldn't you?

Patrick is also eccentric. His original job in Dublin was to take Flann O'Brien home each evening from the pub in a wheelbarrow. Then Rodney sent him to Argentina to get a very rare collection. To make matters more complicated this was during the Falklands War. Only a nutter like Patrick would have taken the job. He kept telexing endless requests for money, c/o the Concordia Hotel, but never acknowledged receipt. It turned out he was in the Concordia Hotel all right, but in Rio de Janeiro not Buenos Aires. Yet he got the books, so there's method in these people's madness.

In searching for books I discover things that sometimes blur the boundaries between business and my personal life. They say that death is the last taboo, but it isn't. Since the spread of AIDS many people have friends who are dying, often very young, so that taboo is breaking down through personal experience. I have discovered the last taboo, and it's adult bedwetting. Adult bedwetting has changed my life, and all because a customer wanted a particular book about it. The trouble is it's impossible to get anyone in the business to deal seriously with the subject, from the British Library to the corner bookshop.

Now, I don't like to accept defeat. I'll get this book eventually. Yet for a long time I thought I'd have to do it alone as it's a subject no one will discuss. Then, while I was searching, I had myself placed on the Eligible for Marriage register in Southall. You see, I have this compulsive attraction towards Indian women, especially in saris. I'm listed as an Antiquarian Bookdealer, which many of these women think is an accountant, a bookkeeper, very respectable; and in the photo I'm wearing one of my most stylish suits so I look like the ideal mature bachelor.

I made a rendezvous with an Indian woman who'd replied. She was breathtakingly beautiful, and in a ravishing sari. But she turned out to be entirely mercenary, just wanted to know my income, what car I drove – I ride a bike – and how big my house was. There was no meeting of minds and conversation soon dried up. In desperation I told her I was researching adult bedwetting and suddenly her attitude changed. She said, 'That's why I won't sleep with men at night.' Which was my cue, because I'm an insomniac and only lie down on a bed during the day. So now we have a daytime arrangement, but she still won't see me after dark. I'm on the horns of a dilemma: the so far unsuccessful search for this book has led me into liaisons of which I'd previously only dreamed, yet I'm professionally compelled to find the book which I suspect will probably bring these adventures to an end.

Yes, sex and books is a messy combination. I don't mean wanking. I doubt that books are common aids to masturbation compared with magazines, though I do have in my collection a Victorian pamphlet entitled *My Single-handed Fight Against Self-abuse*.

Once books and romance intermingle there's usually trouble. Years ago I used to collect telephone directories from all over the world, obtained free from business libraries when they were annually renewed. In dictatorships like Bolivia they list people's numbers by military rank. In India, with millions of Patels, it's done by street. The Navajo telephone directory was only two pages because they have a different form of conversation to us, whereby neither party must interrupt the other and they must show respect by waiting for a long pause before replying, which makes for very long and expensive telephone calls, and therefore because they're poor people the Navajo don't have much use for phones.

Thus I assembled what I gradually realized was a unique collection of telephone directories. No one else was interested in collecting them. I cornered the market. I could get £100 for a Russian directory at the height of the Cold War when telephone directories were not widely distributed inside Russia. They were classed as state secrets: there were no telephone exchanges in offices, you had to know the direct line to each individual person. It was a means of controlling communication between people, so a directory was a prized possession. I sold a pre-war Latvian directory for a sizeable sum to a lawyer because it established who was living in Latvia in 1938, and they could claim property ownership.

At the time I was collecting the directories, of which I now had hundreds in my flat, I became infatuated with an American woman who had come to London to sign up with lots of doctors on the National Health. She was a total hypochondriac, with an allergy to practically everything. But she was gorgeous, as fragile and delicate as a china doll. She eventually agreed to come and live with me, but insisted on cleaning and redecorating my flat beforehand to eradicate all the germs and allergic substances. I went away for a week and when I came back I could hardly recognize the place. In the kitchen there were two fridges, one for food and one for the medicines. The walls were all painted white; the carpets taken up and the floorboards sealed and polished; the curtains removed; no furniture except a Mies van der Rohe chair; everything gone including the telephone directories. The best collection in England given to the dustbin men! I wept tears of rage and that was the end of a beautiful relationship.

I went to the business library to see if I could restart the collection, and got friendly with the library assistant.

For a little light relief I delve into *The Reluctant Mechanic*, the last book my late husband gave me. It must have been a cheap offer from somewhere.
(A MASS-OBSERVER)

She was poor but aspired to better things and asked me to get her university textbooks she couldn't afford. This I did, in return for sexual favours in the store cupboard at the back of the library. Fondling for the paperbacks, groping for the hardbacks; I had no shame. Prostitution for books. One day I got her two huge hardback volumes and these were equal to 'all the way' according to my sordid values. She was so small she had to stand on these books in the cupboard for me to fuck her. Just as I was about to come someone knocked on the door. Panic-stricken, I pulled out and came all over the books. Then I hid behind some coats. She pulled her knickers back on, and to hide the evidence she tried to wash off the sperm with the dregs of an old cup of coffee, but the librarian forced open the door before she'd finished and the poor girl got the sack.

I felt a complete shit because it was my selfish lust that had lost her her job. I never expected to see her again. Then many years later a woman came up to me on a station platform and asked me to help her read the train timetable. She said, 'You don't recognize me, do you? You're the one who lost me my job in the library.' We spent the whole journey back to London chatting amiably. She was poised, well-dressed, self-assured, a successful businesswoman and now a director of the publishers of the very same university textbooks which she had 'bought' off me. What marvellous poetic justice!

Yes indeed, seek and ye shall find.

(drif field)

Cushion

Ilford isn't India. I was born in a corner of London where the shores of South Park Lake had to hold all the mysteries of the Brahmaputra or the Ganges. Two words that only came alive in other people's mouths, words I longed to fill with meaning. Meaning that could help establish my Indianness against the grey rain, the hysterical laughter of my tight circle and the unspoken siege the grown-ups rarely named but tightened around us.

I was bursting to read a welter of tall graffiti daubed in white paint that suddenly appeared on the regular brown bricks. Rows of suburban houses at last interrupted by street life. Someone with something to say. I read it slowly, excited to make out all the rough letters: SAVE COAL BURN PAKIS. I looked round. The street was quiet. On our back gate a smaller message appeared, scratched on with a pair of compasses. When I tried to wash it off the patch became cleaner, more legible.

'Oh super, you're going to India for the first time, like V. S. Naipaul.' I'd no idea what the comparison could mean but hated it instinctively. The headmaster's wife obliterated any uniqueness my schoolboy notions might have had without needing to know me.

Under the vivid green-blue of a Kovalam sky he was there, an area of darkness, but seemed too tight. I couldn't see what he loved though there was enough hatred for the both of us. In his displacement he mapped out another India. It was simpler for me to delight in uncovering India from imagination than to ask if I'd learned to look the other way. He didn't. Perversely, he wouldn't. He started to hang around, not quite read, not quite forgotten, waiting for me to tire of clichés, waiting for me to ask, with polite radicalism, if perhaps they were a diversion. Was there something else?

He'd find a dog waiting to eat the diarrhoea of a baby held above the open sewers he smelled everywhere in Indian life. How could I be proud? He picked open Indian wounds that I generously absorbed as cuts on my skin. But my body was strengthening. My hair grew and my skin deepened to a honey brown. I glowed in the reconnection of generations scattered across Asia, Africa, Europe. I tasted the relief of reversing the flow of rivers of white people with brown.

Brown on brown. Browns that travel from the gentlest glow and green eyes to deep purple-black. Browner in more ways than the single word could ever suggest in London. Browns that blossomed, not stopped dead by the little word 'Paki'.

Naipaul's book opened like the folding doors of the British residencies, stubbornly rectangular, everywhere resisting the flow of Indian curves. Old armchairs were still held out for the imperial bottom, but portraits of Gandhi now hung where the viceroy was honoured. I tried to read him in their grand and dusty embrace. The slow fan above skewed against its flimsy mounting, gently turning the pages in its breeze. But he was too hard to read. Two pages were enough. He asked difficult questions.

January in England and I was cast in a play, not as Mowgli but as him. He was at a conference in Bombay and challenged, then seduced, into defending his books. The other side had the politics and much of the argument. But he struggled to see truth, to ignore the convenience talk of politicians who wanted him silenced. I stepped into his cerebral shadow in a debating chamber on the rolling Sussex Downs, posing as Bombay. His brown skin came off mine with foundation cream I didn't need. I mimicked him. His Mimic Man. I watched his hatred but secretly thought him more alive than the others.

I found myself checking second-hand bookshops for his novels. If there were none I'd be angry at his neglect. If there were, the anger would turn inward. I collected more of his books but learned not to read much of them: my subconscious bargain. I still wanted his words there, if they'd only keep silent. He spoke the unspeakable: we're a result of colonial history.

I lay, on my side, like a bend in the river, curling my body into an angular *s*. This way there was space. People like Mr Biswas *made* space for me to lie down, though there didn't seem to be room for another body at Ujjain Station after the full moon of Kumbha Mela. Two million people were trying to leave town today.

Eight years before I'd carried one. Now there were three, *An Area of Darkness, India: A Wounded Civilization* and

India: A Million Mutinies Now. In the heat my mind atrophied to no more than mere awareness. The book seemed to say, 'It's enough'. If one leg touched the other, sweat sealed me instantly. The two thicker paperbacks made a pillow, slightly softer than the marble and dust floor. His words spun out in a mystery of motives. He cannot reach them or the idea of India or of Indians. He can only pierce but recognizes that. He speaks my furies, laughs at Indian Britishers and dares to find a voice, however alienated. His eyes are open but do they meet you? Sometimes I suspected they were staring into the interior.

'He's hated here, particularly by progressives,' an Indian friend assured me later. Among literature professors his name was enough to earn the derision saved for seers. In his words I could escape 41 degrees and dysentery. Only to reconnect the alienness around me with his fears and insights. India seemed to threaten me less but was more intelligible with him. As his bloodless revulsion grows his outsider's eye appears more precious.

A Million Mutinies has a shiny cover. It was easily available at five-star hotels but not at local bookshops. My ear flattened into his name and grew wet. He supported my head. I took up the third book, still unfinished from when I first brought it to India eight years before. I read it and drifted, sleeping, with the book held firmly in my outstretched hand, open on the last page. Waking in the thick air I caught myself wondering if I'd melt against him.

East India Dock Road cuts through the East End of London. Into Commercial Road. Take the switchback up to Ilford, Essex, and here I am, back in Ilford Town Hall at my sister's schoolfriend's sister's wedding. My link is stronger than most. A panoply of saris display the community's largesse. All the reds, saffron, Gujerati orange and browns take their places by plaques commemorating the fallen of the Boer War. 'Who are all these people?' my sister's friend asks. 'So many Pakis,' we joke.

Under the baroque façade and proscenium stage Naipaul's conviction, in his travel writing, of Indians as

My friend Poonam swears blind it's true that a friend of hers asked in the public library if they had anything in Urdu and was led to the hairdressing section.

(CHRIS PROCTOR)

inherently inferior, unable to heal their civilization, rubbed up against the casual hatred offered Asians here in Ilford, where a range of fascist groups thrive. How dare these hybrid people aspire to a new identity?

Today the children call each other in Hindi–Cockney accents. The view from my old bedroom shows graffiti now worn away. You can just decipher a message in the limbs of broken letters: AVE OAL AKIS.

(PRATAP RUGHANI)

Marginalia

Coming across things written in the margins of books fascinates me. In a minimal but very real way they evoke the presence and character of the person who wrote them.

Once I stayed in a run-down hotel which was old-fashioned enough to have books in the sitting room. I found an anthology, *The Poet's Quair*, whose margins were covered in notes. The book had been used by five people, all of whom were in class s4: Betty Dopward, Jill Unwin (red ink), Sheila King (very neat), Kim Duffy (backhand) and Isobel Robertson (obviously the one who'd nicked it from school since her name was the only one not crossed out).

Having been both a teacher and a pupil I could guess the circumstances of the scribbled notes. I could almost hear the teacher and see the pupil condensing and writing beside the poem: 'The sonnet deals with love, death, time, war, etc, etc'. On the next page: 'The Elizabethan age was the summer of history'. Beside the ballad 'Get up and Bar the Door' the one word: 'humerous'. I see the boredom of the last period of the day in Yeats's 'Among School Children'. Was it Betty or Sheila or Kim or Isobel or Jill who painstakingly filled in each *o* of the text with pencil so that the page looked like it had been peppered with grape shot? Beside 'Sailing to Byzantium' is jotted the sum '.66 + .66', with no answer. Beside 'The Wild Swans at Coole' a note says of poor Yeats: 'He is growing old and losing the happiness of life and does not have any feelings about anything'. Thomas Hardy gets one word written beside his name: 'pessimistic'. T. S. Eliot gets two: 'very religious'. In 'Morte d'Arthur', against the line 'They sleep, the men I love' is an attempt to spell 'euphemism' that peters out into a series of *m*-like squiggles and the observation: 'They kicked the bucket'.

Most frustrating is the entry beside 'The Twa Corbies': 'This knight has had a good life because he used to go and . . .' What was the distraction at this point? The bell? A good-looking window cleaner? Or the first big flakes of snow which might lead to the school closing early? Whatever it was, the secret of how to achieve the good life has been lost forever.

(BERNARD MAC LAVERTY)

Without the Gannet

A copy of *The Fifty Worst Rock and Roll Records of All Time* by Guterman and O'Donnell, purchased in a Notting Hill charity shop for £2. I flip through it in trepidation, fearful that a record I appeared on might be listed. I *do* find a couple I am perversely fond of – Van Dyke Parks's 'Song Cycle' and 'Philosophy of the World' by The Shaggs – but none that had me on them.

On page 51 the entry for Phil Collins's 'You Can't Hurry Love' has been obliterated by horizontal and vertical felt-tipped lines, evidently the previous owner's work. I immediately assume that the latter was a young woman. Maybe it's due to years of finding Bay City Rollers/Bros/Kajagoogoo records in the same charity shop with the name and address of the female owner felt-tipped across the sleeves.

Page 66 has a section devoted to Mike and The

Mechanics' record 'The Living Years'. This is similarly obliterated, now using big crosses as well. I note that Mike and The Mechanics did not include Phil Collins, although they were members of his group Genesis.

The pattern is developing. Page 92 has an entry for Genesis, under the rubric of 'Personnel Changes That Flopped', scored through with horizontal lines. There are no further references to Phil Collins or Genesis until page 244, where P. C. appears as runner-up in the 'Worst Rock and Rollers of All Time' category. The previous owner – I have now decided that her name is Melanie Shillingford, after something I recently saw on the wall of Highbury and Islington tube station: 'Whoever hates Melanie Shillingford sign here', followed by a long list of names – has given up on the dark blue felt tip and has resorted to a stapler. The pages dealing with Mr Collins's mediocrity are clipped together. I have an image of Melanie brutally grasping the large format paperback, almost breaking the spine in her fury, and applying her Bambi stapler to the offending pages with beetle-browed determination, her pink tongue sticking out of the corner of her mouth as she vandalizes the book I have just paid two hard-earned pounds for. And now that blood drips on to the mutilated pages because I've lacerated my index finger on one of her fucking staples I decide that I too hate Melanie Shillingford. Tomorrow I'll be legging it to Highbury and Islington to add my name to the list.

(STEVE BERESFORD)

Thanking Franz

I want to tell you about books that have been important to me. I'd be about thirteen or fourteen when I discovered Fry's *Pantographia* in the Glasgow Public Library. It was alphabets of all the languages of the world. It was enough to get a growing lad growing. The thing that stuck in my mind was a South Sea Island alphabet. There was an *o*, and there was another vowel which was two *o*s, and then there was another one which was *three o*s. That ties up with a story I heard from a Japanese friend who had travelled from the warm south of Japan to the cold north of Japan on the railway, and at every station they stopped newspaper sellers would come out and shout 'Shimboon!' (which means newspaper). When it was away down in the south they'd go 'Shiiimboooon!', and in the centre it got to 'Shiimbooon!', and then way up in the north it was 'Shimboon!' The theory that people have come to is that the colder it is the less one wants to keep one's mouth open. But this South Sea Island alphabet was tropical stuff and they could make it a three *o* job.

Book number two is something I discovered at about fifteen years old: A. S. Neill's book about Summerhill. It was like fairyland to a guy brought up in Scotland, with all the strapping. As a result of reading it, when I became a teacher in Scotland I soon wanted to leave, I'd had enough. I wasn't understood in my own country. People thought I was an idiot and of low intelligence. I wrote to Neill and asked if I could go and teach there and to my delight a fellow called Bill McKinnon, who was a sports master and who was teaching arithmetic in an appalling way, very old-fashioned, had left and they were looking for a new junior teacher. So they sent the dad of one of the kids to interview me and I passed and went down to Summerhill to teach for £2 a week and all found. My last act at the school in Glasgow was to take my belt – the kids thought I was a softie for not having a belt and I had to buy a bloody belt – and I got a razor blade. There were fifty kids in the class and I sliced the belt into fifty pieces and gave every kid a bit. Summerhill was an inspiration and I learned a lot there about how to relate properly to kids. Then I went to London and tried to change it! I worked in a London school and the head-mistress took me to one side and said, 'Mr Cutler, I hear you're rewarding the kids for being naughty.' I had to teach the children tables. We were doing the nine times. I said, 'It's easy, I could do it standing on my head', and I

My father often put his head into my room at night. 'Have you got a good book in there for me to read? I'm trying to get to sleep.'

(NOEL SHERIDAN)

got down and did a headstand, reciting the nine times table as all the money fell out of my pocket.

Book number three: at about the age of sixteen I came across Sinclair Lewis's *Arrowsmith*, about an idealistic doctor. That was me, wanting to heal the sick, and so I decided to become a doctor. Except I had two brothers: one was a medical student and the other was going to be a doctor as well. My dad thought, crumbs, can't have all the kids doing that, who's going to run the business? (My dad was a manufacturer's agent, a middleman.) He said to me – I was a humanitarian vegetarian at the time; I wouldn't even sit at the table if they were eating meat – 'Look, if you're going to become a doctor you've got to

'And so was his grandfather' from Francisco Goya's Los Caprichos, *1799*

get a frog, hold it by the legs and smash its head against the wall, then dip it into a bath of acid feet first. Its legs will move and try to rub off the acid. This'll prove the directions are coming from the spine and not from the brain.' And I said, 'All right, I'll *not* be a doctor then! I'll become a journeyman and go to Russia.' I don't know how my dad kept a straight face with all this stuff. I went and joined Rolls-Royce and became an apprentice fitter and after a year at engineering I realized I was the world's worst. I enjoyed it and I loved the aesthetics of mechanical engineering, but I made very expensive mistakes. They'd gawp at how stupid I was. I thought I'd better get out of there so I joined the Air Force. I had a choice between being a pilot or a navigator. A pilot's no better than a bus driver, I thought, so I became a navigator. I was so dreamy. When I'd come down and show my plot they'd sit and judge it. I'd take a star sight and find myself 400 miles behind where I'd started. They sent a couple of fellows up with me and they said, 'Do you mind if we take photos?' I said, 'No, help yourself', and of course they kept an eye on me. They'd see me sitting there with the chart and I'd go to the window and take a drift so as to ascertain which way the wind was blowing and then tie that in with the aeroplane's course. I'd just sit there and gaze at the marvellous clouds for minutes on end. Alas, you can't pull the brake on a plane ... Being that kind of age, seventeen or eighteen, I also thought, 'Flying, oh, what a nice way to commit suicide.' I'd had my first shot at it at sixteen: six aspirins! My medical student brother brought home this sample of aspirins and I looked at the label and it said: Maximum dosage, two. I thought, 'Right. Six, that ought to do it.' I woke up in the morning feeling great.

Number four: Olaf Stapledon, *Last and First Men*. A knockout, because it just opened my mind to a lot of general things. He came to Glasgow Art School – I did evenings there – and he spoke. It was philosophy he was talking about. Way over my head. I'd wanted to be a philosopher when I was a kid, with a great big beard sitting at a table with an enormous book. That was my idea of what a *man* should be. I had a shot at reading the philosophers; I even went to evening classes. And fell asleep.

The next one is Kafka's *The Castle*. I'd begun to write humour, sixth-form or undergraduate stuff. Then I came across Kafka. I suppose in a way it was the most important book I ever read, because I didn't know what was being communicated, all I know is that after reading it my writing changed dramatically. I would describe it as getting my unconscious in on the act, bypassing the intellect and going straight from the unconscious to the page. With Kafka it was the first time I'd come across the situation where everywhere you go, whatever you do, there's some bugger preventing you from doing it. And I look back on my life as a seen-to-be eccentric – I'm not your conventional type – and people, just because I irritate them I suppose, or I make them feel insecure, make sure I don't get into any position where I can do more damage than I'm already doing. Before the Kafka revelation I hadn't published anything. I'd started writing songs like, 'I've a hole in my head/ Dentist, please stop it up with teeth/ Put some teeth in the top, dentist/ And another set underneath.' Primitive beginnings. I took it to my mother and said, 'Mammy, I've written a song,' and she listened. I could see, bless her, she was trying to approve, but she finished listening, and she couldn't help herself, and said, 'Ivor, why don't you write something nice?' All the way, everybody, family and fellow teachers and so on, just thought I was an idiot. So, that's Kafka.

Number six is Herbert Read's novel *Green Child*. It starts off, I think, in Patagonia, and the child dives into a stream and there's a cave and he finds himself underground where a whole civilization is going on. Their aesthetics and philosophy are based on crystals. In front of each cave dangle some crystals threaded on string, say six or seven, and the wind blows them about and you get this unique kind of chime. The inhabitants had to go through an apprenticeship to make the crystals and they were allowed then, as journeymen, to make their own sets of chimes. I was good at maths and this kind of thing appealed to me and I found how all these things tie up. I have gone back to *Green Child* and wished I hadn't. If you're lucky enough to get the right book at the right time then you're in clover really. What's good about it is that first experience. To reread something like that is like getting hold of a medicine that cured you once and even though you're not sick you think, I'll take the medicine again, it did me good.

The last book is really full circle, I suppose. It's Diringer, a professor at Cambridge, and his big thing is the alphabet. He has every alphabet in the world in his book, and its growth and development. It had me studying Chinese and Japanese, not to learn to speak them, just this magic of making marks on a white sheet. I was cycling home one day and I passed a very grimy white van and there were four words written in the dust: 'Also available in white'. I love the way people have found so many things to write on. And codes: I did morse code in the Air Force and when my friend Phyllis King discovered I had a morse buzzer she said, 'I've always wanted to learn morse.' The number of evenings we spent across the kitchen table, two grown people passing messages in morse! While I was at it I taught her the Russian alphabet and the Greek alphabet and the Hebrew. I didn't know what was going in, but later she sent me a letter, all in Hebrew, and it was Irish jokes.

The book that gives me the most aesthetic pleasure today is not an art book at all, it's T. Makino's *A Concise Pictorial Flora of Japan*. Diagrams, coded language – it's written in Japanese – precision: the whole thing is thrilling, better than sex. That reminds me of when I was in Rolls-Royce. Each apprentice was given a block of steel and a ruler that measured hundredths of an inch. We each had to measure our block. Then we all read out our measurements. This fellow called out '3.461 inches.' The whole class gasped and the teacher thought 'drama' and he said, 'Right.' He took his Vernier micrometer and measured it: 3.461 inches. He gasped too and he said, 'How did you know?' We're talking about one thousandth of an inch here. And the fellow said, 'Well, I thought it looked a wee bit more than 3.46.' With Makino I try and translate the Japanese captions. It's absolute hell. Languages are idiomatic and you'll stick one word down and then the next one, and you have these two words together and you think, it doesn't make sense. Really I'm a terrible masochist. I go to bed with a few dictionaries and I try and work things out. Sometimes you're lucky.

(IVOR CUTLER)

From the Rabbi's Dream Book

At the end of the sentence. The dot. A stop. A black circle. Its edges rainbow like petroleum like linoleum like bubbles blown out of plastic hoops. The period. The end. A stop.

Black round sphere on the page. Black dot holding all the alphabets and words inside itself.

Did you ever see the angel who wears a curved and no doubt jewel-powered device of glass and metals looped about into mad scientist spires and gyres and all of it hooked to transistor batteries worn around his arms like snakes? He puts his mouth on a tuba mouthpiece and blows four notes which you can see moving up the tubing, turning into one black dot rushing up through loops and hoops of metals and glass. The black dot goes up to the top shaped like an upside-down ice-cream brass cone and out it goes. Into the air. Straight to the open book's blank page and it lands right in the white centre.

Black dot in the centre of a page surrounded by white. The period. The end. A stop.

Another angel who wasn't in the room before appears through the roof in a flurry of splashing light like overflowing fireworks. And lands before the large open book and shuts his eyes and slowly lets his wings fold together. Light remaining from his flight falls on to the floor where it dissolves like snowflakes.

In the Second World War microdot messages in the form of full stops were planted in standard Red Cross Bibles, one of the few items allowed to POWs under international law. The Red Cross knew nothing of what was going on, or that I was a full-stop doctor.

(CECIL H. WILLIAMSON)

I am the Angel of the Alphabet, he says to the open book.

The book says nothing.

But the black dot widens in the page's centre and opens like a yawn like an apple sliced into many sudden wedges. And the Angel of the Alphabet seems pleased and flutters his wings like a helicopter and arises to the ceiling and soaks through it like sunlight.

Period. The end. A stop. The room is empty again. Its walls as white as blank pages in the book. There is nothing in the room. Period. Except the book which is on a round table made from sturdy wood and engraved and carved with stars, moons, alphabets, hieroglyphs, petroglyphs, runes going around the edges of the table.

Letter into letter into letter. The black dot splinters into black shapes of lovely designs. Flowers quickly blossoming. People walking. Each letter as it forms itself looks like something remembered from life. An ox, a coathook, a dancer, a room, a staff, a pitchfork, a stem, a seed, a weed.

Letters appear on the page and meet each other to form words. They stand in groups and sing. They discuss each other's meanings. They remember and they forget.

A black angel spreads his black wings through a wall of the room and enters. He is happy to see the page of the book alive with his blackness. His shadow is like a letter on a white wall.

A white angel, entirely white, spreads his wings and enters through a wall as if breaking through water after diving deep into a lake and then pushing up and up to where sunlight wobbles and shatters on the water.

The two angels stand side by side before the book. Their black and white shadows.

And we know that the black angel shuts his eyes as if asleep and all the letters and words float to him and he inhales them as if smelling a stew. And we know he turns an eye-blinking white from head to toe, dazzling.

And we know how the white angel smiles to see the book page suddenly empty of marks. And we are ready when he shuts his eyes and the pages of the book turn faster than a cartoon and become a small snowstorm which the white angel inhales and, to our amazement, turns a magnificent black.

And later, when the sun and moon and stars have turned inside out into letters and pages and words and books, and a century of amazing seconds has gone, and it's hard to know what's happening, but nobody's worried, a comforting voice says to you or me or to nobody in particular that the black dot is the planet of the alphabet. The alphabet atom. All alphabets live in harmony in the period. The stop. The end.

And the blank page, white and empty, is the alphabet's sky.

And sometimes what has been said seems to be true. The letters and words are stars in the white sky of the page. Or the white page is part of a huge letter with dots and spots of black sky poking through it.

And now what do you say if we start all over again?

At the end of the sentence. Dot. Stop. Black circle. Beginning again.

(DAVID MELTZER)

Inpu the Divine

As a young bride in March 1964, just arrived from Paris to London where I was to make my home, I started a double love affair, one with a man who became the father of my son, the other with a particular heraldic light which became the root of my passion for Egyptian hieroglyphic texts. As life went on I found out that both these amours were the carriers of particular hopes, one on the level of my human dream, the other on the level of certitude. On that March morning the tree behind my window shimmered in the early springtime light and the sparrows, blackbirds and blue tits knowingly insisted that winter was over. I believed it too. Although it was still too cold to go coatless the light was there and I saw it and I walked into it.

Years before, as a child I loved to snuggle down between the cushions of the velvet sofa with a bag of boiled sweets and a huge black leather-bound French book, *L'Encyclopédie du monde*. There was a photograph in it of Yehudi Menuhin in his teens with his violin. It covered a whole page. I was fascinated by the exquisite features of his face. I loved the inspired and sad look in his grey eyes as he seemed to gaze at the opposite page littered with images of machines, tools and workshops. One of these showed a mass of people at the gates of a factory. There was a disturbing contrast between the boy's huge face and the shrunken figures of the men and women on the page opposite, squeezed against one another, their featureless, eyeless faces looking like enlarged dots. I felt he was an angel meant to watch over them, but he had only a violin to do so and these tiny people, crushed by the mechanical sounds of the industrial enlightenment, could not hear his music. I never forgot his face. It became engraved in my memory, like a translucent alabaster seal lit within my heart.

When I started school I fell in love with a boy who had a similar face but was not a violinist. One morning I wrote a poem: 'I am in love with a boy. His blue eyes, deep like the sea, touch my heart.' My grandmother found the page under my breakfast tray and smiled. I felt that my deepest secret had been desecrated and buried my face in my pillow. I would not get up. I refused to go to school. It took a long time before I set foot in the playground, and the crowd of noisy children, my friends, made me think of the crowd of people with enlarged dots instead of faces. The sturdy school building, with its bleak windows, became a factory. And as the piercing bell rang and the children ran inside I stood alone, staring at something that did not exist. Yet I could see it: it was the boy with the violin.

Thus I would say that a childhood encyclopaedia had something to do with Egypt because it forged for me an

I read through meals. Food just isn't the same without the sauce of print.

(A MASS-OBSERVER)

icon of the lone individual facing a mechanized world. Later in my life that icon became the emotional pedestal for my vision of the ancient Egyptian god Inpu who was the symbolic redeemer in man. It is true that Inpu had a dog's face, but nevertheless it all fitted, because the dog is a mystical animal gifted with love, and as such it seeks a master, just as the priest seeks the Lord. For mysterious indeed are the ways of the dog. Inpu represented for me a form of spiritual vision which balances heart and reason just as our physical sight balances our left and right eye. The way to such balance is far from simple chronology. Nothing warns you of the deep holes hidden within the very texture of your being, of mirrors luring you into chasms where each of your sighs resounds like an object tumbling into the cavelike depths. I have been through them. I have stepped sideways and fallen into the gap between my soul and my reason.

It was like trying to grab hold of something that has no eyes, no ears, no mouth. Something slippery and ungraspable, whole like the Earth itself. Something unreal, like the other side of night. It was like staggering through deserted corridors, through dark streets, through huge empty buildings, like holding on to floating pieces of paper, sobbing, trying to find the answer to a question one had forgotten long ago. It was like giving up, like closing your eyes with a sense of exhaustion and fear. I nearly died.

Then a glow appeared in my mind's eye. It was a half-open door. It was not lit but it shone and gave light. I walked towards it. I balanced over the edge of my being. All the way to Egypt.

Most people think that hieroglyphs, an arm or an owl for instance, tell a story about an arm and an owl, that these pictures are writing in terms of logical chains of words. We may think that the picture of a house next to a walking man is a story with only two possible meanings: a man has come out of a house or a man will go into a house. Had such pictures only these concrete meanings the language would be limited to basic practical situations. This is not the case. An implement such as a plough would, for instance, only refer to agriculture. On the contrary the image is also used in an abstract sense, that is, in connection with spiritual labour. Mythical ploughing refers to the whole process of the preparation of the ground for the seed and the crop, and symbolically to the foundation rituals in connection with the temple and with the mind itself. In her writing Egypt used parts of man, animals and plants, agricultural tools or cosmic bodies familiar to all. The intellectually evolved priesthood, the practically minded merchants, the intuitive farmers or workers: all took from the writings what they needed according to their own practical level.

Each hieroglyph was a letter and, like the acupuncture needle, an evocative door to subtle paths of the natural and the cosmic life in man. For instance the glyph of an arm is the letter *a*. It is also a word with several meanings: doing, responsibility, act, deed. On a different level it represents a mathematical unit of measure called *remen* which in sacred geometry refers to the principle of individuality. Such versatility of meaning is only possible because the pictures are not just concrete projections of daily objects or animals but are also the symbolic evocations of functions which knit verbs, nouns and abstract concepts into one living structure. In reality hieroglyphic writing is the most astonishing philosophical language ever conceived by man. The thinking that radiates from the sacred books of ancient Egypt is a visionary one, like poetry. A true poet spontaneously thinks as a visionary. This is why poetry is a great healer.

When I was fourteen years old I was living in Ankara with my parents. I remember the morning when, lonely and depressed, I ran into the garden. Our rose garden was exceptional because it had two thousand roses planted in big squares according to colour. I was following the paved footpath that separated them when a tiny lizard crossed my way. He hesitated slightly before disappearing under a rose bush. For a brief second I thought I saw his eyes. A poem came to mind: 'Rarely, rarely comest thou, spirit of delight. Like the lizard with the shadow of the trembling leaf, thou with sorrow art

dismayed.' I remember clearly how intensely I watched
the rose bush while saying these words, as if my eyes
understood something concerning my life that my reason
could not grasp, something that could not be understood
in a straightforward verbal way. I felt that this shy quick
lizard, so terrified of shadows, was my own trembling,
sorrowful self. I became that lizard hidden under the rose
bush. And, as in a dream, I saw the rose bush growing
into a tree. It was not a rose bush anymore, it was an oak
tree full of roses.

I felt shaken by this vision and sat on the path, basking
in the sun. I remembered our oak tree at home in
Belgrade. As a child I had always felt safe lying beneath
it, even at night, looking at the stars through its leaves.
Now, in response to a poem uttered in the middle of the
Anatolian desert where such trees did not exist and
where sprinklers kept the gardens alive I found my oak
tree in a rose bush and took refuge from sadness under it.

Sitting on a bench in Battersea Park many years later I
remembered that rose–oak tree. Looking at the children,
the dogs, bored mothers and jobless youths, I whispered,
'To whom shall I speak today?' It was October 1978. My
newly published book *Rebel in the Soul* lay on my lap. It
was the translation and commentary of a sacred text
from Egypt in which a man, intending to commit philosophical suicide, argues with his soul. Unlike Hamlet,
this three-thousand-year-old pessimist eventually capitu-
lated in the face of a stronger argument, and what began
as a poem of despair ended as a poem of hope containing
despair as a captain contains his experience of a storm at
sea in his weatherbeaten face. That afternoon, however,
my soul did not argue with me as I watched the barges
slowly making their way on the muddy river, while
contemplating what effect that mud might have on the
dignity of my appearance if I were pulled out of the
water.

I would like to be able to describe being enamoured of
hieroglyphic texts in a smooth and logical account, but it
didn't happen in that way. It happened in a series of
contradictory steps, untraceably I would say. It was a

life-saving operation. I was drowning. Somebody threw me a lifebelt. Who? I could see Shelley, and behind him the boy with the violin, and behind him Inpu, the priest of redemption. I remember exactly how dark my thoughts were as I stood up from that bench and walked towards the river. For a while I stood there watching the hungry gulls. They were intense and solitary like me, and as they glided in wide circles over the river their cries seemed to surge forth from my own heart. Their unrestrained flight contrasted with the precision of their landing. This attracted my attention. It reminded me of something, but I could not remember what. To my right were a few ravens, very shiny against the new grass. One of them insisted on walking towards me in a most ungainly manner. 'No bird can walk well,' I thought. Then I concluded, 'Neither can a poet.' I closed my eyes, my heartbeat steadying. I leaned against the back of the bench. It was not logical, but I saw the rose–oak tree in my mind. I was not alone any more because there was an order and I belonged to it, like the gull and the raven. That order was the rose–oak tree, containing the Earth with all the lizards, all the leaves, and the heavenly rose.

Something had happened at the associative level. The poet had taken over. I remembered my heart's own forgotten story. Crucified between time and space, it was their uniter: for time is the kingdom of chronology (like rationality), and space is the kingdom of image (like intuition). My heart was the altar of their duality and yet a single drum. With every beat it knocked at its own door, like the solitary hand of a lost dethroned ruler, wandering through the stormy night. I was the stormy night. I opened my eyes. I may have been looking at Albert Bridge, but in reality I saw the boy with his violin, his face in the sky watching me. I was still at the gates of despair, but then the boy became Inpu, the dog-faced priest, and I walked towards him.

Such are the irrational ways of living intelligence that builds itself from itself. Its ancient Egyptian name is the shepherd's crook. Through its agency an image that came to my mind when I was fourteen became the lifebelt in my drowning mind thirty years later. This was only possible because that stored image had been activated at a given moment of despair and brought to its rightful place, like a key to a lock. A mental acupuncture, based on an evocative image, had restored my wholeness.

(BIKA REED)

The Magus (or Celestial Intelligencer)

Heneage Street, Whitechapel, shares its name with one of the shadier Elizabethan spymasters, a bookkeeper whose covert payments funded a network of spooks and gulls. A sculptor, who had for years fantasized about taking possession of a property in the area, found himself unexpectedly the subtenant of a spacious but bleak set of rooms in this obscure tributary. A Sickertian bolt-hole: the authentic whiff of poverty and illegitimate assignations. David Rodinsky, the vanished caretaker, is recorded as attending a bar mitzvah on the premises. It was his last public sighting.

The sculptor, call him Joblard, had barely got his feet under the desk before he presented me with a gathering of loose sheets which he described as photocopies made from a magical primer, *The Magus (or Celestial Intelligencer)* by Francis Barrett. Not altogether comfortable in their company, I locked them away, until that day came when I needed, urgently, to consult the missing pages, the pages which Joblard had decided *not* to copy. A fiction I was struggling to complete would not go forward; I was forced to check a sentence that hovered on the brink of revelation, but which I was almost sure I had not yet read.

The original book, which I had never seen, was no longer in Heneage Street. It had been returned to the man who lent it to Joblard. And was now safely back on the shelf at the London Library. The sculptor, obligingly, made enquiries. The book was no longer available. The library denied that they had ever possessed such a title.

Inevitably, as you will have guessed, the copies had also disappeared. A BBC crew, shooting a documentary sampled from the tale that launched my search, had mislaid them. They were not to be traced among the cutting rooms, the store cupboards, or the spongy corridors. They were available for splicing into any random apocalyptic footage.

Freed from all prompts, the sentence came to me. 'And often the spirits do come although they appear not visible (to cause terror to him who calls them), either in the thing which he uses, or else in the operation itself.' The book existed only in its absence. It was made up from those pages we read in our sleep, but are forbidden to transcribe.

Months later, outside London, in a gallery filled with knotted bones, eel weavings, heron casts, I exchanged a few words with a local painter who was recovering from plastic surgery. There was a book, given to him years before, of no practical value, it should be passed on.

Electric specs for reading in bed. Photo: IN-Bild/Keystone © Camera Press

The conversation was brief, oblique, but I hadn't quite forgotten it when I received a message from the gallery

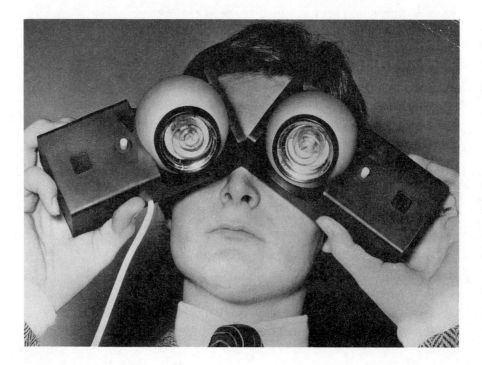

owner. The book was in his office, awaiting my next visit. It was, of course, *The Magus*. The painter had left an inscription in pencil on the flyleaf. 'As promised at the Shamanism exhibition – more use to you than me.'

The fiction I was working on was almost complete, I was racing through the final chapter, when a Jiffy bag arrived with the missing photocopies. The meaning of my entire novel seemed threatened by this benevolent intrusion. I became convinced it was impossible to retain both book and copy. A way had to be contrived to rapidly dispose of the duplicates.

Another fragmentary film was under way, shot in the warren of streets around Hawksmoor's Christ Church. I arranged for the crumpled pages of cabbalistic calculations to be dropped in the gutter on the corner of Princelet Street, where David Rodinsky had lodged, and where the graphic novelist, Alan Moore, would now stoop to retrieve them. Once safely in Alan's hands they would stick. The token was passed.

(IAIN SINCLAIR)

The Dreambook

There is a book that will always be there for the writing. Maybe we might begin, all of us, to write it right now, letter by letter, page by page. Maybe this is the book's very first word, the chapter that begins the writing. It is vital it be done; all we need do is understand the dream of a dreamer who has deserted us for ever. More than to understand: to incorporate ourselves in the dream, so as to keep it alive – awake? – as the dreamer knew how to keep it alive while he lived himself. His is an unwritten book, invisible. I am going to try and open it.

One grey November day in 1983, which, it transpired, was to be the last November of his life, Julio Cortázar arrived in New York to speak before the Standing Committee of the Disappeared. I went to look him up at his hotel; we were to spend the whole afternoon together. I found him tired. He confessed he wasn't feeling well.

'I must take a sabbatical,' he said, after a drink had been put in front of him. 'Because I want to write a novel. I've done what I can for Central America. I should be able to take my sabbatical soon and write my book.'

'Take it right away, Julio, don't wear yourself out completely,' I begged him.

'No, they still need me. I've promised to go to Nicaragua and to a writers' conference in Cuba, afterwards I have to be in Mexico and in April I'm off to Argentina. I too want to celebrate the return of democracy. My sabbatical will begin after that and I'll get hard into the novel. It's been so long since I've written fiction. I really want to immerse myself in the writing and to do only that.'

'Literature does help, thank goodness,' he had written me in an earlier letter. 'They want me for interviews, collaborations, and I tell them, yes, of course, and send them a text on Central America. Both they and I would prefer it to be a fantastic story, but we put up with it, what else can we do?'

I asked Julio to talk about his next book if he was willing to, and in addition I asked him if at the beginning of a new novel he had a clear idea of the plot, if he followed a specific path or plunged straight into the unknown.

'You know I don't like to talk about what I'm doing or about my plans. Like Gabo García Márquez, who believes that plots elude him if he divulges them to other people, I'm superstitious. But the truth is I never have a clear plot in mind. Barely an idea, a sensation or phrase. Though in this case something unusual has happened: I have a very precise notion that the novel is there in my head, that it's finished, and yet I haven't the foggiest idea what it's about. But I know it's right there, ready to be born. I often dream of the novel and I wake up from the dream very happy, but it's nothing I can explain to you, much as I would like to. It isn't superstitious fear at work. What happens in the dream is that

The bedtime story was tired. It had been read too often.

(LES COLEMAN)

the publisher hands me the brand new book, hot off the press, and I take it and open it and admire it, there it is, my novel, the best I've ever written, and I leaf through it and I love it and find it clear, pristine, coherent, exceedingly intelligent, I'd say. And it doesn't bother me in the least that it has been written with geometrical shapes. There is neither word nor letter in this book, only geometrical shapes that, in the dream, are for me absolutely logical, totally coherent, they tell the profoundest and most poignant of human stories. When awake I understand not one iota of geometry, but in the dream it is so, and I know that in this book I have finally attained perfection.'

'Don't procrastinate any longer, Julio,' I urged him that November in 1983. 'Take that sabbatical now.' But not too long a sabbatical, not like the eternal one he ended up taking the following ill-fated February. What a way of overdoing things, Julio.

The recognition of the menace behind supposed perfection was Cortázar's trademark. Nothing is what it seems; geometry perhaps least of all. Of that Julio had already had a premonition. If not, why then did he call a book of stories *Octahedron*, simply because it contains eight key stories? The octahedron is in fact a pyramid mirrored, thus a double, self-contained figure, a precise talisman against what we might call compartmentalization, manias, 'squares'. 'But these are not manias, thought Martin, rather a response to death and nothingness, freezing things and times, establishing rites and passages against a disorder full of holes and stains.'

Except that disorder is more tempting than order, it offers the possibility of infinite orderings in which the octahedron multiplies itself by eight and acquires the sixty-four facets of the diamond or the sixty-four hexagrams of that other book, almost dream, almost geometrical: the *I Ching*. Like a print by Escher, one of those images through which Julio circulated so comfortably, unique in knowing how to confront stairs that go up and down simultaneously to lead to the exact point of departure or to all the other points. As in the city of daydreams

through which the characters of *62: A Model Kit* repeatedly saunter.

A city that is a book, or a dream where book and city
are intertwined, a city 'which is like the bastion of an
infinitely deferred death, of murky investigations', where
appointments can sometimes be kept, and where what is
cloudy becomes crystal clear – geometrical – in the
instant of crossing the threshold. Or of turning the page.

(LUISA VALENZUELA)

Beckoning

It was my first day-trip down south to the big city. To
see the sights, go round the galleries, browse in the
bookshops, buy a book. I'd saved up.

The bookshop was huge, three times bigger even than
the Co-op department store in our town. The method of
payment was also different to the Co-op. There, a bill of
sale was written out, then sealed inside an iron container
with the money and dispatched down a hydraulic tube
to the unseen nether regions of the accounts office, from
which the iron capsule eventually returned containing
the receipt and change. Here, I joined a queue to present
my chosen book, with my cash, to an assistant seated in a
glass-walled kiosk like those in the entrances of cinemas.

Came my turn and I stared in wonder through the
glass at the most exquisite young woman I had ever seen.
Her bobbed, golden hair shone like silk, framing liquid,
aquamarine eyes above high cheekbones over which was
stretched alabaster skin as smooth as a sugared almond.
As if an identikit of beautician's clichés had been used to
assemble the perfectly structured face. A stylized beauty
so different from the faces in my home town, where
women still wore headscarves and curlers until Saturday
night. How could it be that this flawless face was a shop
assistant's, looking blankly out through the window of a

cramped kiosk instead of from the cover of a fashion magazine?

I pushed my pound note through the grille and she slid her right arm languidly across the counter to take it. The bare, slender arm, its skin as unblemished as the face, tapered in perfect proportion from the soft flesh above the elbow, down past the almost imperceptible wrist to a handless single finger, at the end of which was a long, red-laquered fingernail. The prehensile finger hooked my note, tightening around the Queen's neck.

The kiosk woman's inscrutable blue eyes met mine, which had widened as a flush of giddiness passed through me. Embarrassed, I looked down at the book in my left hand, from the cover of which Franz Kafka's high-cheek-boned face looked at me with hypnotic eyes and a little half-smile which seemed to say: 'Welcome to the city, my friend, welcome to my world.'

(IAN BREAKWELL)

The author Raymond Rous-sel designed his own tomb: a stone him ponders a stone volume from his stone library

In Stygian Shop Forlorn

When I started up as a publisher I knew so little about the book trade that my first call on my first sales trip was to the first shop I came across when I got off the bus in Leamington Spa. To soften up its proprietor I bought a quarter pound of humbugs before plonking my display pack on his counter. This simple act unhinged him. He muttered that he sold only confectionery, tobacco and the Sundays and said he'd never cared much for books.

After all, he went on, what earthly use were books except maybe when you stood on a pile to reach up to a high shelf? Books couldn't be sucked, chewed or smoked. Also he'd heard that some books could change your life and he was happy enough as he was. And weren't books best left standing as trees?

He asked me if I stocked soap and said he wouldn't mind subscribing a small carton of scented soap even though he didn't sell soap. Had never heard of anyone immersing himself in books. Anyway, his lady assistant was into Green Thinking and had warned him some books left a dangerous residue.

I couldn't find words to counter this. After all, there isn't much one can do with a book except read it. So we stared hopelessly at each other. The chap's nerve broke first. Said he'd take a couple of 50 pence John Miltons. Wasn't he the chap who lived in a graveyard? Recollected something about cows in a poem and Mr Eshelby had told the class that the poetic word for 'cattle' was 'lowing herd'. So he'd have one Milton to keep his mind from being sucked out of the window on his next package flight. And the other Milton for his sister-in-law. His brother had told him that a bit of poetry livened her up last thing at night.

I can't remember anything else except that he paid me cash from the till. And winked at me.

(J. L. CARR)

Cheek

Walking along a London street in 1974 I spotted Lawrence Durrell in a bookshop, engaged in a signing of his
latest novel. I couldn't afford to buy the book but fancied
getting closer to the author of the Alexandria Quartet, a
seminal work for me as a late adolescent. So what might
I ask him to sign instead? All I had with me was a tatty
London A–Z, much too shabby to present to the great man
for signing. But, lo and behold, approaching me along
the street was a couple of American tourists bearing a
Nicholson's Street Finder in what appeared to be mint
condition. So on impulse I stopped them and asked if
they'd do me the great favour of swapping their atlas for
mine, explaining that a famous author was close at hand
but, owing to unfathomable eccentricity, was only prepared to sign copies of Nicholson's. The tourists were so
bewildered by my appeal that they agreed to the transac-
tion. And shortly afterwards Durrell was too much of a
gentleman, or perhaps too glazed by incessant signings,
to decline to honour what was put in front of him.

(NEIL HORNICK)

I, Rupert Schweik

You are what you read, and for a long while I was
Rupert the Bear. I took him along with me from New
Cross, London, to Hadlow Down, Sussex, when I was
evacuated, and Mrs Woods, my surrogate mother, taught
me how to fit the words to the pictures, how to read.
The woods around Hadlow Down were ideal for playing
Rupert. There was a conscientious objector charcoal
burner with a very sharp axe that had a leather cover for
its head which we weren't allowed to touch, and a lot of
soldiers on manoeuvres, mostly Americans and Canadi-
ans, who used to leave empty jars of peanut butter on the

ground when they left. We, being perpetually hungry bears, liked to lick out the last traces: our first taste of transatlantic life.

The conchie wasn't very popular in the village, although to us he seemed very kind, whilst the soldiers were all sorts. So between them, the deserters, the Military Police, shot-down fighter pilots whom we never quite got to arrest, nuns disguised as spies and so on, there was a vast supporting cast for Rupert adventures in which everyone in our gang, which had a quorum of five, got to play Rupert.

Then one day I won a prize at school for cheating. It was presented to me by the local squire, Sir Somebody Hamilton, to whom people in those days still used to touch their forelocks. It was a beautifully bound Victorian book entitled *Britain's Heroes*. With its steel engravings and stirring tales it immediately cast Rupert from the woods into the wilderness and I was able at a stroke to become a multiple hero, right up until I became a multiple anti-hero. Thus at any one time I might be an amalgam of Alfred the Great, Richard Cœur de Lion, Robin Hood and every one of his Merry Men, Henry V, Marlborough, Nelson and Wellington, plus all those who'd won the VC at Rourke's Drift.

The war wore on and reading wore off. I gave up books for quite a while, although I followed the war maps in the newspapers intensely. The dropping of the atom bomb on Hiroshima was announced on the wireless and I was gleeful until Mrs Woods, who instilled chapel socialism into me, rapped me metaphorically over the knuckles and told me that even the Japanese were human beings. We all went home to New Cross. Uncle Alan came back from a Japanese camp. I had never seen anyone so thin before. He lasted a couple of weeks, and I had my doubts about the humanity of the Japanese.

Rashly, I ventured into my brother's room one day. He had floor-to-ceiling bookcases filled mainly with Penguins. I found the pattern of the rows and the order of it all fascinating but unfortunately my brother caught me and, after roughing me up a bit, imprisoned me under his bed for half an hour. I spent the time reading Penguin spines. Two titles caught my attention, *The Good Soldier* and *The Good Soldier Schweik*. I determined to pinch one of them – at that time I was pinching quite a lot, mainly totally useless things from Woolworths – and for no good reason, but luckily, I chose *The Good Soldier Schweik*.

If I had chosen *The Good Soldier* maybe I'd have gone to a university rather than an art school and my life would have taken a different course. Reading *Schweik* coincided with Saturday morning cinema, and Johnny Weissmuller. This meant that until I gave up Saturday morning cinema altogether I was walking around in the body of Tarzan, with the head of Schweik on its torso: a remarkable change in visual and mental style, Schweik's head and mouth both being much more expressive than Weissmuller's.

The end of Saturday morning cinema was the beginning of adolescence, the abandonment of heroes and the start of rebellion. In those days this meant the bold wearing of a blue aertex shirt to school instead of the regulation white cotton one. Schweik's subversive innocence provided me with the perfect persona. From then on I read and read, hiding behind the Schweik mask. It needed no further adjustment until years later when I read another great twentieth-century war novel, *Catch-22*. Then the mask received a few refinements from a further great survivor, the pilot Orr. Orr, I imagine, would have looked rather like Schweik, although by keeping small apples in his cheeks he deliberately made them round and rosy to go with his eyes, whereas Schweik's came naturally. Schweik did what he did naturally; Orr knew what he was doing. In either case each survived; and so with their help did I.

(JOHN FURNIVAL)

Memorials

Meandering beside the perfumed river, through the badly lit streets of Ho Chi Minh City in the late evening, there amongst the parked cyclos and dilapidated Russian limousines, I came across a dark and musty bookshop packed with second-hand volumes presided over by an aged uncle, who seemed happy to test his antique French and explain that he had worked as a journalist for Associated Press in Saigon under the *ancien régime*: 'I've seen too many things in a long life.' His extended family lie around on benches and couches at the back of the shop, drinking iced tea.

Dry paperbacks, their crisp pages coarsened by dust, yellowed and made brittle by age and heat, have inside covers inscribed twenty-five years ago by passing American soldiers on their way to a war. Cheap novels scribbled with their names and regiments, inscriptions like the engravings on the Zippo lighters sold next door:

VUNG TOU 1967

NO ROSE WITHOUT A THORN

Several shelves are crammed with a mixture of cheap science fiction and gory war novels. A crumbling copy of *The Guns of Navarone* was apparently published in the Readers' Enrichment Series. Jammed in with this a story of Poland and the Second World War succinctly entitled *To Live and to Kill.* On the lower shelves there are other incongruous juxtapositions: a thin and macabre illustrated booklet showing the gravestones and memorials available from Emilio Biagini e Figli next to an unexpected sociological tome, *Understanding Political Variables* by William Buchanan (read, by a Cptn Shirleys 2769331, rather too late in the day in 1972). Also *Whitman: Poet of Democracy* – 'I chant a song to you O sane and sacred death' – held by a young soldier on his way to mortal combat:

WHEN I DIE I KNOW I AM GOING TO HEAVEN
BECAUSE I HAVE SPENT MY TIME IN HELL

Mr Hong suggests that it has only been possible, politically, to open such a bookshop in the last year. 'It is painful for me to part with any of the thousands of books I've collected over the years, but then I will have to say goodbye to them sometime soon. I'm seventy-one now and they would be too much of a burden on my family.' The books are piled on to shelves from floor to ceiling; an array of dim light bulbs are erratically switched on from the back of the shop. Some shelves exhibit the traces of an earlier French colonial habitation: *Les Ammanites et leur culture* next to *La Condition humaine* by Malraux. Members of the family occasionally bestir themselves and wander across to offer a new pile of pirated volumes: a curious collection of photocopied books rebound in leather with gold embossed covers. Felix Greene's *Vietnam! Vietnam!* originally a Penguin paperback sold for twelve shillings and sixpence in 1967, is now 165,000 Vietnamese dong or $15.

Mr Hong moves among the shelves, amongst the six thousand books he has accumulated in a lifetime, arguing about the soul of his country, the necessity of spraying the books against moths twice a year, the 'unnatural' nature of communism and the art of a rural culture. He is like Dominguez, a character out of Graham Greene's *The Quiet American* (sold for $6 in the photocopied version). He glances at the open doorway and mutters about the Hanoi government. 'I'm afraid that everything is off the record.' The phrase of an old journalist.

PLEIKU 64–65
THERE IS NO GRAVITY
THE WORLD SUCKS

(ROD STONEMAN)

Have Book, Will Travel

In 1989–90 I cycled overland from London to Australia, a
twenty thousand kilometre journey that took nine
months. Before departure, as I compared 'essential' equipment with the small space available for it, it seemed as if
books would be squeezed out of my pedalling life by the
harsh constraints of two panniers and a handlebar bag. In
fact they ruled my ride in remarkable ways.

Embarking on such an enterprise required a philosophy and an example, and two inspiring travel classics
which I read before setting off set out the alternatives.
Dervla Murphy, the patron saint of long distance cyclists,
described her epic 1947 ride from Dublin to Delhi in *Full
Tilt*. Put your trust in the people, they will see you
through was her motto, albeit in her case with a revolver
in her saddle-bag. And Geoffrey Moorhouse, describing
his attempt to cross the Sahara overland from the Atlantic
to the Nile in *The Fearful Void*. 'Trust no one' seemed to
become a self-fulfilling prophecy as he struggled east.
Unashamedly I decided to become a Dervla Murphy
man, and never was a role model more powerfully

vindicated. One bicycle pump, taken in France, was the only breach of that trust.

There was room for only one volume among the camping gear and spare parts, exchanged like a relay baton as I rode. Isabel Allende's *Eva Luna* ended up in Darwin as Salman Rushdie's *Midnight's Children* after enough reincarnations to reach a Hindu heaven. Protecting the value of my investment was crucial: never swop down-market was the rule. The traveller's favourite, fantasy, was an ever-present trap to be avoided like the plague: I wasn't going to exchange my good reads for fairy tales.

Sometimes I disappeared into Sargasso Seas of bike-clogging density, and my single volume became a life raft to escape from the public domain. Toiling up the Indus Valley Tom Wolfe's *The Bonfire of the Vanities* fulfilled this role, my signal to the nose-to-the-pane, wall-to-wall inspecting eyes to avert their gaze. On reaching the Karakoram I baton-changed with a returning trekker emerging from the high mountains as I was going in. He was as desperate for the bright lights of the big city as I was for solitude and paradoxically Tom Wolfe had to satisfy both requirements, *Bonfire* swopped for *The Right Stuff* at Rawalpindi Station.

Sometimes my single volume acted like garlic to ward off the vampire of chauvinistic Islamic misogyny. Marge Piercy's *Gone to Soldiers* kept south-east Turkey at bay. In Bangkok, on the other hand, it was good to have Anaïs Nin's *Delta of Venus* in my saddle-bag to help resist the sexual blandishments of a city that is like a set on which *Emmanuelle* and *The King and I* are being made at the same time.

In 1989 the world was turning on its axis as I rode and sometimes books felt like political depth-charges. None more so than *The Satanic Verses*. I didn't take it – possession would have been an even surer passport to jail than whiskey in some of the places I passed through – but liberal Muslim people continually quizzed me about it. In many countries along my route Communist Parties were illegal, and I took particular pleasure in ostenta-

Each day the walk home from school was different, depending on the book. One day I was deep in tropical forests with gorillas, the next day hunting the black tulip, breathing the scented air of the Scottish highlands or sailing wild seas. I read oblivious to my mother's calls, curled in a deep armchair. I read into the small hours by candlelight, and when the flame had died, by moonlight. I climbed into the leafy hideaway I had made in the great weeping ash tree and whisked myself to far distant places.

(A MASS-OBSERVER)

tiously reading Lenin in Sumatra as a gesture of solidarity with its political prisoners. Mentioning Toer, the great Indonesian writer who has spent much of his life under house arrest, to a hotel owner in eastern Java was the key to finding someone prepared to talk about the massacre that everyone wants to forget, when supporters of General Sukarno butchered over half a million Communists in the greatest cover-up in twentieth-century history. 'You know Toer?' the hotelier asked incredulously. In pidgin English he told me of those terrible days. 'Here, how many killed?' I asked. 'Many, many footballs,' he replied. An awful vision of decapitated bouncing heads flashed across my mind, but he meant football teams: of eleven people.

In Iraq, when the temperature reached 120°F in the shade, I drew enormous inspiration from Puig's *Kiss of the Spiderwoman*. The main character, imprisoned in a South American jail, faced far more serious problems than I did, but his psychological make-up was similar. He favoured organizational solutions to life's dilemmas. From his gay cell-mate he comes to realize that these are not enough. The only escape route lies through imagination. Beneath the sun's sledgehammer I learned the same lesson.

Apart from the dreaded fantasy, *Lonely Planet* guides are the traveller's favourite read. I enjoyed describing myself as a 'tourist'. Nothing irritated me more than the snobbish distinction between 'traveller' and 'tourist'. To the locals we are all tourists, period. They know that the scruffy denims hold plastic capable of releasing a wad of notes from a hole in the wall, and a passport that can push aside visa restrictions that would inhibit all but the wealthiest of their own land. Best recognize that we're all tourists.

Maybe I've been too hard on fantasy. The great liberating discovery of my ride was to discover that the words 'Meester, what is your name?' are not in fact a question but a friendly greeting, the only words of English the speaker knew. At a stroke my world changed. Perhaps one day old men across Europe and Asia will be telling their grandchildren of the day John le Carré or Graham Greene came cycling by.

(DAVE COOK)

Magnet

I was due to catch the train to Cardiff where I was to photograph identical twins. I wanted to visually symbolize the telepathic thought transference that exists naturally between twins, an ability we non-twins may also have had in childhood but which, without the permanent kinship of a *doppelgänger*, becomes blunted as we progress through life. I planned to photograph each twin reading

Cheryl Thomas reading 'One of Twins' by Ambrose Bierce, watched by Meryl Thomas. Photographed for Ian Breakwell by Dave Daggers

the same book. It didn't matter what the book was, but it might as well be one I could read myself on the train journey, and small too, since my holdall was full to the brim and the only remaining space was in a little side pocket.

I stood on a pair of steps and reached up to the top shelf where the miniature books were. My eyes panned along the row. There were *Collins Gem Dictionaries* and phrasebooks in French, German and Spanish, including the one I'd used on my first visit to Madrid in 1982. It dated from 1957 and was full of useful colonial phrases like 'Clean my shoes immediately'; 'Fetch my trunks from the station'; 'Bring me some sealing wax now.' Even when I got the translation right I got the pronunciation wrong. I would discover in restaurants that my meal hadn't arrived because I was trying to order a main dish of windscreen wipers or a side dish of sunglasses. One of my most ambitious sentences turned out to translate as 'The orchestra is playing too fast, where is the communication cord?'

With the phrasebooks were some of the delightful booklings by one-man publisher J. L. Carr, a gent of the old school who issued mini volumes of the English poets Donne, Milton and Arnold, together with equally tiny dictionaries of Curates, Prelates, Eponymists and extraordinary English Cricketers. On the back cover is J. L.'s byline: 'These books fit small envelopes, go for a minimum stamp and are perfect for cold bedrooms. Only one hand and wrist need suffer exposure.' They adjoin another series of little books which, in a different way, were also intended to be read with one hand: *Meet the Models*, published in Birkenhead, probably in the late 1950s judging by the frilly frocks the models rapidly cease wearing. Measuring 13 × 10 cm, each book has an oval cut-out on the front cover which frames the lipsticked, pouting face of the featured model who in the subsequent pages performs a quaint Dance of the Seven Veils in a sequence of photos accompanied by a first person commentary in rhyming couplets: 'I frankly feel it's time to peel. I've lots to show, so here we go!'

Nestling next to the models is a clutch of Hanuman Books which feature post-punk New York writers, obscure tracts from the Beat Generation and writings by artists. The books have an endearing Lilliputian format: 10 × 7 cm, with candy-coloured covers like Hindu prayerbooks, typeset in India by printers who speak no English, then handsewn by local fishermen. Hanuman's most substantial volume, *The Collected Writings of Willem de Kooning*, placated my impatience while waiting for a bus, and I read Francis Picabia's *Yes No* in its entirety while boiling an egg.

No good, I needed something more substantial for the journey. The last time I caught this train it got stuck in the Severn Tunnel. My eyes eventually alighted on the last book in the row, a squat blue hardback by Ambrose Bierce: *Can Such Things Be? I didn't remember it; must be* thirty years since I last came across it. I took it down, blew off the dust and opened it at random. At the title

Meryl Thomas reading 'One of Twins' by Ambrose Bierce watched by Cheryl Thomas. Photographed for Ian Breakwell by Dave Daggers

page of a short story entitled 'One of Twins'. Of course. There is a predictability about coincidence that never surprises me. Nor was I surprised that the book exactly fitted the pocket in my bag. Merely inevitable.

(IAN BREAKWELL)

Lost in Europe

I'm in a seat by the window, but a streaky sheet of grime shuts out the landscape going past. I'm on a train heading north to Prague from Bratislava, but the book my nose is in takes me to Trieste. It's John Berger's *G*: 1915, not 1974; Slovenia, not Slovakia ... which is darkening anyway, beyond the dirty window.

One of those journeys where you're thrown into your imagination all the more, not because there's nothing new to pull on your attention, but because the strangeness around you is lulled; not like being on a plane, though, where you're thoroughly dislocated yet too much intruded upon by your nowhere surroundings just to drift off. Planes are distraction, not absorption; snooze, not reverie. A train travelling through the night is the space of a dream.

There are four of us in the compartment. A blank-faced, fidgety youth occupies the far corner seat, next to an old woman who sits with her eyes closed. She is peasant sturdy and wears a headscarf and a wide black skirt, and a basket encrusted with hardened soil is planted between her feet, in it a huge pair of shears loosely wrapped in newspaper. They got on the train at different stations and in the hour or two since haven't uttered a word. Gillian and I occasionally look up from our books and exchange the odd remark, in English, and neither shows any sign of noticing this foreignness.

I bury myself deeper and deeper in *G*: Slovenes, Italians, Austrians, riot and resistance, the Habsburg empire in terminal spasm. In this novel time is a fraud, 'now' and 'then' collapsing into each other. Trieste itself is riven by history: a city on the cusp of shifting frontiers, languages, cultures. One of those fictions where place and time have a mutual instability. Where am I? When am I? Just the ticket for a ride across the map of Middle Europe.

We started out in Venice. Gillian had arrived along with another friend, Jan, a Czech, who had then gone back to London, leaving us a list of Czech friends we were to look up along the way, in Vienna, Bratislava and Prague. He and Gillian had brought me a bundle of recent paperbacks from London, among them *G.* My holiday reading.

Through the cracks in Vienna's surface dullness, its suspect air of propriety, the past sends silent screams. At least so it seems in the fevered state I've entered with the onset of flu. Schönbrunn, Prater, the Kunsthistorisches Museum are all perceived through a thickening of reality as my temperature climbs; faintly hallucinatory, like the overfriendly Czech architect who gives us hospitality for two nights, the Polish–German couple who are the other house guests, all of us in a prolonged haze of slivovitz and schnapps. Then there's the heat and the babble of languages in the long queue for visas at the Czech embassy. At this point I get dizzy and faint. Where am I? Against all the odds we get our visas before the office closes, and my head clears on the bus to Bratislava.

Bratislava is too subdued and rural, too centreless to be taken seriously as a city. The country market, the red carpeted hush of the Lenin Museum, the high-rise flats on the outskirts where we spend a night, warmly received by two more network names: all seem just a rehearsal for our real destination.

But on the train Prague gets further away. Anticipation is in abeyance. Inhabiting Trieste, I find myself reluctant to arrive elsewhere and journey's end drags me too abruptly out of fiction's living words and sentences into the void of the waking world. On the ill-lit station platform the here and now remains obscure. The deserted late night station, the silent forecourt and the greyness that seeps towards the rest of the city give it only provisional substance. As we straggle after other passengers in the direction of the tram stop I bend Gillian's ear, eager to talk about *G* now that I've had to stop reading it.

I'm still talking about it as the long-awaited tram jolts us off towards the centre. Everything is as dark as an East European city could be back then in the seventies, and how are we to know where to get off, and how to locate the student hostel we're supposed to stay in?

The driver, impervious to our mangled attempts at pronouncing Czech street names, waves us back along the aisle when we approach him. People stare, there are some murmurs of interest at our plight, then a middle-aged woman rises and speaks to us in English. We show her the address we want to find and she assures us she'll tell us when we reach the right stop. Smiles all round.

Then she asks are we from London. Well, yes ... She has a daughter who went there in '68, and she hasn't been able to see her since. The daughter must be our age she thinks. And she goes on talking, becoming more emotional as the tram lunges on through the still undifferentiated darkness. More people stare at us now, then at the woman, then they look away. She speaks softly.

Just as we get to the stop she scribbles an address. 'Please come and see me,' she says, as if our encounter has really mattered to her: perhaps she found in us an echo of her exiled daughter. 'By the way, I have an English writer staying at my flat. Perhaps you will meet him if you come. His name is John Berger.'

'Look!' I blurt, just before we leap off the tram. 'I'm reading one of his books.' I pull *G* from my bag and wave its red cover at her. She smiles again, as if she hasn't heard me, and gives us a wave of her own.

'Fancy that!'

And off we trudge into the dark, to have Prague claim us for itself and get us lost and send us wandering round in circles, tired and bedless until, around 1 a.m., it takes pity on us in the form of complete strangers on their way home. It falls to the lot of a young woman who works as a make-up artist at the television station to give us a roof for the night. In her tiny flat she houses a splendid collection of platform shoes that have entered the country from the West, we infer, courtesy of a German boyfriend.

We think about the woman on the tram a few days later and wonder whether to pay her a visit. Our meeting had, after all, seemed fated. Odd enough even for us to doubt its reality. Just imagination maybe. So one afternoon we track down the address and climb the stairs of a sombre narrow building that has two flats to each dim-lit landing. There's not a soul about, not a sound escapes from behind any of the identically heavy panelled, firmly closed doors, all with solid brass nameplates.

We find the right floor, the right name. We ring the bell, whose thin tinkle barely penetrates the hush, and when nothing stirs on the other side of the door we knock, several times, hard. No one answers. We loiter for ten minutes, thinking that a neighbour might appear and gather up the loose end we now feel left with. But no one does.

(LIZ HERON)

I never read pornography even though it was available when I was stationed abroad. I could never see any point in getting myself excited for nothing.
(A MASS-OBSERVER)

Fortunata

Intercity. Lancaster to London. I'm reading *Sexing the Cherry* by Jeanette Winterson. A woman in her early sixties enters the crowded carriage. She has a strong presence. She looks directly at me as she approaches, a broad smile on her face. She's about to speak, maybe sit next to me. I look away. She decides on the seat in front and sits down with her back to me. I get back to my book.

As I read she sings softly to herself. I hear the occasional snip of scissors. Through the narrow gap between the seats I can see that she is doing something with a length of coarse string. I wonder what it is. I think she's Dutch or German. I get back to my book.

La-la-la. She's still singing. The string becomes taut. Snip. It slackens. La-la. Taut. Snip. Slack. I lean forward. The gap between the seats widens. I see her fingers pulling deftly as she cuts the string and ties it back together again, pulling each knot tight before moving on to the next cut about a foot farther along. I don't understand. La-la-la. Snip. Aware that she's being watched, her head starts to turn. I get back to my book, where I read about Fortunata, the youngest of twelve dancing princesses. She was so light that she could climb down a rope, cut it and tie it again in mid-air. I put the book down. The woman gets off the train. At Milton Keynes.

(JOHN SMITH)

Et in Agadir Ego

By the time we reached Agadir I had only one book left, the Sahara being no place for a speed reader. It was a very old edition of *Brideshead Revisited*. An orange Penguin, which had once cost 3/6, it had a dismal etching of a stately home grimly encircled with barbed wire on its cover. Paradise lost, where love had died for Charles Ryder. On a romantic quest myself, in search of literary ghosts and additionally on my honeymoon, I read of Ryder's loss, disillusion and spiritual regeneration. It was a mistake.

Morocco has a place extraordinarily like Crewe, a sort of happy shunting ground called Sidi-Slimane. And there, in a hot railway carriage, love could have died for me too. Inexpressibly moved by Lord Marchmain's death and with the strains of '*Quomodo sedet sola civitas*', that 'beautiful chant', echoing in my head I felt the unmistakable stirrings of a Catholic conversion. Each ineffable spiritual convulsion, every labyrinthine argument for the

Tridentine form was interminably relayed to my partner, a North London Jew and hard-line Darwinist, cross-eyed on rough Moroccan Ricard. The trains coupled and uncoupled all night. The marriage seemed doomed ...

Fortunately the English bookshop in Tangier provided my 'twitch upon the thread' so central to Waugh's book and restored me to my usual self and all the dull bibliophile concerns of the Charing Cross Road. Powers, popes, principalities, romance, lace, minarets and roses: I packed a new case of books.

We came home, got a cat and didn't go on holiday again for fourteen years.

(ELIZABETH YOUNG)

Thursday's Child

If we are to believe Paterne Berrichon, the brother-in-law who never knew him, then within seconds of his birth Rimbaud was strutting around the room with Gargantuan self-confidence and reading aloud to his mother to reassure her. To reassure her of what? My own modest feat of reading a story to Jennifer Styles and Georgina Skaif while we sat on the red concrete steps of the flats was a fraud, accomplished by turning the pages and reciting the memorized words I had heard read to me so many times as I lay under the heavy eiderdown in my grandparents' bed. There was a story of a foolish prince who destroyed his headgear in order to pay for sweets costing half a crown. Another illustration showed a small boy on a scooter, who propelled himself enthusiastically past a road sign that pointed in opposite directions to London and Edinburgh. Thursday's child has far to go, the caption read. It was the one that rhymed with woe.

We lived in a council flat in a small block of which we were amongst the first tenants. Three floors, three flats to a floor, the whole arrangement doubled on the other

*Roland Miller adjusts the
pages of his perambulating
book, which revolve as the
wearer walks along.*
Photo: Julian Smith

side, making eighteen flats in all. It was surrounded by
sand at first, soon replaced with grass and a pair of
splintered saplings. A girl from elsewhere on the estate
told me that the site used to be an orchard. She and
other kids from the prefabs had tried to sabotage the
building of the block by nicking tools and bricks and
smashing windows.

Now it seems an almost attractive example of late
fifties' council architecture, small enough that everyone
knew everyone else. In winter we'd all meet in one of
the kitchens, my mother standing before a blazing oven
with her skirt hitched, lighting another Senior Service
off the ring while Billie Skaif, Freda, Tish or Mrs Styles
drew breath and my mother closed one eye and dipped
her head to one side as she exhaled.

I remember her doodles, always of the same face: a
woman from a line illustration in a fifties' magazine
advertisement. She'd draw them for hours with eye-liner
pencil, self portraits with impossibly long lashes, show

them for approval, each one, and I'd try to copy them but couldn't. The only person I could draw was Fred Flintstone.

Later I started scribbling violently over the paper, which Miss E. liked, and out of that I started to learn to draw. Miss E. tied her hair back with bootlaces, ate Trill, and had begged off American tourists in Tangier. She encouraged me in everything, even had a friend who used drugs for 'experimental reasons'. She lent me books by Rimbaud. Moonstruck, I dogged his footsteps to Charleville.

I found a room in the junkie-infested attic of a local doctor's house on the rue du Petit Bois, at the end of which had been the wood where the adolescent Rimbaud used to loaf around with his friend Delahaye. The wood had been uprooted to build a municipal stadium, now a crumbling monument with futurist bicycles on the bas relief above the gate, the cyclists paced by a 1920s' motorbike.

I retrace my steps after all these years in the shadows of the trees along the stadium wall and the front of the lycée. On the far side of the school are derelict warehouses and factories. I wander across a disused railway line, a patch of waste ground, and the curl of the Meuse is there, almost above me, glittering, fast, narrower than I remember. A road climbs a stair of shuttered houses on the far bank. Further along is a footbridge, and painted on one of its supports: MORT AUX ARABES.

I cross the bridge and follow the river to the steep wooded slopes of Mont Olympe and gaze down at the municipal campsite and the floral clock. The opposite bank is now quai Rimbaud, where I raced to get Isabelle to school on time as she clung behind me on the carrier of her black Solex. And as I think of her now, just killed on her way home from work on the mountain roads above Grenoble, it isn't nostalgia that brings tears to my eyes, but the indifference of these revisited places, the lying futility of memory.

(JOHN MUCKLE)

Our neighbour, an indolent farmer, spent hours inspecting as we unpacked our belongings in our new French home. He was Monsieur Dupe, he told me, Olivier. 'Wait,' he said. He trotted off, to return with the local phone book. Laying it on the case I'd been emptying he gravely turned the pages. Then, with a cry of triumph, he pointed with his *merguez*-red finger. 'There,' he proclaimed. '*Je suis là*. There I am.'

(CHRIS PROCTOR)

Home to Roost

When an author sends a book out into the world it's like a message in a bottle: you never know who it will reach and what it will mean to them.

One day I got a letter from the Hebrides, sent on from a Glasgow publisher. It asked if I remembered, which I didn't, giving a lift to someone hitch-hiking down the A1 twenty-five or so years ago and talking with him about books, poetry and poets. In fact the letter writer had forgotten my name until he came across it on a pamphlet of imitation 'translations from the Gaelic' in the library at Benbecula. Liking the poems, he had ordered a copy for himself from the publisher. Noticing another book of mine, also listed, he'd ordered that as well. This was a prose journal, written long after I had forgotten our meeting, with an entry for each day of the year, and it happened to start and end on a day in October. He had enjoyed this also, but what he really wanted to ask was why had I started and ended it on his birthday?

But it works both ways, and many years before, in Canada, when I was still young and foolish enough to occasionally do something wise, I visited a friend who showed me a small book by a young American poet. He was then mostly unknown, although I had already seen a few of his poems and been intrigued by them. It was a particularly attractive production by a small press in San Francisco and I was further impressed and gripped by the poems so I sent off for a copy. On an impulse I ordered two, thinking that eventually there would be someone who might appreciate the extra one. Shortly after this I travelled back to Britain, and later I spent some years in southern California, but that extra copy never happened to find a new home. Even more surprisingly perhaps, it did not vanish as much else did along the way. I had corresponded regularly with the poet but we did not actually meet until ten years after that original purchase, and in New Mexico. There was much talk on many subjects, eventually including the way in which books, like other possessions, vanish, and the various reasons for this, chiefly our respective nomadic existences and the habit, one might say dangerous addiction, of 'lending'.

He then remarked, 'You won't believe this, but I don't even have a copy of my own first book.'

'You won't believe *this*,' I was able to reply, 'but I have been saving one for you all these years.'

(GAEL TURNBULL)

The Two Macs

like collapsing bookshelves the stone slabs hung back from the sea.
Annabel Nicolson

Like professors, poets are renowned for their absent-mindedness, something that sets them apart from us mere mortals. One such is the great Gaelic bard Sorley MacLean, or Somhairle Mac Gill-eain as he is known to those who can get their tongues round it. Once, stopping

overnight in a hotel, he wondered why there wasn't a dialling tone coming from the phone in his room. Perhaps it was because he was holding a hairdryer, some smart alec suggested.

On another occasion MacLean was attending the Writers' Weekend in Paisley. Billed to read with his fellow poet and long-time friend Norman MacCaig, the pair of them made an undramatic entrance into the lounge bar where the reading was due to take place. It was a few minutes past the hour at which the programme was to start. The audience of about a hundred fell into an expectant hush, for they were about to hear Scotland's two greatest living poets.

MacCaig, tall and angular, folded himself into a seat in the front row. MacLean, a terrier with a nail-brush moustache, took up his station in front of the audience and began to riffle through his papers. The silence was sepulchral. A minute passed, then another. MacLean continued his search for the elusive poem. More agonizing minutes passed. By now the audience was stiff with suspense. Suddenly MacLean found what he was looking for, and he began to peruse it with studied intensity. Yet more minutes went by and still the poet refused to acknowledge his audience. Someone sneezed; another coughed. Thoughts began to turn towards the bar and the fact that it might at this rate be closed before the reading was over. And then, when all had seemed lost, MacCaig piped up in a musical voice, 'I knew Sorley was going to read tonight, but I didn't know it was to himself.' At that MacLean awoke as if from a deep sleep and began to recite.

(ALAN TAYLOR)

Amateur

No one expects anything from me, but I think positively. It is very important to be cheerful, to look on the bright side. If anything goes wrong I have only myself to blame. But I am organized and I provide all my own entertainment. It's best to be selfish. If everyone was positively selfish like me the world would be a better place. If only everyone could see that their happiness lies in their own hands. I admit I've been lucky, I don't have to work any more and that was due to a bit of foresight. I'm not rich but I've enough to pay for my modest needs.

You have to be a certain type to live on your own and spend your days without boredom and petty worries. For a start you must not take any notice of what the neighbours might say about you. People on their own, especially where I live, are thought to be a bit queer, unnatural. The neighbours may even feel offended that you are not interested in them, so you've got to rise above all that. My books and my music keep me in a state of mind that I'm very happy with. For a long time I've loved music, although I have to say that I'm no more than an amateur. I passed my music O level, just, so my knowledge is limited but I can follow the score when I listen to my favourite pieces. What I particularly enjoy is to follow one of the instruments that is partly swallowed up by the rest of the orchestra. Tracing the notes is like chasing the light of an aeroplane through a sky of stars.

My books and my music supply me with all my most entertaining diversions and have done for most of my adult life. Early on I used to go to concerts, before I got to dislike crowds, and I used to know people who played music. I even had a girlfriend for a while; she played the viola with the Thames Ditton Ladies' Sinfonietta and she introduced me to French music: Debussy, Franck, Satie and Ravel were her particular favourites. She was very sexy when she played the viola; the way she clutched the instrument, her breasts swaying beneath the crisp cotton blouse, was very arousing. Unfortunately she was not to be aroused, at least not by me. Our association ended because she did not accept my advances and that finished me with women. Well, not quite, because I did go to a prostitute the week after we broke up, but that was a horrible experience that I'd rather not recall. I'd

At the moment I have two library books out, both medical. The reason is to find out things. *Goodbye to Arthritis* because my girlfriend is a sufferer. And *Sex and Your Health* because I worry.

(A MASS-OBSERVER)

wanted to revenge myself but my viola player never knew and I would not want her to learn of the terrible indignity I underwent. So after that I learned to keep my relationships with others on the level of acquaintance rather than friendship. There have been occasions when I've been sorely tempted to go out looking for a whore again but, what with AIDS and my first unfortunate experience, I have developed my own solace.

This is what I meant about looking on the bright side. I had to turn my natural desires and their fulfilment into something that was truly positive, it's no good masturbating and being ashamed of it. I had to make it into something special. At first I used to fantasize, especially about my viola player. I used to imagine fucking her while she was playing the viola. She would sit on my lap and all it took was the drawing of the bow across the strings while I caressed those splendid breasts. That kept me satisfied for a while but as she slipped more into the past I found I was less and less excited by the prospect of another session with an imaginary instrument, even though I put on some appropriate music, usually *Shéhérazade*.

The next phase in my development towards a more complete self-sufficiency came out of my reading. I love a good read, the sort of novel that really absorbs you, sagas and family histories, that sort of thing. For a long time my favourite book was *A Horseman Riding By* by R. F. Delderfield. There were so many characters to follow and they were all interesting. It is a very long story, the book has one thousand, one hundred and fifty pages and there are five scenes of an erotic nature. The first, on page 276, is quite charming, has nothing about it to remind me of my viola player and even less of the coarseness of my expensive disaster. It takes place on an island in the middle of a lake, without any vulgar descriptions but with tantalizing phrases such as 'embracing him with a kind of zestful gaiety' and 'she carefully unhooked her skirt'. It left me room to imagine my own ideal anatomies but the fifth scene was for me the most exciting, where the imagination is left to decide what to do with the desirable anatomy described. On page 823 the squire 'sat absorbing the strength and symmetry of her body ... appraised every part of her ... the glowing health of her skin, the smooth sweep of her hips', enabling me to conjure up an ideal vision supported on 'the sturdy columns of her thighs'. But gradually I became tired of this account and found the description inconsistent, a nagging feeling that gave way to a sense of absurdity which kills erotic tension. The reason for this lies in the list commencing with her sturdy thighs 'balanced by wide buttocks and a long straight back, her full firm breasts, her strong neck and powerful shoulders offsetting the curious smallness and neatness of her head'. The squire was sitting in front of her while she 'stood quite still', which made nonsense of him seeing her breasts and buttocks in one sweeping glance and was made even more ridiculous when he says, '"You're not just Rubens' model, Claire, you're Velázquez's"', while I was seeing something grotesque by Picasso.

Gradually I abandoned novels as my source of sexual excitement as the language failed to provide me with an image that was not tarnished in some way. It was a search for perfection, and like at the end of my relationship with the viola player I went a-whoring, but this time with pornographic magazines. And as with the prostitute I was disgusted and felt degraded by the grossness of the material and humiliated when my member became engorged at the sight of oiled labia, engorged when my sense of shame was equally swollen.

However I never lost my love of music and foolishly I nursed fantasies about becoming a conductor. I even attended music appreciation evening classes for a while but soon realized that my poor O level pass and an enthusiasm was insufficient grounding for such a career. Even so there was nothing to stop me, in the privacy of my own sitting room, in front of the stereo, conducting the Hallé, the Berlin Philharmonic or the Cleveland. Gradually I collected a library of musical scores and I bought a lovely antique lectern which I used as a music stand. The musical preferences of my ex-girlfriend

I like bookshelves with glass doors to keep the dust out. But I like to get a book from the shelf without opening the door, so the problem's insoluble.

(A MASS-OBSERVER)

remained mine. Durand SA of 215, rue du Faubourg St-Honoré, Paris, provided me with most of my music books. The most expensive are the conductor's scores which are in large format so that you do not have to turn the pages so often. I did not buy myself a baton, preferring to use the elasticity of my hands and fingers to pluck the notes out of the air as my eyes raced along the staves.

Picture, if you can, an evening in November. I have just drawn the deep red velvet curtains that cover my french windows, the television is set to channel 8, but the video is not switched on so that the screen is just glowing and representing my audience. My Bang and Olufsen CD player is alight but not yet playing and I walk slowly, with a quiet dignity, to the music stand upon which rests the conductor's score for Ravel's *Bolero*. On the cover lies the remote control. I pick up the handset and hold it in my right hand while I open the score with my left. I bow to the television and then to the stereo, I point the remote control and toss it on to the sofa behind me. The music begins. Of course I was dressed very formally, these were special occasions for which I used to hire a suit with tails, a white bow tie, a white shirt with stiff collar and cuffs, cuff-links, black trousers with the black ribbon down the outer seams and a pair of highly polished black patent leather shoes. Later I acquired my own, I even bought myself some white silk socks.

Let us return to that November evening. I can see myself, white cuffs protruding from my black sleeves, my hands poised above the first page of *Bolero*, the words 'à Ida Rubinstein' making a chain link between my forefingers. My hands flutter as the two snare drums begin the irresistible and insistent beat that will not change, no matter how many more instruments swell the orchestration. But it is not my business to stay with the quavers and triplets of the tambour section, I must pay attention to the flutes, first and second violins, violas, cellos and double basses. Fleetingly I regret not wearing white gloves, but I can turn the pages more easily with my

fingers, the skin slightly damp, fingers that gently tap the air as an encouragement to the flute while keeping time with the snare.

The flute has one tune to itself, answered by the clarinet. The second tune is played very high by the bassoon and answered in its turn by the E flat clarinet. By this time there is a feeling of suppressed panic, I have to keep up with the music, to turn the pages, to follow the notes without losing track for one moment. I have to remain fully conscious of what is happening as it is happening. By the time I reach figure 4 in my score the second violins playing pizzicato have joined the violas, the notes falling softly. Their strings steadily, rhythmically plucked, the violas play monotonously. The panic in my belly is softening, growing warmer as the oboe d'amore's delights disappear behind the trumpet which, by figure 10, is playing senza sordine. This dropping of the brass's mute is a call to my bodily energies, a summons demanding more than yet another rehearsal, more than even a dress rehearsal. I am glad I am not wearing gloves. I turn another page, I unzip my flies.

By the time I reach figure 11 there is only room for four bars per page, so many instruments are contributing to the temperature. This means that I have to turn the pages more rapidly, continue my conducting and coax the slowly enlarging member through the vent in my underpants. Actually, once it is free I hardly need to touch, the music is exciting enough to keep me in a state of delight, with the gathering of flutes, oboes, cor anglais, clarinets, bass clarinet, bassoons, contrabassoons, horn, trumpets, saxophone, snare drums, harp, first and second violins, violas, cellos and double-basses. The glow of the television reminds me that I am being watched, my performance must be perfection itself. In the snowy particles on the screen I fancy I can see the coming applause, the ticker tape that will rain down when I make my final bow. The fourth horn, first trumpet and snare drum are exactly in step, the quavers and triplets have a stiffness, around which slides the unguent of the strings. But what's this? The second violins are also exactly in step, the quavers and triplets tight and slippery, yet we are barely half way through the music.

Mercifully there is a change, not in the rhythm, which is as insistent as ever, not in the alternating tunes, but in the balance of instruments, which heads off a premature conclusion and gradually moves around the orchestra allowing each principal its own time and space. The unrelenting percussion becomes louder and, relative to the rest of the orchestra, quieter, gathering up the collective energies, raising them to a pitch before moving on to collect from another combination of instruments. To maintain my timing as well as I can there are moments when I have to follow a minor sound, an instrument buried in the orchestration. If I succeed in following by eye and catching the sound of perhaps the contrabassoon between figures 12 and 15 I can then allow myself a heightening of excitement for a couple of pages and, holding the score in one hand, step to one side of the lectern and pump myself hard, not in time to the snare but to the kettle drum, or pluck in keeping with the harp. This requires swift changes of hand, always in rhythm, so that I can turn the pages. But this is not possible for long and I return the turquoise mock leather covered music to its stand and resume conducting with, I hope, the same dignity as Herbert von Karajan, who is credited with my recording.

The instruments I have not mentioned, which are the ones whose call is the most urgent and irresistible, are the trombones, which make their appearance along with the tuba at figure 14 in my score. But at the moment they are just potential, the lubricious strings have me in their power. So much so that I can no longer pretend that I am Karajan, and I fling my jacket behind me to join the remote control. Generously wide as they are I am able to step out of my trousers and, still keeping time with the madness of the music, I kick them to the sofa, quickly followed by my trunks. I missed two bars in that last regrettably unaesthetic manoeuvre, but this is more than made up for by the sense of freedom and the approach of a glorious finale. Strings are wonderful things, they keep me tensile, expectant and excited; drums are reassuring, reminding me of the immediacy and physicality of my music; the wind section is sweet, it toys with me; but the brass, the brazen trumpet, the worldly saxophone and the shameless trombone, rasping and rubbing, bring me to my knees in front of the electronic audience regarding me with its shivering cornea. Leaving my score up on the wooden stand, open four pages before the end, I gently stroke myself, eyes closed, as that final raw glissando of trumpet and trombone achieves for me a magnificent yet tremulous approach of delicious sensation.

That was one evening, one November, when a new independence dawned for me. I admit that there are times when I have to make a special effort to look on the bright side, but I just remind myself that I have much to be thankful for, and there are many more scores to be learnt. Recently I have had my *Bolero* rebound, this time in real leather, and I've bought myself some white gloves.

(DAVID CUTHBERT)

Heckles and Hackles

1986. Performance theatre at the Royal Albert Hall. Jan Fabre's company is on stage. The event has been heavily hyped and as the evening progresses it becomes clear that the majority of the large audience are not getting what they came for. The performance is very minimal and extremely slow. It will continue for several hours.

The first signs of restlessness are slight, just a few more coughs than you might expect, but after an hour and a half people are leaving and the heckling is in full swing. The performers are tense, working hard, totally committed. It is very serious. The audience is laughing. It is excruciating.

After two hours the performance has become even slower. There is no visible movement on stage and the heckling is now almost constant. The Royal Albert Hall has turned into the Colosseum. The audience want blood and the performers are dying for their art. I want to die too.

Just when I can't stand it any more a man's clear, powerful voice rises above the mob. '*Shut up!*' it booms. The heckling stops abruptly. At last, the voice of reason. He repeats his impassioned plea, 'Just *shut up* ... I'm *trying* to read my *book!*'

(JOHN SMITH)

Resting Thespian

After the books were dressed on to the set I would look along the spines. The majority were old but dull acquaintances, appearing as they did week in and week out on the shelves and tables of different television productions. Tired and generally shabby, their backs to the camera, they seemed to have no interest in the dramas played out around them. Perhaps they'd seen it all before and I looked right past them for the odd interesting newcomer that I could save from this treadmill to become a proper book again. Luckily not too many other technicians were engaged in this activity or if they were there was no clash of interests. Each hunter had his own field. For instance a friend of mine had collected over the years an almost complete set of turn-of-the-century encyclopaedias. Full of references to the lost Empire, the volumes, scattered in storage through dozens of tea chests, would turn up every now and again until, in the end, only one still eluded him.

The set for Christopher Hampton's *The Philanthropist* consisted of the book-lined rooms of a university lecturer. Books from floor to ceiling, shelves and shelves of them, all waiting for their big break. Unfortunately the vast majority of them were the usual imposters, just there for show – what was *Rabbit Breeding in Norfolk* doing in a professor of philology's study? – but it was still a gold mine. The rehearsal and recording of the play would take three days in the studio so I had plenty of time to pick and choose. On the first day my friend, after a detailed search of the upper shelves, found the last missing encyclopaedia and at home late that evening he reunited it with its eleven companions. I was in no hurry but early on the second day, while the action continued on a side set, I found what I was looking for. It stood out from the others in its bright yellow dust cover, a fat book full of knowledge, *The Fabric of Existentialism.*

I don't think there were actually any clues in the script to let me know that later that day as the scenes

I remember reading *Jude the Obscure* in hospital waiting to give birth to my daughter, and sobbing as Jude's child committed suicide as I sat in a ward of howling babies and chaos.

(A MASS-OBSERVER)

progressed the main character would rise from his desk, walk across his study and take down from the shelf *The Fabric of Existentialism*. By this time only the conspicuous yellow jacket remained. Inside was one of the imposters, *The Cultivation and Distribution of Watercress*, an undeserving extra promoted to this leading role through a simple change of clothes. I could feel the real book deep in my bag struggling to get back on the set, its big moment slipping away. I did feel guilty for a short time but in the end it really wasn't much of a moment in acting terms, the bright yellow wrapper had the main part, the actual contents didn't matter at all. I knew instinctively that the path to true happiness for this particular book meant leaving the precarious theatrical life, the uncertainty of always waiting for someone to pick you up, and settling down with my other books on a quiet shelf.

(JOHN CHRISTIE)

Vortex

Piano stools, if present at all, are seldom the right height for upright pianos. They certainly were not when I was out in the wild, performing live in all sorts of pubs, clubs and dives. And anyway $1\frac{1}{2}$ ins. (or 37 mm) had to be added to the sedentary ivory tickling height adopted in the home or studio for that extra downward thrust in wild performing necessary to startle audiences. I might even have had to start with a kiddie's school chair.

I talked the language of phone books. 'One phone book!' or 'Three phone books should do it!' I would shout. It didn't matter whether they were of urban or rural thickness. I welcomed the introduction of a certain random control element over my spontaneous pianistics. Occasionally, when run out of tone clusters, or run off the end of the keyboard, I would even read from the phone book, usually by shouting a funny name. This provided me with the necessary jolt back on course, and the audience with a chance to return fire with even funnier names.

If the piano was good enough – maybe one of those big German ones with child-bearing hips – I would be moved to fine adjust the seating height by tearing a phone book in half, down the spine not across, mind you. This would enrage the management and, in turn, engage the audience as we careered helter-skelter towards the climax of another essentially daft evening.

Now that I'm seldom out in the wild, but instead send out wild thoughts from office and studio, the phone books rest on their British Standard steel shelving ready to find me, well, maybe a bookbinder who can put my Edgar Allan Poe's *The Tell-Tale Heart* in a bulbously purple heart, or set Lin Yutang's *The Importance of Living* in half an inch (13 mm) of well-resined plum blossom. Which reminds me that when I received *The Reader's Digest Repair Manual* it fell from its cardboard packing and divided into two on the floor. Another ploy to increase readership! The first thing I had to do with it was to refer inwards to repair outwards.

We will skip past the time when I hurled an Evelyn Waugh paperback out of the train window, through the lattice-work of Hungerford Bridge and into the Thames, silently screaming that nobody should even have the chance to borrow it. We will move on to further destruction, and I mean that in both ways.

In the last few years, having saved up enough supreme relaxation coupons to treat myself to a bath, I have lain there anticipating that extra sensuality of the tingle of sweat, an excretion once too often accelerated by my anger at the sight of a Christmas gift called *The Toilet Book* wedged in the top bathroom shelf and covered in talcum powder dust. Since I've dropped the preaching to practise the enjoyment and, since this cheap lavatorial humour never really amused anyone in the house, I leapt out of the foam like a monster possessed and wrenched *The Toilet Book* from its shelf. Having used some of its pages for the most appropriate purpose, I pulled the chain to send the volume back where it belonged. As it

The Toilet Book *goes down the vortex.*
Photos by Ron Geesin

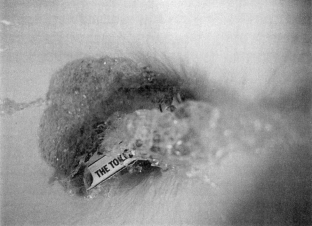

whirled down the vortex I too was so flushed with a surge of nostalgic adrenalin as to proceed immediately to the music room, seat myself, warm, damp and pink, on a very normal piano stool and play a swirl of ecstasy. Very gently.

(RON GEESIN)

Mulch

I had written my first novel. I wanted to lend a sense of occasion to its dispatch and decided to walk to the nearest post office, three kilometres from the French farmhouse where I lived. The sun shone on this bright morning. I was almost bursting with pride and self-importance and couldn't help telling the clerk it was a book I was posting. My book. A book I had written. And now I was sending it to London.

'No you're not,' she said. 'It's over two kilos. We don't take anything over two kilos.'

'So what do I do with it?'

She shrugged and suggested I cut down the length.

Out I staggered, amazed at a world where editing started at the post office, and suddenly I began to fear that I had been overconfident about the whole work. The first droplets of rain fell as I began the journey home. By half way the heavens had opened. Under my arm was a slab of wet paper rapidly turning into pulp. Premature recycling. I stuffed the manuscript further under my coat, but that too was so sodden that the deterioration continued unabated. Ex-paper began to slop into the puddles at my feet. There is only one litter bin in Les Essards. I stood by it and dropped in the remnants of paper that hadn't adhered themselves to the lining of my coat.

On reflection I'm proud of that book. No publisher ever rejected it.

(CHRIS PROCTOR)

The Information Man

It would be nice if sometime a man would come up to me on the street and say, 'Hello, I'm the Information Man and you have not said the word "yours" for thirteen minutes. You have not said the word "praise" for eighteen days, three hours and nine minutes. You have not used the word "petroleum" in your speech for almost four and a half months, but you wrote the word last Friday evening at 9.35 p.m. and you used the word "hello" about thirty seconds ago.'

This Information Man would also have details as to the placement and whereabouts of things. He could tell me possibly that of all the books of mine that are out in the public only seventeen are actually placed face up with nothing covering them while 2,026 are under books in vertical positions in libraries and 2,715 are under books in stacks. The most weight upon a single book is 683 pounds and that is in the city of Cologne, Germany in a bookshop. Fifty-eight have been lost; fourteen totally destroyed by water or fire; while 216 could be considered badly worn. A whopping 319 books are in positions between 40 and 50 degrees and most of these are probably in bookshelves with the stacks leaning at odd angles. Eighteen of the books have never been opened, most of these being newly purchased and put aside momentarily. Of the approximate 5,000 books of Ed Ruscha that have been purchased, only thirty-two have actually been used in a directly functional manner. Thirteen of these have been used as weights for paper or other things. Seven have been used as swatters to kill small insects such as flies and mosquitoes and two have been used in bodily self-defence. Ten have been used to push open heavy doors (probably, since they are packaged in tens, one package was used to push open one door). Two were used to nudge wall pictures into correct levels, while one was used as a wiper to check the oil on an auto dipstick. Three are under pillows. Two hundred and twenty-one

My mother, worried that I never responded to her when I had my head in a book, took me to be tested by the Schools' Audiology Service. I had to bang with a spoon when I heard the *Queen Mary*'s foghorn. I was ear perfect.

(A MASS-OBSERVER)

people have smelled the books' pages, probably most of these on the original purchase.

Three of the books have been in continual motion since their purchase over two years ago, all of these being on a boat near Seattle, Washington . . .

(ED RUSCHA)

Dear Diary

You made me an offer I could never refuse, day after day, days you kept safe, kept full. You taught me tricks, tricks like writing in code so the family wouldn't know if they spied that the perfect schoolgirl who played hockey and dreaded exams was rife with romance and riddled with fear. If I missed an entry there was a hole in my life. You taught me to write it in next day. Sit down, you said sweetly, open the book, write the date and make your day, make mine. There are so many ways, try this one. Your page was always smooth, the curlicues flowed. I changed my handwriting in your honour. I bound, signed and sealed you with a loving kiss, like Anne Frank, who gave me the idea of days into volumes and volumes into hiding. Her Secret Annexe was my secret too. For her there was no life after diary, no unopened packet of five on the shelf. There was no such time, no such shelf.

It was a very small book at first, red, ruled feint, one inch by four per day. It was weakly bound, the cover warped. I got as far as February. The next, three years later, was also small, green, with a white-capped pencil in a channel down the spine. This time I sprawled into March. Then in 1961 a bigger blue book, well sewn, unruled, and a new blue Biro. I wrote every day. I lived in anticipation of what I'd write that night and when I wrote the day was appeased. Soon it was a series: the red and green moiré effect covers, pages ruled and unruled, quarto then A4; several large files, furry at the edges; the

Paris volumes, hand-done covers plastic wrapped, with Métro tickets and tarot cards stuck in. Then for years it was the blue books, quarto, classico, ruled feint, hard covers, endpapers; followed by the brown books, plain pages, quarto, then A4. In 1982 they changed the cover colour to yellow. They come in packets of five.

Twenty-five years at a page or more a day made ninety volumes on the shelf. Safe and full our carapace, safe and full. A loose holiday page was lost in 1966 and another left blank in mourning. A half page was torn out in 1967, in love and embarrassment. A week left blank in 1974. An extra white file came in at the end of a year in America, 1981. In 1984 I tore out one sheet to write a letter. I felt the rending but you didn't scream. You're not a screamer, are you? You sit tight on your shelf, spine after dated spine. You wouldn't scream if you were buried alive, or if I were.

You grew in silence beyond my arm span, beyond the oxygen line. All the years I imagined getting you out first if there was a fire, and how do you repay me? Tick-tock, you reply, keep taking the pills, follow those curl-icues wherever they go, there are patterns everywhere, there've always been enough analogies to sink an ark, there are new truths every two hundred yards, eat them all.

For a season we managed an uneasy peace. Then war. I wrote a word and you threw it back. Entire entries went on the rampage. I scrawled and stamped. Your pages shone. I threw the book across the room but carried you around when I went away. I always knew where you were in the house, you had your particular pen, I had my breathless moments. I could still feed in a day now and then, feel the recent past dangle when the book was closed and rock on my knees in my head. Where's the day? Put away, the day is gone, gone, and you are still quivering.

The crunch came on a cliff top with my friend Dixie. We'd gone out for the afternoon, found a sunny place on flat rock, sat there for hours, talked and stared. Dixie's very preoccupied with babies at the moment – it's a long story. She was throwing stones into the water. 'These are my babies,' she said. 'What would you like to throw?'

Dear Diary, the moment was yours. I soon ran out of stones on the cliff. I loved the trial by air, the cool trajectory before we dived in.

Yours etc.

(JUDY KRAVIS)

Three Moments

One. Suddenly my head twisted back and round so as to snatch a glimpse of the book passing through the air. The heavy, dark covers spread wide, their pale pages rustling and flapping as the book worked the dry class-room air, like a slow and serious bird. It seemed to pause in mid-flight above my head, an image of knowledge in transmission. I seemed not to see the book complete its trajectory but I do remember the noise the boy made when it hit his face. There was blood. But there was no further memory of the teacher who had thrown the book other than a rumour of his dismissal from the school.

Two. 'I'm going to put your name in my little black book,' the voice announced in a heavy authoritarian tone. My inner voice whispered, 'He doesn't know your name, he doesn't have a book, and he probably can't write. He only knows about making you afraid.' In fact, there was no evidence of any such book. Nevertheless, years later when buying an address book, I felt compelled to ignore the wide variety of choice in the shop and go straight for the one book that immediately caught my eye. It was thickly serious with a heavy, waxy, black cover. 'This is a real book for keeping names,' my inner voice told me. But then I uncomfortably recognized a forgotten memory moving within my action.

Three. As the flesh of the flower flattened between the closing pages of the book a sticky juice oozed out, seeping into the paper, moving out to the margins and on to my fingers. I awkwardly wiped my hands on my school blazer. She silently looked into my face, distaste and attraction mingling incredulously. 'Is that a promise?' she asked, as a smile began to form. I returned the smile awkwardly and with a sense of embarrassment where in later years there would be irony.

(TIMOTHY EMLYN JONES)

Marbled Halls

Since my release from prison on St David's Day 1977 hardly a working hour has passed without my being obliged to offer my explanations about allegations and condemnations, be they false or true, written by authors giving their versions of what they believed to be the truth about the 'Poulson affair'. So each day I am brought to book.

I remain a believer in the adage 'publish and be damned', expecting only in return that the price for that legitimate freedom is that what is written can be substantiated in all circumstances. My protesting plea is not that authors wrote books about the Poulson affair but that too many of their sources were tainted. Then false, inaccurate and misleading words are addressed to the reading public, the people who make up juries.

Unlike the prosecution in court, authors' published allegations culled from newspaper reports and magazines find their way, edited or expanded, into books that eventually appear on the shelves of public libraries. There they have the weight of authority that newspapers, here today and gone tomorrow, can never have.

The power of the book is one I have been aware of since early childhood. My very first book was called *Lost Toby*: large print, well spaced, thick, easily turned pages.

Shortly after being given the book on my fifth birthday my best friend, an only child who lived upstairs from us, scalded himself to death. My religious mother attributed the coincidence of her buying me the book to an all-knowing God's prophecy. My friend's name was *Toby* Scott and he is permanently etched into my life.

My mother was a militant Christian socialist, unending in her use of biblical quotations of both religious and political significance: 'whipping the money changers out of the temple' and 'crumbs from the rich man's table' were typical citations. For her, loving your neighbour might be possible were it not for the power and dominance of 'the merchants of death' who stood to gain from the cruel destruction in war of millions of lives, on both sides, who had little or nothing to fight each other about. Those who had survived the First World War were rewarded by returning to the poverty and homelessness they had left behind, while those they mourned were forgotten, and the wounded begged until the next charity flag-day.

A Sunday School prize added *Robinson Crusoe* to my small collection, and first lifted my eyes beyond Wallsend High Street. Of a Friday evening, my night to have a bath while my mother was out office cleaning, I imagined myself with a Man Friday on the desert island I created from chairs and towels – vegetation and trees – in the middle of which was the tin bath. The sea was filled from the hot tank at the side of the coal fire. Why, I think now with the logical mind of the adult, did the island surround the sea? Only the child I was then could tell me.

When Roy Plomley invited me to be one of his 'Desert Island Discs' castaways I chose for my special book *Italian Landscape* and for my luxury item a huge block of stone I intended to create a piece of modern sculpture from. Those choices reflected my interest in architecture and the arts. They in turn are rooted in my house-painting career and the three-nights-a-week night school classes, two nights 'practical' and one night 'Fine Art'. On my fourteenth birthday I got a job as a painter.

For the first few months I endlessly pushed the barrow to and from jobs. Vans were rare in those days. I was competing against horses. The main craft skills required me to imitate in paint the grains of a range of hardwoods and marbles to match the real thing, as both hardwood and marble fireplaces, door frames, architraves and pillars still figured in large houses. I wanted to be the best grain painter in the North-East and pored over every book that might help. I read about the origins of forests and rock formations and then learned the geology of the areas that determined the nature of the wood grains and the flows, when molten, of the marble, and the nature of the shades of the marble so intermixed and translucent, as if still in molten flow and yet icy cold to the touch.

I couldn't see the wood for the grain of the trees until I came across another kind of book: John Reed's *Ten Days That Shook the World*. That made the link between my 1920s' and 1930s' childhood and youth and the nature of European history. I lived in a caring, intelligent and well-managed family, but in an environment awash with the inheritances of inadequate sanitation, waves of deprivation, killing diseases, poverty, unemployment and wasted skills. John Reed made me understand the manifest power over all lives of the bosses: the owners of the mines, steel mills, shipyards, engineering works and building sites into which we were poured like water from time to time, or shut out according to the whims or harsh demands of those who owned them. The bosses expected us, the majority, to sacrifice, kill and, if necessary, die to perpetuate our underprivilege. It was the rent collectors, the weekly-payment-club collectors and the penny-a-week insurance men who were their bread-and-water plimsoll line. Why, I asked myself, were those responsible for the brutalities of life never brought to book?

Instead they threw the book at me.

Until I did three years of a six-year sentence I would have been hard to persuade that prisons had a single virtue. I now confess that not because, but in spite of the

At boarding school I devoured accounts of Second World War escapes from prison camps. Inspired by these bloody-minded myths a group of us decided to break out. After a few weeks digging, in the guise of a garden club, we were under the wall. Only to emerge in a padlocked toolshed. Warned of the dangers of incontinent literature, we were soundly thrashed.

(IAIN SINCLAIR)

prison system, during my years inside I was able to grasp educational opportunities denied me as a child. Once I'd adjusted my mind and body to the realities of a prison cell, and given unlimited time and no pressure, it seemed like 'a heaven-sent gift' – the prison chaplain's words, not mine – to lift the veils of ignorance. Suddenly the six-year sentence seemed too short and I doubted that, with my parole deducted, I would have time to read all the books I wanted to. There were holidays to arrange: self-created prison holidays declared by myself for myself, that required me to read ancient and modern travel books ranging from the Holy Land to the Himalayas. I took out my paints and accompanied Tolstoy to Borodino, braving the winter cold to paint a scene from his description of it. My guide books were *The Oxford English Dictionary*, *The Dictionary of Idiomatic English* and *Roget's Thesaurus*. With their aid there were no prison walls, gates, barriers or boundaries to bar my way to walking, climbing, marking, learning and mentally escaping. I was lucky. For a high proportion of my fellow prisoners the inability to read denied them any escape. There was no book to bring them to.

(T. DAN SMITH)

Miss Hobson

It was a moral choice. I was nine, at a rough old school in Peckham and I'd won the school prize for Art and also for Religious Knowledge. The headmistress called me to her room. In one hand she held a Bible bound in black leather and shining gold leaf edges, in the other a box of Reeves watercolours, open and showing squares of glistening colour, plus tubes of black and white paint and two fat paint brushes.

'You have to decide between them as there aren't enough prizes to go round.' I thought of my battered tin

of Woolworth's paints at home, so it didn't take long, I chose the paints. 'I knew you would,' she said contemptuously, tossing the paintbox at me and dismissing me from her presence. 'If you had said the Bible you'd have got the paints as well.'

(JACKIE STANLEY)

Herbert the Storyteller

Young Herbert was fortunate. His mother was interested in books and in writing. She had herself thought of becoming a writer, as she once sighed with the self-dramatization that was an integral part of her character. So Herbert was not brought up in a household where books counted for nothing. Nor was he plagued by having 'a lady novelist', as they were called in the thirties, for a mother. He had a parent who encouraged him to write as soon as he could read, and to make books. Those first books, full of drawings and scribbles, were lovingly bound by his mother in gaudy wallpaper covers. How pleasing for a three- and four-year-old! He knew then that books were an important part of life, and of love. Curiously, they conveyed another message: that books were an extension of private forms of communication, a family affair, and not necessarily for the eyes of everyone.

Young Herbert grew up with these misunderstandings planted in his subconscious. He wrote for the family, or later for his class mates. It was not until he was thirty years old that he attempted to reach a wider audience. Even then the good old messages still sounded like distant hunting horns through a wood, saying 'Don't try to write for money; write what you most enjoy.' Not surprisingly those messages brought great happiness with a long writing career. Novelists need many gifts: a clear eye for character (or caricature), a pleasure in narrative, the ability to criticize one's own shoddy work, an independent mind, and much else besides. These gifts are fertilized by the accidents of which life is largely composed. One grows by 'luck or cunning', to quote Samuel Butler.

One piece of luck Young Herbert enjoyed, though it was far from enjoyable at the time, was that his family moved into a house that proved to be haunted. He was possibly eight, his sister, Young Liz, only four. The house, in fact, was very haunted. None of your odd chance appearances every Michaelmas. None of your ghosts spoken of but never glimpsed. None of those funny knockings heard by an uncle in a distant cupboard. Oh no, Bessie, as the family called the ghost, was always on the move upstairs, particularly in the front bedrooms overlooking the lane and the churchyard opposite. Bessie was frighteningly active, always heard, sometimes seen. No faint footsteps for Bessie. She travelled with a policeman's tread across the bedroom floors. And it seemed she hated the children who tried to sleep in those bedrooms. A cause of extreme terror for Young Liz and Herbert.

(Reader, dear reader, infidel reader, you may doubt the reality of ghosts. Let me confirm, in a parenthetical paragraph, that they do exist. Young Herbert did not doubt it. Now that he is Old Herbert he still worries over the question, as experience wars with intellect. Intellect tells him there cannot be such a thing as ghosts. Experience argues otherwise. In the eighties this loathsome apparition was still active, even though the house had, for that very reason, ceased to be a domestic residence. It is now council offices, into which the staff are terrified to go at night. The local vicar was eventually called on to perform an exorcism. He did so. With a mighty bang the apparition was gone. A year later Bessie was back. This is no fiction, dear reader. This is what we call real life, without in any way understanding the import of what we say. The moral of which is, we have to believe our own experience, however unacceptable it may be. That is the course of sanity. Close brackets.)

In the days of Bessie, Young Herbert was sent to boarding school, and in boarding schools he was incarcerated for ten years. Boarding schools are, or were in the thirties, like prisons, except that the food is worse, justice more arbitrary, corporal punishment more frequent. The nights are the worst, as Young Herbert found out when he was first trapped in one of these institutions at the age of seven and a bit. But you *don't blub*. This is Survival Rule One. Blub, and you're done for. Young Herbert found a creative substitute for misery: storytelling.

After Lights Out cunning little Herbert turned the experience of Bessie to good account. With an artistic touch here and there, devilish pauses, diversions, tiny frights, squeaks, he could make of the haunting a terrifying saga, culminating in the true (more or less) moment when his mother came face to face with – this in the sickly daylight of a dreary autumn afternoon, sun going down as if for ever into mists creeping over the graveyard – with Bessie herself. She ran screaming into the lane.

© BIFF

Where she stood for two hours fearing to re-enter the house until father came home ... 'Stop it! No more! Shut up, you sod!' some of the other inmates cried, diving under the bedclothes. What praise! What greater confirmation could a little tacker have of the power of narrative?

That is no rhetorical question. Greater confirmation was to come. In those distant days before Nanny Television came along and ruined the nation's reading habits, good boys' magazines flourished, darkly illustrated, containing plenty of juicy reading material. The best of these was *Modern Boy*. It formed Young Herbert's weekly reading. He read it from cover to cover, all except the stories about racing at Brooklands, which somehow never appealed.

By this time Young Herbert was sent to a bigger boarding school, a penitentiary in Suffolk, for which he has never had a good word to say, except for the following: that there he learnt to tell a long consecutive story under conditions of extreme hazard. Well, life itself is hazardous. No great religion promises us that life is going to be a picnic. That large dormitory, filled with thirty aggressive little monsters, was ample illustration of the hard facts of daily existence.

Rules were strict. After Lights Out came Survival Rule Two: *no talking.* However, misery still lurked in the dark. New boys in particular were victims of the school system. Many of the masters were bullies and sadists; the boys merely copied them. We needs must love the nastiest when we see it. And the test or initiation ceremony for new kids – 'new ticks' – after Lights Out was to stand up on their beds in their pyjamas and *tell a story.* If the story was no good – the rest of the dorm waited for it to be no good – shoes were flung at the new tick. Out of fifty-eight well-aimed shoes several were bound to reach their target. Not a single shoe reached the target of Young Herbert's person. He had the story of Bessie to protect him. It slayed them. From then onwards he became the champion storyteller of the dorm.

Many were the excellent stories in *Modern Boy.* They generally ran in series or serials. There were spy stories (the Second World War was already looming, and the senior boys were put to digging air-raid trenches in the prison grounds), stories of Ken King of the Islands (set in the South Seas), and stories of Biggles by Flying Officer W. E. Johns (*Modern Boy* was where Biggles began). For some reason, over half a century on, Old Herbert still recalls individual sentences from Biggles stories: 'So they drove on through the night'; 'He watched the water drain away without regret'. Immortal prose? Well, yes, as far as Herbert is concerned ... What particular magic did those ordinary sentences hold, that they should be remembered across fifty years?

But the best serial stories featured Captain Justice. Captain Justice stories were written by Murray Roberts, the pen-name of Robert Murray Graydon. Captain Justice lived in the mid-Atlantic on a metal island, in the near future. With his loyal team, and in his invisible airship *The Flying Cloud*, he fought various menaces which the Great Nations could not deal with: a great dictator with mesmeric powers in Darkest Africa, huge frog beings from the Sargasso Sea, giant robots, mad scientists. And he visited the runaway planets that ploughed through our solar system with monotonous regularity. These stories were meat and drink to Young Herbert. He made them his lifeblood. These were the stories he told every night in the dorm, doing different voices, pausing, adding sound effects, diversifying and in general accentuating the positive. And he would always stop on a cliffhanger, with Justice struggling in the grip of a thought-powered machine.

Young Herbert had won his first audience, his first success. That success had bitter rewards. For there happened to be a spy hole by the dormitory door. A listening-post, one should say. One of the typical, mean, sneaky devices of tyranny. The housemaster would listen in from the corridor, fling open the door, enter the draughty barn of a dorm, dash on all the lights and stand there twitching his cane.

'Who was talking?'

Survival Rule Three was even more demanding: *always own up*. So Young Herbert would raise his hand. He would be made to get out of bed and bend down. There in his pyjamas, in full view of everyone, he would be given six cuts of the cane. This was known euphemistically as 'dabbing'. Survival Rule One was useful here. Sometimes he would be taken down to the housemaster's study, where the punishment would be more formally administered. Sometimes the six would be delivered before the previous dabbing had healed.

There was an obstinate streak in Young Herbert which developed in the face of adversity. He never stopped telling his serial stories. At a third and better school he

My first book was *Heidi*. In summer I would go into the garage with a lump of cheese and toast it over burning newspaper, just as Heidi's grandfather toasted the goat's cheese. And the white rolls of our Scottish breakfasts were available for me to fantasize with. Poor Heidi's rolls went mouldy with keeping. I had the same experience with a pork pie bought for me by my grandfather from Liverpool.

(A MASS-OBSERVER)

made up original stories and wrote them down, charging a theoretical penny a read.

Beyond the three iron rules already mentioned lay a fourth: *never tell*. One never did. But to this rule Young Herbert once made an exception. At the end of a winter term it happened two dabbings had coincided. One dabbing overlapped the other, giving his backside the appearance of a noughts and crosses grid. In this state he went home for a brief respite (called a holiday) before the next gruelling term began. In the safety of his bedroom he was able to look in a mirror at the battlefield. The chief flesh colours were blue and black, set off by yellows and touches of red which fringed the fresher stripes. Young Herbert felt very proud. Hearing his mother on the landing he broke the rule. He called her in to view the damage. She looked and fainted away.

Possibly this was another instance of her tendency towards self-dramatization. If so, it appeared satisfyingly authentic at the time . . .

Such is the power of storytelling. Herbert, now Old Herbert, has survived many a dabbing from the critics. However, early training enables him to bear their strictures with stoicism. It's a useful quality for any writer.

(BRIAN W. ALDISS)

Chump

I got my formative education from Hollywood so I had difficulty separating illusion from reality. I imagined the only need of literature would be as a catalyst for my first date at art college, when a Doris Day look-alike would ask me to carry her armful of books down the college steps and on to the campus lawns. In preparation for the day I gave my mother a pattern for an Ivy League jumper, the type with a large initial on the chest. She dutifully knitted it for me.

Came the day of enrolment and I discovered that

there were no campus lawns, no steps, students didn't carry piles of books, nor lindy hop on desk tops. Instead they wore duffle coats, sandals and beards. I felt like a jam puff in the middle of a plate of wholemeal scones. One beatnik took pity and slipped me a copy of Jack Kerouac's *On the Road.* How could I have been so naïve as to fantasize a sun-kissed sophomore oasis in the middle of a North Yorks industrial town? As I slunk home past the gasworks, shoulders hunched and arms folded over the woolly D on my chest, it seemed as if the eyes of the men in flat caps at the bus stop were staring mockingly at my ludicrous figure.

'And you looked so nice in it,' said my mother, hurt I never wore the sweater again. I couldn't offload it until four years later when I'd left home and was living in my first bedsit. Then I used it for pipe lagging.

(DUDLEY EDWARDS)

Art and Culture

A book called *Art and Culture* – a collection of essays written by Clement Greenberg – having been published in America early in the 1960s, had found its way into the library of St Martin's College of Art. In August 1966, having regard for both the persuasive power of the book among students and for the provocative title, the book was withdrawn in the name of John Latham, and an event organized at his home together with the sculptor Barry Flanagan, who then was in the role of 'student'. The event was called 'Still and Chew', and many artists, students and critics were invited.

When the guests arrived they were each asked to take a page from *Art and Culture* and chew it, after which they could, if necessary, spit out the product into a flask provided. About a third of the book was so chewed, and there was some selective choosing as to the pages. The chewed pages were later immersed in acid – 30 per cent

'My sister threw a book at my head.'
'So what did you do?'
'I bit her nipple off.'
(KAREN ELIOT)

sulphuric – until the solution was converted to a form of sugar, and this was then neutralized by the addition of quantities of sodium bicarbonate.

The next step was the introduction of an Alien Culture, a yeast, after which several months went by with the solution bubbling gently.

Nearly a year after the Chewing, at the end of May 1967, a postcard arrived addressed to Mr Latham with a red label on it saying 'Very Urgent'. On the back was a plea for the return of the book, 'wanted urgently by a student, *Art and Culture*'.

A distilling apparatus was assembled, and a suitable glass container procured for the book to be returned to the librarian. When this was done a label was fixed to the glass saying what it was and together with the postcard it was presented to her back in the school, where for some years John Latham had been engaged as a part-time instructor. After the few minutes required to persuade the librarian that this was indeed the book which was asked for on the postcard, he left the room.

In the morning postal delivery a day later a letter arrived from the principal at St Martin's addressed to Mr Latham. It said he was sorry but he was unable to invite him to do any more teaching.

(JOHN LATHAM)

Shrine

One day the neighbours directly below us placed a small black coffee table outside their back door. Later they stacked six tall piles of books upon the table. It didn't appear that there was anything unusual or significant about this event. My guess was that they were house painting and wanted the books out of the way of splashed or spilt paint.

The books have remained on the table in the backyard for nearly three months. They have been rained upon,

snowed upon, hailed upon, sun baked, frost bit, even a
cat pissed on them. No one has come to take them back
inside. The table covered with books has become a
shrine to a mystery. In the back of my mind I suspect
television.

Now, every day, I look down into our neighbours'
backyard in hopes that the table and its books will be
back inside. So far nothing has changed. I suspect it
never will.

(DAVID MELTZER)

The Third Summer

A Cellophane scrap discarded from a cigarette pack
rolled like a glistening cuticle across the short grass. A
squirrel looped between two trees. A man with a dog's
lead slung like a chain of office round his neck chided
his animal. 'Mind your own,' he said as it bounded up to
the woman who lay reading under an oak. She turned
the page of the dense latinate prose, mottled with leaf
shadows. All afternoon the sun had been trying to break
through. Occasionally an erratic ray, piercing the haze,
would flush the park with brief strident light.

The book lying on the grass before her had the
dimensions and heft of a brick or bible. Its very title
resonated with archaism: *Malleus Maleficarum*, commissioned by the Inquisition to extend the definition of
heresy to embrace witchcraft and supply the witch trials
with their legal lynchpin. *The Hammer of Witches* was in
every sense of the word a heavy book. She'd taken it
from the library shelf with the thought that it would
demand stamina and attitude to read it. For all that
summer she'd had the sensation of edgelessness and
weightlessness, as if she were in the process of disappearing. It was the third summer after Liam's death.

Up till now she'd moved through her grief as through
a corridor whose darkness had enclosed and shaped her.

But this summer she'd emerged into a light that was empty even of his death. Shock, sorrow and rage were replaced by a stupefied vacancy whose only signpost was an obscure sense of shame, as if she'd mislaid some priceless object or failed to comprehend some obvious fact.

Often in the last few weeks, seeking to recharge her grief, she'd spoken aloud the words Billy had used to announce Liam's death to her. But the words 'Liam is dead' telegraphed themselves to her one by one and the more she repeated them the less she could grasp their combination.

She'd been working in a bar when Billy rang with the news. After the call she'd picked up a glass she'd just washed to dry it. It had shattered in her hand. Instinctively she'd clenched the shards, severing the nerves and tendon of a finger which now bore a zigzag of scars from the surgery. She wore the ring Liam had given her on another finger now. The fact it was 'his' finger that had come undone, the one on which she'd worn his ring, was not without a certain comfort. His death had produced other such accidents of symmetry. She treasured these coincidences as stories complete in themselves, anecdotes recountable to people who'd never known Liam. She logged them as evidence of a world incalculably transformed by his disappearance from it.

She'd moved from the flat they'd shared and one by one set aside the friends who'd known him. There was nothing left of him apart from her memories. Except for some furniture she had adapted to her new home. One chair, its green baize bell-shaped seat broken from the swivel stand, was stashed on top of her wardrobe. Its protruding corner was just visible from her bed. His death was no longer something that would always be happening to her. It was over. It had, she thought as she turned another page of *Malleus Maleficarum*, slipped through her fingers somehow. Hadn't he ever. He'd always been fading out before her, often vanishing only to reappear subtly changed. Or simply changing his tune on the spot. Like the way he'd danced to soul, turning on a sixpence. She could no longer distinguish between the trickster fluidity of his character and that of his death. Death seemed merely a yet more elusive disguise, though there was the fact that she would never set eyes on him alive again. And that was all, that was that. A fact she taunted herself with in dreams, when he'd appear in her room to pronounce his eternal absence. 'I'm dead,' he'd tell her gently, giving the words a slightly spurious edge which was so characteristically his tone that it would unfailingly convince her he had indeed returned to her.

Increasingly she rebelled against the embrace of these dreams, dreading to wake with his name on her lips again. She brought all her astuteness to bear in an effort to reduce his phantom to dust. But any attempt to dispel the delusion on its own ground was always undermined by a semblance of his presence before her. Resurrected in her dream he was assigned a funeral so redolent of his life that his death was the freshest part of it, evergreen.

Barely a hundred and fifty pages into the library book and she was already flagging. Its power to appal was soon overtaken by the tedium of its prose. Six-hundred-odd pages of hidebound tedium. Nevertheless she ploughed on, reading after supper as she sat cross-legged on her bed. She found herself compelled, despite the boredom, by something more than diligence. By the drama of good versus evil the text espoused. Plus now and again there was the odd moment of light relief when the thesis of misogyny was illustrated by delirious conjunction:

and sometimes witches collect the male organs, twenty to thirty at a time, and put them in a box or shut them up in a bird's nest where they move among themselves like living members and eat oats or corn as has been seen by many and is a matter of common report . . .

Looking up bleary-eyed from this passage she saw a grey insect flit past her nose. That was the sixth one in the time it had taken to read the last four pages. She lifted the open tome and slammed it shut on the moth. They were prolific that summer, the humidity being conducive to their breeding. She'd tried more scientific measures against the moths' occupation. She'd laid down mothballs and sprayed a whole can of Doom, assiduously following the small print which bade her pay 'special attention to the edges and folds of carpets and the tuck-ins and webbings of upholstery'. But its combination of gamma HCH and tetramathin, though virulent enough to lay out a large alsatian, had failed to fulfil the promise of lasting protection. The moths continued spinning themselves out of thin air. She sniped at them with the book, whose leaves were now spattered with moth corpses, their smudges of wing dust reminiscent of the marginalia of illuminated manuscripts.

The book, lowered after its latest catch, seemed heavier than before. *The Hammer of Witches* slid from her hands as her head lolled in a doze. She was dreaming she was in a restaurant at a small round table. The meal was over. Surrounded by, but apart from, the bustle of waiters and diners she sat suspended in a world of hushed linen and glittering cutlery. A pair of gloves, mint white, appeared on a plate before her. They were both crystalline and waxy. She stared as the gloves pulsed. Their gestures outstayed the hands that had left them behind. Identical and replete, they were linked only to themselves. She grasped the pristine shapes at the same time as she rose, released from the table.

She woke early to the squeaking of seagulls over the nearby canal. The first object her eye fixed on was the corner of the green baize chair sticking out from the top of the wardrobe. Watched by the single reproachful eye of an ancient teddy she delved among the hatboxes and broken lamps and hauled the chair seat down from the wardrobe. Veiled in the white down of moth spawn it fitted snugly into the black plastic bag. It was dead light as she carried it downstairs and deposited it in the dustbin.

(KAREN WHITESON)

Blackie Narcissus

As a child I was never allowed to play with my mother's make-up. I discovered that licking the blood-red covers of Blackie books and then my lips made garish lipstick. Suddenly I was an adult. Years later the memory returned when I went to see Michael Powell's film *Black Narcissus*, and Sister Ruth, in massive Technicolor close-up, desperately rebelling against her confinement in the Himalayan convent by smearing her lips scarlet before falling to her death in her sinful red dress from the convent bell. And now today, while watering the kidney beans I notice that the borage is plagued with blackfly. My attention, and the garden hose, wanders until I realize I have watered the old red hardback copy of *Gaston Leroux's Crime Omnibus* which I had been reading on the terrace. As I pick it up the red dye comes off on my fingers. But now I am grown up, Gertrude Jekyll not Sister Ruth, and instead of painting my lips I wash my hands.

(FELICITY SPARROW)

Sister Ruth flaunts the lipstick in the film Black Narcissus. Photo: BFI Stills Library. Courtesy of Rank

Money's Worth

It's quite simple. The most important book is the one you never read.

Every day I would sit on the floor at mum's feet, as she sat in a chair by the window. For ten minutes I would be silent as she brought to life the next few pages of *Green Smoke*. I love that book. That book I never read.

It taught me to separate my mouth from my mind. While my lips chanted my six times table I would day-dream of dragons and coves and miniature horses to be kept in my top drawer and fed on leftovers.

It taught me how to dream up stories to tell my sister, fantastic stories that were mine to give her, just as *Green Smoke* had been given to me.

It taught me how to bring to life zombied words squashed between pages of wood that cry out for their roots.

It taught me that the world should be silent for ten minutes each day so that it can hear its own heartbeat.

It taught me the power of listening, the power and strength in the ability to keep quiet and be told.

It taught me how to communicate, within and without words.

It taught me to tell stories.

Green Smoke cost three shillings and sixpence.

(JANETTE M. SMITH)

Sweet Poison

When I was twelve I bought, or maybe stole, a paperback anthology of beatnik writing from the rotating wire rack in the Soda Shoppe on Main Street in Wytheville, Virginia. It was edited by Seymour Krim. The Soda Shoppe was where I'd discovered the first issue of *Famous Monsters of Filmland*, which became my favourite magazine. It was also Stephen King's favourite magazine. Stephen King and I are the same age, but I don't think he read that beatnik book.

I took the beatnik book home, hidden under my jacket, and kept it in a toy safe made of grey enamelled steel with a red plastic combination lock. It was a bank, actually, with a coin slot in the top. I had to bend the book in half to get it in there, breaking the spine. I knew my mother wouldn't have let me keep it, because she was terrified of beatniks. Not that she had ever seen one, or ever did.

I had some firecrackers, which were illegal in Virginia, in that safe, and a tiny deck of primitive pornographic flash cards, with drawings and jokes. I read 'The City of Interzone' chapter from *Naked Lunch*. I read parts of Kerouac's *Visions of Cody*. I read an hypnotically bad little poem about a beatnik using hydrochloric acid to burn the lock off the gas meter in his New York apartment. The acid went *hiss* when it went through the lock. It went *hiss* when it went through the floor. I think it went *hiss* all the way to the basement.

Reading that beatnik book my youthful soul was poisoned, sullied permanently by bohemian literature. What a great feeling.

(WILLIAM GIBSON)

Clocking Out

Between leaving the Royal Navy after National Service and starting a course in film and television at Bede College, Durham, I read the great classics in my own private study at Carr's of Carlisle, birthplace of the biscuit industry.

Summer in the Export Forwarding Department was hot and hectic as we dispatched biscuits to the sort of places we knew only from the labels: Bulawayo, Sioux Narrows and Tegucigalpa. But when autumn tinted the leaves in the grounds of the cathedral, which we could see from the top floor of our Victorian factory block, and the last of the Christmas orders for bourbons, custard creams and cocktail dainties were loaded on to lorries bound for Liverpool docks, our working days became less frantic. Our foreman was dispatched to a far-flung department and we were left to ourselves. After all the best discipline is self-discipline.

Now there was time for high jinks. A splendid woman from one of the outlying villages would challenge us to Cumberland and Westmorland Wrestling. Her most devastating throw was a beautifully executed cross buttock. Reminiscent of *Chariots of Fire* and those most distinguished followers of the Greek ideal of the scholar–athlete we held races round the perimeter of our work room, which was seventy-five paces long by twenty-five paces wide.

By late October there was no work at all and we were completely free to pursue our 'contemplative leisure', which, rather than work, was what Oscar Wilde recommended in *The Soul of Man Under Socialism*. One of my colleagues actively pursued the lift lady. They made love morning and afternoon after hanging Out of Order signs at the gates of each of the five floors. Those of us who remained loyally at our posts built a magnificent Cardboard City. No one person designed it; like an ancient cathedral it grew through communal inspiration. First there was a passage, which in places was fifteen feet high and composed of small, medium and large boxes packed with tins of biscuits, some of which weighed over fifty pounds. This passage led the occasional straying member of management directly from the room's entrance to the office and to nowhere else.

To gain access to our labyrinthine city you removed a cunningly positioned empty box and entered. Once inside you discovered an elderly short-sighted snuff-taking Salvationist who had put up an improvised work bench to repair watches. Next to him there was the ladies' sewing circle, a café, a gymnasium and what was known to everyone as 'Eric's Library'. It didn't have the imagined

splendours of that in Umberto Eco's *The Name of the Rose*,
it was more of a 'machine for reading in'.

I am forever grateful to the benign paternalism of
Carr's, who paid me, as a grade two employee, seven
pounds fifteen shillings a week to read the great classics.
The company sponsored a literature class run by the
Workers' Educational Association and held in the manage-
ment canteen, where I was given my reading assignments.
I read the classics and much much more.

We would punch the clock at 7.30 a.m. then hold our
regular fifteen minute workout, enjoy a cup of tea and by
eight I was into *War and Peace*. Although bare and
functional at first my library began to take on a certain
character. Someone had painted a fire on a piece of card
and sketched a window with a winter scene and snow. At
Christmas I had a tiny artificial tree, some decorations,
ginger wine and mince pies brought by the Cumberland
and Westmorland Wrestling lady. I read solidly for five
months every year for seven years to the tinkle of watch
repairing, the click of knitting needles and the murmuring voices of those who just wanted to natter. I always
disliked the coming of spring because cuckoos and the
first green shoots also heralded orders from abroad. The
dismantling of our city began and my library was sent
overseas. Reading became an evening activity.

Now everything has gone, the building is demolished
and beloved Carr's has become a busy and thriving
section of an international conglomerate, United Biscuits,
who make, among other products, Ross Young's Pizzas:
'Enough of these were eaten last year to stretch from
London to Los Angeles and back again.'

Shortly before I left the factory – I realized I was
never going to become a Captain of Industry – a young
man, a distant relative of the Carr family, was assigned
to me to set him on the first rung of the ladder which
would lead inevitably to the boardroom. He looked at
the massed rows of boxes and said, 'Right, where do I
start?' I felt sad for him and for me. My reading room
would never be reconstructed and the possibility of his
enjoying a long winter of literature was unthinkable. But

with only a matter of days before my industrial career came to an end I couldn't resist saying, 'The first thing you do is go to Carlisle Public Library and choose a very good and very long book.'

(ERIC WALLACE)

Penguin Factory Christmas Party, 1947

On Christmas Eve there was little work done in the warehouse, which idled. The sorters and packers played rummy, penny pontoon and solo. There was a raffle for a tricycle and a lampshade. At about noon the sorters went down to the Peggy Bedford for a beer, having arranged to meet Fred and Harry there. But Fred and Harry were diverted to fetching chairs for the canteen and never arrived at the Peggy, leaving the group there rather uncertain of themselves. Mrs Riches had a lemonade. Johnny and Nellie were not used to beer and didn't like it, so a quick return was made by bus to the warehouse. Harry later expressed his fury at having to fetch the chairs.

Invoicing had been decorated with cotton wool snow, paper chains, mistletoe and a small Christmas tree. Paper hats were distributed by Mrs Hall, who retained the distinctive one herself, thereby incurring sarcastic comment from a sorter.

At about 1.30 staff from the rest of the building began to assemble in the warehouse. Mrs Hall, who stood with the packers and sorters, surveyed the assembled masses uneasily. 'Let's move over,' she said, but the sorters made no move. So Mrs Hall and Mrs Sansom went over and sat themselves on a bench in the centre. 'We don't want to show ourselves off on a bench,' said the sorters. Eventually they moved over and sat themselves on the far side.

The workers grouped themselves according to department. Only Hans Oberndorfer walked round engaging the different groups in conversation. The Lanes, Jack Summers of Royalties, Olney the Secretary and Holmes of Accounts arrived, dressed in white waiter's jackets with bottles and trays. Allen Lane shook the cocktails in the silver penguin-shaped shaker. The sorters commented on the men, assessing the masculine qualities of Holmes and Oberndorfer with humorous and occasionally bawdy comment.

Christmas dinner was then announced and everyone flocked to the canteen, hung with decorations and with the walls covered with drawings of penguins on roundabouts, inscribed 'The One and Olney', 'The Secco Sisters' and 'Madame Goodenough, the Bearded Lady'. The service hatches were framed with large heads, the mouths allowing the passage of plates.

At dinner there was more mixing of the groups. Menus had been typed on the covers of Homer's *Odyssey* and listed turkey, beer, baked potatoes, beer, concluding with Christmas pudding and beer. Of the production and editorial staff, Hans Oberndorfer, as in the warehouse, appeared to be the only person to sit with 'the others'. As dinner proceeded there was a lot of cheerful talk with *badinage*. The 'waiters' continued to serve and gained additional applause by filing in at one stage and singing everyone 'A Merry Christmas'. Singing became general, but disorganized, with one group competing with one song against another. The sorters and packers struck up a version of 'We're Happy in Our Work', inserting the word 'Penguin' at the appropriate place. This was the only indication at all directly expressed that the management's special arrangements for the staff were appreciated.

(A MASS-OBSERVER)

I notice that every second-hand bookshop I venture into has a copy of the blue Penguin *Plastics in the Service of Man*. I have avoided reading this book since I first saw it in the fifties. I'm going to buy it some day. I fear that it has something in it that, had I read it in time, would have changed my life.

(NOEL SHERIDAN)

The Wall My Sky

The other day I was stopped in the street by a woman with a clipboard who asked me my views on a series of so-called celebrities. 'In your estimation,' she asked, 'is this person nice? Do you think this one would make a charming dinner guest? How about this newsreader? Would you be inclined to take her advice if she recommended something to you?'

'It's ridiculous,' I replied. 'I've never met any of them.'

'But you *must* have seen them on television!' she said.

'There's no must about it. I don't watch television. I read books.'

'But I read books *and* watch television,' she snapped, adding, 'though not at the same time.' I was relieved to hear that, worried as I was that I might be in the presence of a superior being whose only chance of a job these days was to wander up and down the High Street asking people for their views on banal matters.

'I have a view!' I proclaimed proudly. 'I have a glorious view. The kind of view someone like you can only read about in books. The kind of view you'll never see on television.' Alas, she was not interested, so I shall complain to you instead.

Let me tell you more about my view. In the gap between two buildings I can see everything and anything. It changes each time I look, and I am not just talking about the weather. I can sit in my garden and observe an infinite supply of slices of life. You have doubtless heard the cliché, but all human life passes before me, including yours. I have seen drivers trying to find a space to park their cars. People having rows. Children getting smacked by their impatient mothers. I can see the sea and the container ships that bring us precious cargoes of durables and perishables. I have seen an air–sea rescue while storms battered the coastline and I have followed the course of a fire as it consumed the parish church. At night I can see every celestial body the universe has to offer. I watch the lights of the hurrying traffic and see

I don't read books and I don't read newspapers. I don't read at all. I read meters instead.

(A LONDON GASMAN)

05003-15

young lads who have yet to learn how to drink scuffling and chundering in the gutter after the pubs close. Through a grid of parted curtains I have seen couples making love or committing murder and musicians practising with their instruments. And I have often seen people watching television. You might think me foolish for having dedicated my life to preserving my glorious view, but if only you could see what I saw then I am sure you would have done the same.

Then my neighbours built a brick wall to keep their lives out of my view. The wall extended from their potting shed to the very edge of my imagination. I was indignant and determined on a course of action that would result in the demolition of the wall, until my solicitor advised me it was built upon their land not mine. In short I had no rights. I demanded air rights, right of visual passage, the gift of observation, all to no avail.

So I dragged the old tea chest out of the garage and tipped out the books in it, then stacked one atop the other so that I could give myself, by standing on tiptoe, the remains of my view. As though they knew of my plan, they raised the wall, another row of bricks each day until I was forced to scour the charity shops and jumble sales for cheap books with hardcovers to raise my stack a little further. I hoped that sooner or later they would stop building the wall because I was running out of books, and money. I was wrong, for in my absence I swear they measured my pile and raised their wall accordingly until once again my glorious view was possible only on aching tiptoe.

I paused to open one of the cheap books I'd bought. *Structures and Why Things Stand Up* informed me that, to my regret, a wall of single brick width could in theory rise to half a mile in height before the bottom row of bricks began to crack under the weight. It was time to review my strategy. I had been restricting myself to a stack of single books when what I desperately needed was a pile. If I could buy books by the truck-load then my pile could reach the moon if necessary. So I went in search of redundant books: workshop manuals of cars now long reduced to rust; instruction manuals for electronic cameras now smothered with leaking battery acid; hagiographies of pop groups lost to memory; cheap Book Club books; mail order catalogues; unwanted copies of the Maastricht Treaty; vanity publications over-produced by a press left on auto; guides to redundant computers and their primeval software; five thousand old copies of the *National Geographic*; more Book Club books; a Gideon Bible and the Book of Mormon; books about religions that had gone the way of all flesh. I thought better of using the Koran; I do read the papers.

As I dumped another load of worthless books on my side of the wall and prodded them with a shovel I was sure that they would provide me with a stable summit. I climbed to the top and once again found my view visible only on tiptoe. Surely this was not possible, for even if this damnable wall were as high as the Great Wall of China I would have been able to see over it many thousands of books ago. But as I wallowed in self-pity I was startled to see my bricklaying neighbour perched atop a ladder on the other side, a hose in one hand and a box of matches in the other. He grinned and then called to someone down on the ground, and petrol poured out of the hose and began to drench my books. He smirked and asked me whether I wanted to be burned to death. Some question! He was teasing me, letting the petrol soak my mountain as I stood there on my summit, terrified. 'Just remember this!' he said. 'People who burn books always end up burning people!' He never carried out his implied threat, but how was I to know that? For a few days I just stood and waited for him to do his worst, and while I waited I would browse through any book on my mountain that took my fancy. Something with illustrations. Travel books with photos that would remind me of my view. Books full of faces I could no longer see.

There was one book without pictures that attracted my attention. A book on astral projection had a chapter entitled 'How to Pass through a Brick Wall'. It made great claims, suggesting that if I became a believer I could pass through any physical matter with the ease of a lugworm wriggling through mud. Okay, I'll believe, and I did, earnestly. I attempted the feat at the foot of the wall. I was required to lean forward and, supporting the lower half of my body on my knees, press against the brickwork with the palms of my hands. I chanted a few formulae, made a few appropriate pleas to powers beyond my understanding. Nothing happened.

Finally I grew to find fascination with the wall itself. I know it's not mine, but I began to feel as though it somehow belonged to me. When it rained the grey cement turned a blue-black colour and the raindrops blotched the biscuit hues of the bricks. And when the sun shone it dried out and beamed back at me with all the reassuring regularity of a brick wall. I thought I was fulfilled and complete. Me and the wall as one. Why, just a few weeks before the notion of a truce with the wall would have seemed scarcely credible. But there are always other ways to surmount a problem. So forgive me if I sound smugly contented, but I almost am. Were it not for the constantly recurring thought that what happens on my neighbour's side of the wall was somehow better than what happened on mine I was entirely satisfied. Well, almost satisfied. Well, maybe not almost, but quite happy with the arrangement.

You see, I have now found a way to see *beyond* the wall. This has always been our problem. We see an obstacle and we are rendered impotent. Why not, I thought, tell myself that the wall is merely part of the debris of everyday human materialism? A wall is a wall is a wall. Not my wall. My wall became my sky. I could become as the lark, ascending my spiral flight until I soared high above the wall, peering down at the humdrum things my neighbours deemed fit to indulge in.

Nothing of account. Nothing remarkable to tell you about. Nothing, except the hole they have made at the foot of the wall via which they have been carefully smuggling books from under my beak, books they then stack in neat piles to await the application of a machine that transforms them into bricks. It was a revelation, one that I've followed up with assiduous research. Did you know, for example, that ten medium-sized hardbacks make one brick? That the average contents of a town library could provide materials sufficient to build an average semi with an integral garage? That if all the books in the British Library were mutated there would be enough bricks to build another British Library?

Yes, books betrayed me, and I now own a television. Not that I watch it all that much, you understand, just enough so that when I am stopped again in the High Street I can offer my preferences and have a view on which television newsreader I would like to have as a dinner guest. Something quite beyond the scope of books.

(CLIVE PITSILLIDES)

Just Wait

'kinada it's cold! Where's that sodding bus? I've been standing here for twenty minutes now. I've read the bus timetable twice, the spine titles of the videos in the window behind the bus stop, I've even tried to identify all the flowers and shrubs in Joanne's Plantique (For All Your Floral Needs). Now, for want of something better to do, I'm studying the Second World War camouflage markings still visible on the walls of the library across the road.

Those were the days, when it was thought that the library was worth bombing. Before the caretaker went berserk and trashed it. Now the library has been politically corrected and ethnically cleansed, leaving only a motley ragbag of worthy books that lean forlornly on the half-empty shelves, while the library staff twiddle their thumbs and play with their desk-top computers behind the unused counters. A people's university in times gone by, a communal seat of learning, reduced to a moribund amenity, like a doctor's surgery without the patients. Dull and dead as a doornail.

But wait, what's this? Perhaps all life has not yet departed? A man and a woman standing on the library steps are engaged in ever more animated debate, which escalates into raging argument, their voices carrying across the road:

'You'll miss me, mark my words.'

'I'll miss you? You must be joking. I'll miss you like a hole in the head you stupid bitch!'

'Hah! You say that now you plonker, but you'll miss me all right, you'll miss me in the morning, in the afternoon and in the night-time too!'

'Like hell!'

'Yes, too right, you'll miss me like *hell!*'

'Do me a favour you stupid cunt! I'll miss you about as much as bogey from my nose!'

'We'll see! We'll see! You're so fucking thick you'll mess up a good thing, the only good thing you ever had

One of the standard biology textbooks twenty years ago, and perhaps still so today, was written by a certain Professor Slaughter. I would often see this thick tome on shelves. In bold letters the spine spelled out the legend: Slaughter *Living Things*.

(CHRIS PROCTOR)

Termites' nest in library.
Photo: Rentokil

in your whole miserable, self-centred life you cruddy
tosser!'

'Me? Ha! Ha! Ha!'

'Yes you! Tosser! And that's all you'll have left to do,
toss yourself off, that's if you've still got the strength
after you've lain awake night after night thinking what
you threw away you arrogant, flea-brained tosspot!'

'Enough you whingeing bitch! I'm off!'

'Yes, fuck off and good riddance you brain dead
clown!'

'I will, right now! And you can rot in hell you poxy
fucker!'

'Brave words! Big mouth! Pissing in the wind! Just
wait! When you lie sweating in your sleepless bed think
of what you threw away! Think of this!' she screams,
then stubs out her cigarette with a twist of her high-
heeled foot, takes off her fur coat and throws it on the
pavement, followed by her scarf, sweater, blouse, skirt,
bra, shoes, tights and pants, until she stands four-square
and naked, hands on hips and bosom heaving beneath

the library entrance's engraved inscription: 'All ye who pass in quest of happy hours, behold the price at which the happy hours were bought.'

He spits with contempt on the pavement in front of her bare feet, turns on his heel and heads off down the road, up which, praise be and not before time, comes the bus.

(IAN BREAKWELL)

Two From 'Three Library Users'

The narrow but tall house in Westbourne Terrace, W2, is well over a hundred years old. It was built in Queen Victoria's time and is still standing today, more than forty years after the three episodes to be described here.

The most diverse refugee organizations had established themselves all over London. By far the largest, the Austrian Centre, with its youth organization, Young Austria, was here in Westbourne Terrace.

Offices, also a large meeting room for the left-wing core of the organization. But the meeting room served also as a cabaret theatre and as a hall for larger events, and beneath it was a cheap restaurant for refugees, which, however, upheld the best traditions of Viennese cooking, and next to it, a single room, the small lending library.

I was the librarian. Behind my table, and to the right of it, two large bookcases, in front of me the cupboard with a few books to be repaired, which also contained the small amount of money for lending dues and replacement of lost books. On my table, card indexes and papers, warning letters to tardy borrowers, leaflets calling attention to meetings, and all kinds of odds and ends. Books too, of course, which I read when I happened to have a few free minutes.

The books were partly donated by refugees, partly contributed by the founders of the Austrian Centre themselves or bought new; the new books were mostly works by left-wing authors, which were supposed to expand the readers' horizons in this respect. The donated books in particular were of a diversity difficult to describe. Beside a few leather-bound volumes from the eighteenth century, there were more or less well-worn paperbacks from the Weimar Republic, then again fine, but very often incomplete editions of the classics; art nouveau books, art books, historical novels, philosophical treatises, essays, children's books, poetry and anthologies, and in among them old guide books and schoolbooks.

One day, shortly after the outbreak of war, while I was reading I was interrupted by a young woman. Her whole face was beaming. 'Your system worked!' she called out to me, 'I've got news from my mother! Very short only, a telegram. But news nevertheless!'

I was happy for her. The system she was talking about was a fairly simple one. A few weeks before the outbreak of war, I had organized a link via a country that would remain neutral, via Switzerland, that could pass on letters and telegrams. This news was the first case which proved that the link worked. 'Only there's one word in the telegram I don't understand,' said the young woman, 'probably a greeting or something. My mother will have written it in German of course. But in Switzerland they translate it into English, and I don't understand enough English yet. Perhaps you can translate it for me?' She gave me the telegram. The word was 'deceased' and the sentence had only three words: 'Your mother deceased.'

'Do sit down,' I said. Then I tried to prepare her for the fact that the telegram was no cause for joy. At first she didn't understand, then she did not simply weep, but threw herself back and forward in a fit of sobbing, almost like a fish on dry land.

Forty-five years later, in another part of London, in Mill Lane, as I was rummaging through old books which were displayed outside a junk shop, I was asked by an old lady whether I was an Austrian poet. She said my name. When I answered, she said, 'I'm sure you won't remember me any more, but I once brought you a telegram in the library of the Austrian Centre and asked you to translate it for me.'

'Then you are Alice Zoldester,' I said and she was surprised that I remembered. I would never have recognized her again, but how could I ever have forgotten that short translation?

At the outbreak of war, refugees from Germany and Austria were classified as 'enemy aliens', which, depending on inclination, one could understand to mean 'hostile foreigners' or 'strangers from enemy countries'. The description was an encouragement to mistrust. Very many refugee women, who earlier had received work permits only as servants, lost their jobs and were accommodated in hostels hastily organized by Bloomsbury House, the refugee committee. Apart from a bed and modest board they received sixpence a week pocket money, out of which they had to pay for travel, toiletries and similar things, which was of course impossible. Most of them sold or pawned their last pieces of jewellery or surplus clothes, but in almost every hostel there were one or two women who began to earn something extra by occasional prostitution. They then, of course, had far more money than the others, bought their room-mates chocolate, cigarettes or eau-de-Cologne and said to one or other of the young girls, 'Go on, come along to the coffee house and take a look for yourself. You don't have to go with anyone you don't like.' One such girl who came along was Ruth, a member of Young Austria, and a fairly enthusiastic reader in my lending library, beautiful, tall, dark-haired.

When it somehow became known in Young Austria, our youth organization, that she, as the group leader said, 'had gone astray', it was decided to expel her for 'un-Austrian behaviour'. Ruth came into the library weeping, told me about it, and I intervened.

'First, if we have created a youth organization, in order to influence these people politically,' I said, 'then we also have the duty, as a youth organization, to take care of members who have got into difficulties and not throw them out. Second, given the living conditions of these girls and women in their hostels it's no surprise at all. It's more a surprise that many more don't go astray. And third, it's far from being un-Austrian behaviour! Since the beginning of the depression it's not been so unusual at home either. Has it?'

The decision was overturned, Ruth came back to the library to thank me. A girl in the group was to talk to her and take care of her. For a few weeks she really did come regularly to the group evenings and members' meetings again. Then, one evening, she turned up in the library to bring back some books. 'No, I don't want any new ones. I want to thank you once again for having tried to help me, but I won't come again. It's really no use. Most of them ignore me or look at me with contempt or try to sleep with me as fast as they can. Or both at the same time, in that they ignore me in the group but afterwards try to get off with me. I can't bear it any more, I'm not coming back.'

My arguments had no effect. My suggestion, just to come to me if she needed anything, was also rejected with a shake of the head. At the last moment, before she went out, she gave me a kiss on the forehead and was gone before I could recover from my astonishment. Only the smell of her perfume remained for a few seconds.

Years later I read her name in the newspaper. Her skull had been identified from dental work. She had been killed by Christie, the mentally disturbed London murderer who could not be tender to living women, and had been buried in his house at Notting Hill Gate about a week later.

(ERICH FRIED)

After supper the old woman settles in a deep armchair with her favourite novel which she has read over and over since childhood. After two familiar chapters she falls asleep, book in hand. Snoring contentedly, eyes closed, she turns the page.

(GEORGE LITTLEBLACK)

Mister Affcott

On the first day of May in Seville the bullfighter Manolo Montoliu was killed on the horns of the bull Cabatisto. The doctor said that 'the heart opened like a book'.

(MATTHEW TYSON)

It was a bright clear day. The sky was an intense hard blue and everything looked scrubbed clean. Being on the brow of a hill the farmhouse got whatever weather was coming. I was asleep in bed and came to suddenly as I was aware of someone in the room with me. It was Mr Affcott. He was standing at the foot of the bed looking at me with a slightly melancholic expression which was enhanced by the fact that his face was painted gold. I took all this in with my first waking glance and the shock of him just standing there made me yell. This brought Les with his shotgun bursting through the door. He sent Affcott out into the yard behind the house and told him to stay there. Meanwhile we traced his route through the house, which was perfectly easy due to the amount of things he'd broken or knocked over, and this led us back to the library window which he'd smashed to get in. There were traces of gold paint around the frame and the whole thing was hanging from its hinges. He had taken down my copy of Darwin's *The Origin of Species* and left it open on the table. On the left-hand page he'd underlined the words, 'organic beings tend to increase'.

Looking out of the window we saw Mr Affcott disappearing slowly into the woods. The back of his neck was gold too.

(D. K. NIELSEN)

Fix the Word

It all began when he was only twelve. The smell of *Treasure Island* had suddenly overpowered him as he opened the book. It was a brand new copy, and its shining pages reflected the light, as well as the story, back into his eyes. Printed pages and imprinted pupils wrapped around him like silver neon. He lowered his face into the book, buried a twitching nose between the grains of sharp, white paper, and with that became a book sniffer.

For the next ten years this had been enough, but like all addicts his cravings had grown until one afternoon he stumbled across what could be the ultimate fix. How to mainline each individual word, hook up and IV every syllable straight into his bloodstream. But would a vowel be a bigger hit than a consonant, and was the buzz dictated by the number of letters, or did the actual *meaning* of the word play a part? While some junkies took embalming fluid or horse tranquillizers, he decided to shoot the liquid potency of language into a vein linked directly to his brain.

He cut his favourite words and phrases from a much-loved book, shredded each one of them up – making sure to keep each tiny pile separate – and thought to cook the powder up in a spoon just as if it was a more conventional drug. But could the age of the original volume matter at all, and how would the word 'each' from a new, unread page differ from a signed 'Myra' at the end of an old letter? Could he really become *the word* as he forced it into his arm, and what about those amazing cocktails he was already planning?

'If speed does kill,' he said aloud, 'then let me at this bitch!'

A sliver of 'when' slipped though the outer film of his skin, burnt the flesh, and found a small, dark place to curl up; only to be quickly followed by 'I will love you forever. All ways.' They lay fermenting in their own spots like two visions that might never combine or even meet.

The left side of his face became limp as it slid into a state of post-stroke. Both hands clawed tightly as his arm muscles shortened. Images of sharp, grey rocks broke up against distant shores, and sent tiny flints into the sea. A heavy, velvet curtain refused to be drawn. For a moment he was sealed in ice so hard it was tinted blue, and next his body was being licked by perfumed flames. Silent musk enfolded him. The language of his thoughts was suddenly far purpler than any he'd ever spoken. This was the effect of 'when'. Then the 'I will lo' opened the door just an inch, and eased its way into the crooked room.

When he was found later the next day, he had somehow managed to get out of the over-stuffed armchair and was folded up in a corner. His eyes were bright but apparently unseeing, and his face was buried between the pages of a dusty, old book. He rubbed and licked the paper, leaving a trail of slow spit along every line, his nose like the silent fingers of a Braille reader as it scanned and understood each letter and word of his very favourite introduction.

(TONY JACKSON)

Acknowledgements

The editors are grateful to the following people for their help in making this book: Judith Alexander, Pete Ayrton, Peter Bateman, Margaret Busby, Barbara Einzig, John Hampson, Mike Hart, Susanna Robson, Jerome Rothenberg, and Dorothy Sheridan of the Mass-Observation Archive; to Ana Forcada for translating Luisa Valenzuela, and Barbara Wright for translating Marcel Mariën; to Penelope Dunn, Miranda McAllister, Josine Meijer, Caroline Muir and Jon Riley for their editorial assistance, and to the staff of the Photocopying and Post Rooms at Penguin Books.

David Meltzer's poem 'The Fire' previously appeared in *Knots* (Tree Books, 1971); the text here titled 'Shrine' in *Two Way Mirror: A Poetry Notebook* (Oyez, 1971); 'From the Rabbi's Dreambook' was published in *New Wilderness Letter* No. 11, 1982, as was Tina Oldknow's 'Muslim Soup'. John Latham's 'Art and Culture' featured in the catalogue of his exhibition 'State of Mind' at the Stadtische Kunsthalle, Düsseldorf, 1975; Robert Nye's 'Childhood Incident' in *A Collection of Poems 1955–1988* (Hamish Hamilton, 1989 and Abacus, 1991); Matt Simpson's 'The Last Days of Pompeii' in his collection *An Elegy For the Galosherman* (Bloodaxe, 1990); Ed Ruscha's 'The Information Man' in the *Journal of the Los Angeles Institute of Contemporary Arts*, 1975; Anthony Earnshaw's 'Ex Libris' drawing in *Flick Knives and Forks* (Transformaction, 1981); Glen Baxter's drawing of 'Edna Stilt' in *The Works* (Wyrd Press, 1977); Annabel Nicolson's stone wall photograph in *Escaping Notice* (Nicolson, 1977); Lynne Tillman's 'Hole Story' in *The Voice Literary Supplement*; and Peter Finch's poems 'Quiet Day in the Bookshop' and 'Booklifter' in *New Welsh Review*. The extract from 'Three Library Users' by Erich Fried is from his collection *Children and Fools*, translated by Martin Chalmers (Serpent's Tail, 1992). Texts by Mass-Observers are from the Mass-Observation Archive in the University of Sussex. Permission to reproduce all the above listed works is gratefully acknowledged.

Royalties from this book are being donated towards the Royal National Institute for the Blind's provision of Braille and talking books.

Notes on Contributors

BRIAN W. ALDISS's recent books include *Remembrance Day*, a contemporary novel, and *A Tupolev Too Far*, a collection of savage short stories

ELENA ALEXANDER is a writer who travels a great deal but always returns to New York City

KEVIN ATHERTON casts bronze figures in relation to their settings, including passengers waiting on station platforms and galloping horses by railway lines

SYLVIA AYLING lives in Essex, close to where her heroine Sylvia Pankhurst dwelt

ANDRZEJ BADZIAK is a Polish animated filmmaker

WAYNE BALMER is very wary of monkfish dinners in Shepherds Bush

GLEN BAXTER's drawings are immensely popular as funny books, cards and calendars

STEVE BERESFORD is an improvising musician

MARCEL BERLINS opines on legal matters for the *Guardian*

BIFF cartoon strips appear regularly in the same paper as Marcel Berlins

Filmmaker IAN BOURN developed a betting system based on the size of greyhounds' pre-race turds

DAVID BRIERS is Exhibitions Officer of the Ferens Art Gallery, Hull

ANGUS CALDER is the author of *The People's War* and *The Myth of The Blitz*

J. L. CARR published numerous small books for cold bedrooms. Only one hand need suffer exposure

JOHN CHRISTIE is a television lighting cameraman and makes artists' books for Circle Press

Australian DEIRDRE CLARK has a specialist interest in operatic arias in praise of cigarettes and plumbing

LES COLEMAN's waggish aphorisms appear in *Unthoughts*

Travel writer DAVE COOK was tragically killed while cycling through Turkey

Singer, painter and writer KEVIN COYNE lives in Nuremberg. His books are *The Party Dress* and *Show Business*

Painter DAVID CUTHBERT loves books except in tea chests. He used to be a removal man with Pickfords

IVOR CUTLER is a Scottish poet, musician and humorist

Welsh painter IVOR DAVIES was recently intrigued to discover a tail in his soup in China

Artist GREG DAVILLE publishes miniature books in Brighton

TERRY DENNETT runs a photography workshop and archive in London

THEO DORGAN, born in Cork, suffered education under Christian Brothers, died and was reborn perpetrating poems. He is now Director of Poetry Ireland/Éigse Éireann

drif field produces *drif's guide to the secondhand bookshops of the british isles*, a volume that has earned him some notoriety

Artist RIKKI DUCORNET's novels include *The Stain, Entering Fire, The Fountains of Neptune* and *The Jade Cabinet*

ANTHONY EARNSHAW makes witty boxed assemblages in Saltburn-by-the-Sea

DUDLEY EDWARDS was one of the graphic artists who painted John Lennon's psychedelic Rolls-Royce

New Yorker JANICE EIDUS is author of the short story collection *Vito Loves Geraldine* and the novel *Faithful Rebecca*

KAREN ELIOT, a fugitive figure, was last heard of in Tierra del Fuego

The ELLESMERE PORT HOUSEWIFE is an anonymous Mass-Observer

Poet PETER FINCH runs the Oriel Bookshop in Cardiff

ALLEN FISHER is a poet, painter and publisher

JEAN FRASER is a London-based photographer

German poet ERICH FRIED escaped from the Gestapo to London, where he lived until his death in 1988

Artist JOHN FURNIVAL is assembling the world's largest

collection of blue envelopes

Isle of Wighter DAVID GASCOYNE is one of England's greatest living poets

Multi-media composer and musician RON GEESIN's latest CD is 'Blue Fuse' on Headscope

WILLIAM GIBSON kickstarted the cyberpunk genre with his seminal novel *Necromancer* (1984)

BERYL GILROY is known for her autobiography *Black Teacher* – she was London's first black woman appointee – and her children's books, poetry and novels

FRANCISCO GOYA's Black Paintings in the House of the Deaf Man are amongst the world's most intense frescoes

JOHN GUEST is compiler of *The Best of Betjeman*

RALPH HAWKINS writes poetry on the Essex coast

Born in Guyana, ROY HEATH has published an autobiography and eight novels. *The Murderer* won the Guardian Fiction Prize

A Surrealist between 1933 and 1951, MAURICE HENRY drew 25,000 satirical cartoons

Writer and translator LIZ HERON edited *Streets of Desire: Women's Fictions of the Twentieth Century City*

SELIMA HILL's poetry is much acclaimed, as was her collaboration with sculptor Bill Woodrow at the Imperial War Museum

Biblioholic CHARLES HILLDROP hunts for conger eels in deep sea wrecks

CHARLIE HOLMES wrote to the Perth Public Library announcing his intention to steal three of John Buchan's books on the date of his centenary. He was subsequently apprehended and imprisoned

MICHAEL HOLROYD is the biographer of Bernard Shaw

Theatrical entrepreneur NEIL HORNICK also runs Image Diggers Archive

Born of a marriage made in Marks & Spencer, Crewe, artist PATRICK HUGHES was told by his grandmother never to contradict and still does

RON HUNT is an art college librarian and a painter. He once collected vintage hats as a hobby

Poet TONY JACKSON, together with his publisher and one of this book's editors, once comprised the entire audience for a concert by six of Europe's finest jazz musicians in Stockton-on-Tees

TIMOTHY EMLYN JONES is an artist and writer in Stourbridge

JOHN KIRBY is a painter working in the west of Ireland

GOHAR KORDI is the author of *An Iranian Odyssey*

JUDY KRAVIS edits and publishes *Roadbooks* in County Cork

EDWARD THOMAS LANDIS is an attorney-at-law in Chattanooga and an administrator of the Shaking Ray Levi Society

Artist JOHN LATHAM exhibited a book sealed in impermeable plastic in an aquarium filled with frustrated piranhas

GEORGE LITTLEBLACK is a reviewer of sports videos

EDWARD LUCAS writes for the *Independent*

BERNARD MAC LAVERTY's novel *Cal* was made into a memorable film

DAVID MACH's sculpture of a nuclear submarine made of car tyres made national news when tragically attacked by an arsonist

CONROY MADDOX, England's senior Surrealist painter, had his throat cut from ear to ear and lived to tell the tale

MARCEL MARIËN once wrote to the King of Belgium suggesting memorials to the dead be erected *before* the Second World War so that the cannon fodder might have a taste of their future glory

DAVE MARSHALL was expelled from the same London grammar school as Alfred Hitchcock and Edmund Purdom

MASS-OBSERVATION contributors remain anonymous according to the terms of their collaboration with the archive housed at the University of Sussex

DAVID MELTZER is a widely published Californian poet

ROLAND MILLER is adviser to the Minister of Culture of the Slovak Republic

ROGER MILLS wrote *Bad Fun* and *The Tarnished Wings of Angels* for teenagers and an adult novel, *Stand Up For Bastards*

ANOUK MORTIMER believes that the body has its reasons

JOHN MUCKLE wrote a book of short stories, *The Cresta Run*, and co-edits the magazine *Active in Airtime*

GERRY MURPHY the poet lives in Cork

ANNABEL NICOLSON makes books, films, performances and drawings in cloth and fibre

D.K. NIELSEN is compelled by his unnatural interest in surfaces to work as a decorator. He was recently arrested in Portugal for whistling

Poet ROBERT NYE also writes historical novels including *Mrs Shakespeare: The Complete Works*

Marked from birth by books MERAPI OBERMAYER now makes book sculptures in Amsterdam

HUMPHREY OCEAN, former bass player with Kilburn and the Highroads, has painted portraits of Paul McCartney, Philip Larkin and Danny McGrain

TINA OLDKNOW manages a gallery of contemporary art in Seattle

JOE ORTON and KENNETH HALLIWELL lived, loved, wrote and died dramatically together

DES O'SULLIVAN writes for the *Irish Times* and the *Cork Examiner*

Giant worms live in GERALDINE O'SULLIVAN's West Cork garden

Photographer MARTIN PARR made the controversial BBC series 'Signs of the Times'. His latest book is *A Photographic Journey*

For many years JIM PENNINGTON never went into the showers after playing cricket. Now we know why

HENRY PILKE packs 'em in on the Newfoundland cabaret circuit

A committed Europhile, CLIVE PITSILLIDES believes the best place to live is in an English seaside resort

CHRIS PROCTOR's career as a stand-up comedian in working men's clubs ended traumatically after he performed his only act seven nights running to the same audience

Canadian KATE PULLINGER's books include the novel *Where Does Kissing End?*, the compendium *A Gambling Box* and a collection of short stories, *Tiny Lies*

AFSHIN RATTANSI, one-time reporter for Channel 4, has written journalism and five novels. He lives beside the Marylebone flyover, analysing catastrophe risk

Born in Yugoslavia, now based in London, BIKA REED writes books on Ancient Egypt and composes music and poetry

PRATAP RUGHANI is co-editor of the *New Internationalist* magazine and a documentary director for BBC Television

Artist TONY RICKABY portrayed the façades of buildings which are not what they appear to be

J. K. ROBERTSON has a soft spot for marsupials

GEORGE RODGER is one of the famous Magnum photographers

Performance artist NIGEL ROLFE has become allergic to the flour in which he has for years rolled naked

Californian artist ED RUSCHA is famous for his paintings and photo books featuring deadpan wordplay

RUDOLF SCHWARZKOPF has seen the light and loves us all

Painter NOEL SHERIDAN has been Director of the National College of Art and Design in Dublin and the Perth Institute of Contemporary Arts. He is a member of Aosdana

JEREMY SILVER works at Virgin Records. He co-edited *Angels of Fire*, an anthology of radical poetry

Headland did a collection of MATT SIMPSON's poems for kids *The Pigs' Thermal Underwear* in 1993

IAIN SINCLAIR trawls the lore and legend of London in his poetry and his novels *White Chappell, Scarlet Tracings* and *Downriver*

JANETTE M. SMITH is a Community Arts Officer at the Hawth Theatre, Crawley

JOHN SMITH is a filmmaker based in London

Ex-town planner T. DAN SMITH's perceived role in the Poulson civic corruption case in Newcastle haunts him still

CHERRY SMYTH, from the North of Ireland, writes on the representation of women in cinema

FELICITY SPARROW is a producer of short films

FRIDA STAMP is an East London housewife

JACKIE STANLEY is a painter and printmaker in Dublin

ROD STONEMAN has commissioned an impressive array of international films for Channel 4

VÉRONIQUE TADJO is a writer. She lives in Abidjan, Côte d'Ivoire

ALAN TAYLOR is Literary Editor of *Scotland on Sunday*

LYNNE TILLMAN, New York filmmaker and novelist, is author of *Absence Makes the Heart* and *Motion Sickness*

Musician DAVID TOOP is author of *The Rap Attack*

Poet GAEL TURNBULL lives in Edinburgh

MATTHEW TYSON makes artist's books in England and France

After ten years in New York LUISA VALENZUELA returned in 1989 to her native Buenos Aires, an experience reflected in her novel *National Identity*

SHERYL VAUGHAN is compiling a list of bookshops that have toilets

ERIC WALLACE has for twenty-five years been the newsreader for Border Television. His filmed life story, *The One and Only* (dir. Michael Cumming), lasts $8\frac{1}{2}$ minutes

KAREN WHITESON's poetry appears in the Stride anthology, *Frankenstein's Daughter*

CECIL H. WILLIAMSON is curator of the Museum of Smuggling

REBEKAH WOOD is writing a study of Villiers de l'Isle-Adam's *The Future Eve*

KEN WORPOLE is a writer and member of Comedia, an independent research network

ELIZABETH YOUNG's *Shopping in Space* (with Graham Caveney) critically assesses the blank generation of post-punk New York novelists